# The Real

# FRANK ZAPPA

# · Book ·

## by

## Frank Zappa

### with
### Peter Occhiogrosso

Poseidon Press

New York · London · Toronto · Sydney · Tokyo

**Poseidon Press**
Simon & Schuster Building
Rockefeller Center
1230 Avenue of the Americas
New York, New York 10020
Copyright © 1989 by Frank Zappa
All rights reserved
including the right of reproduction
in whole or in part in any form
POSEIDON PRESS is a registered trademark
of Simon & Schuster Inc.
POSEIDON PRESS colophon is a trademark
of Simon & Schuster Inc.
Designed by Awest
Manufactured in the United States of America

1   3   5   7   9   10   8   6   4   2

Library of Congress Cataloging-in-Publication Data
Zappa, Frank.
The real Frank Zappa book/Frank Zappa, with Peter Occhiogrosso.
p.   cm.
1. Zappa, Frank.   2. Rock musicians—United States—Biography.
I. Occhiogrosso, Peter.   II. Title
ML410.Z285A3   1989
784.5′4′00924—dc19
[B]            89-3470
CIP
MN
ISBN 0-671-63870-X

PICTURE CREDITS: Gerald Wortman (p. 81); Doug Metzler (p. 100);
Cynthia Plaster-Caster (drawing, p. 104); copyright © Lynn
Goldsmith (pp. 242, 251); AP/Wide World Photos (p. 260); Cal
Schenkel (drawing, p. 295); Greg Gorman (p. 348).

Illustrations by

THIS BOOK IS DEDICATED TO GAIL,
THE KIDS, STEPHEN HAWKING AND KO-KO.

*F.Z. August 23, 1988 06:39:37*

# CONTENTS

# INTRODUCTION

# Book?
# What
# Book?

I don't want to write a book, but I'm going to do it anyway, because Peter Occhiogrosso is going to help me. He is a writer. He *likes* books—he even *reads* them. I think it is good that books *still exist,* but they make me sleepy.

The way we're going to do it is, Peter will come to California and spend a few weeks recording answers to *'fascinating questions,'* then the tapes will be transcribed. Peter will edit them, put them on floppy discs, send them back to me, I will edit them *again,* and *that result* will be sent to Ann Patty at Poseidon Press, and **she** will make it come out to be **'A BOOK.'**

One of the reasons for doing this is the proliferation of stupid books (in several languages) which purport to be **About Me.** I thought there ought to be *at least ONE,* somewhere, that had **real stuff** in it. Please be advised that this book does not pretend to be some sort of 'complete' oral history. It is presented for consumption as entertainment only.

## SO, A FEW PRELIMINARY NOTES:

**[1]** *An autobiography is usually written by somebody who thinks his life is* **truly amazing.** *I do not think of* **my life** *as amazing in any sense—however, the opportunity to say stuff* **in print** *about* **tangential subjects** *is appealing.*

**[2]** *Documents and/or transcriptions will be labeled as such.*

**[3]** *The epigraphs at the heads of chapters (publishers love those little things) were researched and inserted by Peter—I mention this because I wouldn't want anybody to think I sat around reading Flaubert, Twitchell and Shakespeare all day.*

**[4]** *If your name is in the book and you didn't want it to be there (or you don't like my comments)—my apologies.*

**[5]** *If your name isn't in the book and you feel 'left out'—my apologies.*

The Real

# FRANK ZAPPA

## ·Book·

# CHAPTER 1

# How Weird Am I, Anyway?

*"I never set out to be weird. It was always other people who called me weird."*

Frank Zappa (*Baltimore Sun*, October 12, 1986)

This book exists on the premise that somebody, somewhere, is interested in *who I am, how I got that way, and what the fuck I'm talking about*.

To answer Imaginary Question Number One, let me begin by explaining **WHO I AM NOT.** Here are two popular **'Frank Zappa Legends'** . . .

Because I recorded a song called "Son of Mr. Green Genes" on the *Hot Rats* album in 1969, people have believed for years that the character with that name on the *Captain Kangaroo* TV show (played by *Lumpy Brannum*) was my 'real' Dad. No, he was not.

The other fantasy is that I once *'took a shit on stage.'* This has been propounded with many variations, including (but not limited to):

**[1]** I *ate* shit on stage.

**[2]** I had a 'gross-out contest' (what the fuck is a **'gross-out contest'?**) with *Captain Beefheart* and we **both** ate shit on stage.

**[3]** I had a 'gross-out contest' with *Alice Cooper* and he **stepped on baby chickens** and *then* I ate shit on stage, etc.

I was in a London club called the Speak Easy in 1967 or '68. A member of a group called the Flock, recording for Columbia at the time, came over to me and said:

> *"You're fantastic. When I heard about you eating that shit on stage, I thought, 'That guy is* **way, way out there.'** *"*

I said, *"I never ate shit on stage."* He looked really depressed —like I had just broken his heart.

For the records, folks: **I never took a shit on stage, and the closest I ever came to eating shit** *anywhere* **was at a Holiday Inn buffet in Fayetteville, North Carolina, in 1973.**

# More Important Information for People Who Wonder What I Eat

I wasn't crazy about most of the food my mother made—like *pasta with lentils*. That was one of the most hated dishes of my childhood. She would make enough to last a week, in a big pot. After a few days in the icebox it used to turn black.

My **favorite** things to eat then were blueberry pie, fried oysters and fried eels—but I also used to love *corn sandwiches*: white bread and mashed potatoes with canned corn dumped on it. (Every once in a while, we'll come back to this fascinating topic, since it seems to matter so much to certain people in the audience.)

# The Boring, Basic Stuff

*"Be regular and orderly in your life so that you may be violent and original in your work."*

Gustave Flaubert

How 'bout that epigraph, huh? Peter, you're cracking me up already. Okay, here we go. . . . My real name is *Frank* Vincent Zappa (not *Francis*—I'll explain it later). I was born on December 21, 1940, in Baltimore, Maryland. When I popped out, I was all black—they thought I was dead. I'm okay now.

My ancestry is Sicilian, Greek, Arab and French. My mother's mother was French and Sicilian, and her Dad was Italian (from Naples). She was *first generation*. The Greek-Arab side is from my Dad. He was born in a Sicilian village called Partinico, and came over on one of the immigrant boats when he was a kid.

He used to work in his Dad's barbershop on the Maryland waterfront. For a penny a day (or a penny a week—I can't remember), he would stand on a box and lather the sailors' faces so his Dad could shave them. *Nice job.*

Eventually he went to college at Chapel Hill, in North Carolina, and played guitar in some sort of *'strolling crooner'* trio. (I still get birthday cards from the insurance company owned by Jack Wardlaw, the banjo player.)

They used to go from dormitory window to dormitory window, serenading coeds with songs like "Little Red Wing." He was on the wrestling team and, when he graduated, he took a job teaching history at Loyola, in Maryland.

Both my parents used to speak Italian in the house so the kids wouldn't know what they were talking about—which was probably money, since we never seemed to have any. I guess it was convenient for them to have a *'secret code'*—but not teaching the kids the language may have had something to do with their desire to assimilate. (It was not fashionable to be of 'foreign extraction' in the U.S. during World War II.)

We used to live in the Army housing facility in Edgewood, Maryland. There was a family—the Knights—to whom my Dad referred as *"that hillbilly bunch over there."* One day Archie Knight got into an argument with my Dad, and the next thing I knew, Dad was running toward the house, shouting, *"Get the gun, Rosie! Get the gun!"*

That was the first time I knew that he had a gun (a chrome .38 pistol, stuffed in a sock drawer). My mother was pleading with him not to shoot the guy. Fortunately, he had the good sense to listen to her.

Because of that incident, I knew where the gun was. I took it out one day and remember thinking: *"This is the best-looking cap pistol I've ever seen!"* So, when nobody was looking, I used it to shoot *single-shot caps,* and the 'blue dots' I had chopped off the end of some wooden kitchen matches.

My parents were disturbed when they discovered that I had gummed up the firing pin.

My mother's parents had a restaurant—also on the Maryland waterfront. She used to tell a story about a guy who came in and started a fight. I believe it was my mother's Dad who took one of those big forks they used for taking potatoes out of boiling water and stabbed the guy in the skull with it. He didn't die—instead, he ran off, with the fork sticking out the top of his head like an antenna.

My Dad's Dad seldom bathed. He liked to sit on the porch with wads of clothes on. He liked to drink wine, and started off every day with **two** glasses of *Bromo Seltzer*.

My mother's mother didn't speak English, so she used to tell us stories in Italian—like the one about the *mano pelusa*—the hairy hand. *"Mano pelusa! Vene qua!"* she would say in a scary 'grandma voice'—that was supposed to mean *"Hairy hand! Come here!"*—then she would run her fingers up my arm. This is what people used to do when there was no TV.

My first memories of childhood include wearing a little sailor suit with a wooden whistle on a string around my neck, going to church all the time and kneeling down a lot.

We lived in a boardinghouse one time when I was very little. I think it might have been in Atlantic City. The lady who owned the boarding house had a *Pomeranian* and the *Pomeranian* used to eat grass and vomit things that looked like *white meatballs.*

Later, we lived in one of those row houses on Park Heights Avenue in Maryland. We had wood floors, heavily waxed, with throw rugs on them. The tradition in those days was that you waxed everything until you could see your face in it (remember, there was no TV, so people had time to do stuff like that)—and the other tradition was: *when Dad came home from work, you ran to meet him at the door.*

Once, when Dad was coming home from work, my younger brother, Bobby, ran faster than I did, and arrived **first** at the door. (It was a door with little panes of glass in it.) He opened it, hugged Dad, then closed it. I came running and skidded on the throw rug, crashing my left arm through the glass. I heard them talking about how they should get a doctor to stitch it up. I complained so much they didn't stitch it up— just stuck a bunch of Band-Aids on it and I wound up with a scar. I can't stand needles.

I had horrible teeth, so my parents used to take me to an Italian dentist who had a unique piece of equipment—a cross between a chainsaw and a sewing machine. He'd stick the thing in my mouth and it would go **voodn-voodn-voodn-voodnnnnnn**—no *novocaine.* I learned to dread the sound of the word **'dentist.'**

My parents felt that they **had** to go to an **Italian dentist**— because they couldn't trust one of those 'white-person' [*possibly-related-to-some-sort-of-hillbilly*] dentists, and so it was that I made the acquaintance of the nefarious **Dr. Rocca.** He would have been sensational as an evil monk in *The Name of the Rose*.

## My First Space Helmet

My Dad was employed as a meteorologist at the Edgewood Arsenal. They made poison gas there during World War II, so I guess it would have been the meteorologist's job to figure out which way the wind was blowing when it was time to shoot the stuff off.

He used to bring equipment home from the lab for me to play with: *beakers, Florence flasks, little petri dishes full of mercury* —**blobs** *of mercury*. I used to play with it all the time. The entire floor of my bedroom had this 'muck' on it, made out of mercury mixed with dust balls.

One of the things I used to like to do was pour the mercury on the floor and hit it with a hammer, so it squirted all over the place. I **lived** in mercury.

When **DDT** was first invented, my Dad brought some home—there was a whole bag of it in the closet. I didn't eat it or anything, but he said that **you could**—it was supposed to be 'safe,' it *only killed bugs*.

Sicilian parents do things *differently*. If I said I had an earache, my parents would heat up some olive oil and pour it in my ear —*which hurts like a motherfucker*—but they tell you it's supposed to make it feel better. When you're a kid, you don't get to argue about it.

I spent the first five or six years of my life with cotton hanging out of my ears—*yellow,* from olive oil.

19

Along with my earaches and asthma, I had sinus trouble. There was some 'new treatment' for this ailment being discussed in the neighborhood. It involved stuffing *radium* into your sinus cavities. (Have you ever heard of this?) My parents took me to *yet another Italian doctor,* and, although I didn't know what they were going to do to me, it didn't sound like it was going to be *too much fun.* The doctor had a long wire thing—maybe a foot or more, and on the end was a pellet of radium. He stuffed it up my nose and into my sinus cavities on both sides. (I should probably check to see if my handkerchief is glowing in the dark.)

One of the other wonder remedies that had just come out then was *sulfa.* Winter was freezing cold in that house at 15 Dexter Street. The walls were so thin—it was like a cardboard house. We used to wear flannel trapdoor pajamas. In the mornings, to get warm, we stood by the coal stove in the kitchen.

On one occasion, the trapdoor on my younger brother's pajamas caught fire. My Dad came running in and beat the fire out with his bare hands. Both his hands and my brother's back were totally burned. The doctor put *sulfa* on them and neither of them got scarred.

My Dad used to help pay the rent by volunteering for human testing of chemical (maybe even biological) warfare agents. These were called *'patch tests.'*

The Army didn't tell you **what** it was they were putting on your skin—and you agreed *not to scratch it, or peek under the bandage*—and they would pay you ten bucks per patch. Then they would take it off after a couple of weeks.

My Dad used to come home with three or four of those

things on his arms and different parts of his body every week. I don't know what the stuff was, or what long-range health effects it might have had on him (or on any of the children that were born after the time that they did it).

There were tanks of mustard gas within a mile of where we lived, so everybody in this housing project had to have a gas mask in the house, for each member of the family.

Mustard gas explodes the vessels in your lungs, causing you to *drown in your own blood.*

We had a rack at the end of the hall with a family's worth of masks on it. I used to wear mine out in the backyard all the time —it was my space helmet. One day I decided to find out how it worked, so I took a can opener and opened up the filter (thereby *ruining* it). In any event, I found out what was inside it—charcoal, paper filters and different layers of crystals, including, I think, *potassium permanganate.*

Before they would squirt mustard gas onto a battlefield, they had some other stuff called *chloropicrin,* a dust that induced vomiting—they called it *"puke stuff."* The dust would creep around the edges of the soldier's mask, causing him to vomit. If he didn't take his mask off, he could drown in his own spew, and if he did—*to let the chunks out*—the mustard gas would get him.

I was always amazed that people got paid to figure out how to do this stuff.

## The Second Part of My Childhood

The second part of my childhood (are you **sure** you want to know this stuff?) takes place mostly in California, when I was about ten or twelve. First, I'll tell you how we got there.

I was sick so often in Maryland, Mom and Dad wanted to move. The first time I managed to escape from the state was when my Dad took a job in Florida—another civil service position, this time in *ballistics*, something about shell trajectories. It was still World War II.

## MY MEMORIES OF FLORIDA INCLUDE:

[1] Opa-Locka had a lot of mosquitoes and if you left the bread out overnight, green hair grew on it.

 [2] Every once in a while we had to hide under the bed and turn all the lights off because somebody thought the Germans were coming.

[3] My Dad 'made margarine' by squeezing a red dot sealed inside a plastic bag with white stuff in it which, when smushed up, caused the white stuff to turn yellow, giving the illusion of 'butter.'

[4] My brother got a boil on his butt, and my Dad had to squeeze stuff out of it (margarine training probably helped), and there was a lot of screaming.

 [5] I was told to watch out for alligators because they sometimes ate children.

[6] Everything looked like it was in Technicolor compared to Baltimore.

[7] I got to play outside a lot, climbing trees, which eventually led to a fungus on my elbow.

[8] Except for that, my health improved, and I got about a foot taller.

**[9]** My mother got homesick and, since I was taller, figured it was okay to go back to Baltimore.

**[10]** We went back to Baltimore and I got sick again.

Edgewood, Maryland, was sort of out in the country. It had a little woods and a creek with crawdads in it, just at the end of Dexter Street. I used to play down there with Leonard Allen.

Even though I was sick all the time, Edgewood was sort of fun, but when we moved back to Maryland, we didn't go to Edgewood—we moved into a rowhouse in the city and I hated it.

I don't think my folks liked it very much either, because the next thing I knew, they were talking about moving to California. My Dad had gotten another offer to work at the *Dugway Proving Ground* in Utah (where they made nerve gas), but we got off lucky—he didn't take it. Instead, he took a position at the *Naval Post-Graduate School* in Monterey, teaching *metallurgy*. I had no idea what the fuck that meant.

So, in the dead of winter, we set out in our *'Henry-J'* (an extinct and severely uncomfortable, small, cheap car manufactured then by *Kaiser*), via the Southern Route, to California. The backseat of a 'Henry-J' was a piece of plywood, covered with about an inch of kapok and some stiff, tweedy upholstery material. I spent two exhilarating weeks on this Ironing Board From Hell.

My Dad believed (as I'm sure everyone on the East Coast did) that California was all sunshine and warm weather. This led him to stop the car somewhere in the Carolinas and present, to a somewhat amazed black family standing near the highway, **all** of our warm winter clothing, convinced as he was that we would **never** need any of that shit again.

When we arrived in Monterey (a coastal town in Northern California), it was freezing cold, and it rained and fogged all the time. Oops.

## Chemistry in Northern California

Because of my Dad's work, I switched from school to school fairly often. I didn't enjoy it, but then, I didn't enjoy much of **anything** in those days. A 'weekend outing' of that period occasionally meant piling into the 'Henry-J' and driving toward Salinas, a place nearby where they grow lettuce, and following the trucks, waiting for some to fall off. When it did, my Dad would stop the car, pick it up, brush away the asphalt chunks, toss it in the backseat with me, take it home and *boil* it.

I didn't enjoy being poor. It seemed like everything that I wanted to do, that would be *fun,* cost too much money—and when you're a kid and you can't do *fun stuff,* you're either going to be bored or dissatisfied or both.

For instance, I would have loved to own a chemistry set. In those days if you got the large-size *Gilbert Chemistry Set,* the booklet that came with it would teach you how to make stuff like *tear gas.*

By the time I was six years old I knew how to make gunpowder—I knew what the ingredients were, and I couldn't wait to get them all together and make some. I had all that chemical paraphernalia around the house, and I used to *pretend* to mix ingredients—dreaming of the day when one of my little concoctions would actually **explode.**

Once I thought I had come up with a formula for a new poison gas when the liquid potion I was working on (based largely on Windex) came in contact with some zinc.

My Dad wanted me to be an engineer. I think he was disappointed that I didn't have an aptitude for arithmetic and the rest of the stuff that was required.

They used to give kids in the sixth grade something called

the *Kuder Preference Test.* You had to stick a pin in the page, in boxes that you selected. The test was supposed to determine *what you would be best suited for, in terms of employment, for* **the rest of your life.** My test results indicated that my destiny was to become a secretary. I scored highest in 'clerical.'

My biggest problem, throughout school, was that the things they were trying to teach me tended not to be the kinds of things I was interested in. I grew up with poison gas and explosives—with the children of people who built these things for a living. Did I give a fuck about algebra?

## The Stuff in the Old Garage

We moved from Monterey to Pacific Grove, a quiet town nearby. I spent my recreational hours building puppets and model planes and making homemade explosives from whatever ingredients I could find.

One day, a friend said, *"See that garage across the street? It's been locked* **for years.** *I wonder what's inside of there."*

We burrowed under the side wall. There was a pile of crates, full of fifty-caliber machine-gun bullets. We stole a bunch, removed the bullet heads with pliers, and extracted the *'gunpowder'* —only it didn't look like *'gunpowder,'* it looked like little greenish-black sequins (I think it was called *ballistite*). It was a member of the smokeless powder family (nitrocellulose)—I'd never seen any of that before.

We put it in a toilet-paper tube and stuffed it into a mound of dirt in the middle of a vacant lot and lit it, using *gimp* for a fuse (that shiny, flat plastic stuff you make keychain holders out of in summer camp).

When loosely packed, *ballistite* produces a shower of little yellowish-orange fireballs.

The other thing that turned out to be rewardingly explosive was *powdered Ping-Pong balls.* We used to spend hours filing Ping-Pong balls into dust with a rat-tail file. I got the idea when I read about a guy who escaped from jail by making a bomb out of playing cards. The article said that the playing cards were coated with some kind of cellulose material, and the convict had scraped it all off and accumulated a *plasticized dust.*

The casing for the bomb was a toilet-paper roll wrapped with tar tape. He blew his way out of a jail with it, so I thought: *"There's a clue here somewhere."*

 ## How I Almost Blew My Nuts Off

You used to be able to buy *single-shot* caps at the hobby store. These were better than the ones on the little rolls because they had more powder in them and made a bigger bang. I spent hours with my X-Acto knife, cutting away the extra paper, saving the trimmed charges in a jar. Along with this, I had another jar full of the semilethal Ping-Pong dust.

One afternoon I was sitting in our garage—an old rickety one with a dirt floor, like the place with the machine-gun bullets. It was after the Fourth of July and the gutters in our neighborhood were littered with *used fireworks tubes.* I had collected a few, and was in the process of reloading one of them with my own *secret formula.*

I had it propped between my legs, filling it with a layer of this and a layer of that, packing each layer down with the butt end of a drumstick.

When I got to the layer of single-shot caps, I must have pressed too hard and the charge ignited. It blew a large crater in the dirt floor, blew the doors open, and blew me back a few feet, balls first. Why, I could have *almost* escaped from jail with that one.

# The End of My Scientific Career

I continued to be interested in stuff that went **boom** in spite of that incident.

I had a friend in San Diego around 1956 who was also interested in explosives. We had been experimenting for about a month, finally collecting a quart mayonnaise jar full of stuff that was a combination of *solid rocket fuel* (fifty percent powdered zinc, fifty percent sulfur) and *stink-bomb powder*.

On Open House Night, we hitchhiked to school with the jar, borrowed some paper cups from the cafeteria, poured the powder into them, passed them out to our friends and started little fires all over the school (while everybody's parents sat in the classrooms, reenacting their offspring's daily schedules).

The next day, I found my locker (where I had stored the jar with the leftover formula) wired shut.

A short time later, in Miss Ivancic's English class, I received an invitation to visit the dean's office, so that I might be introduced to the fire marshal.

They threw me out of school and were going to put me on probation, but my mother pleaded with the probation guy (who happened to be Italian) and explained that my Dad was about to be transferred out of San Diego to Lancaster—and they let me go. This concluded Phase One of my scientific career.

# CHAPTER 2

# There Goes the Neighborhood

Around the age of twelve (1951 or '52) I started getting interested in the drums. I guess a lot of young boys think the drums are exciting, but it wasn't my idea to be a rock and roll drummer or anything like that, because rock and roll hadn't been invented yet. I was just interested in the sounds of things a person could beat on.

I started off with orchestral percussion, learning all the *rudiments*—things called *flams, ruffs, ratamacues* and *paradiddles*. I had taken a summer-school group course in Monterey with a teacher named Keith McKillop. Instead of drums, he had us practicing on wooden planks. We had to stand in front of the planks and practice the *rudiments* used in Scottish drumming.

After that I begged my parents to get me a snare drum, which I used to practice on in the garage. When they couldn't afford to rent the snare drum anymore, I started playing on the furniture—beating the paint off bureaus and things like that.

By 1956 I was playing in a high school R&B band called the Ramblers. We used to rehearse in the living room of the piano player, Stuart Congdon—his Dad was a preacher. I practiced on pots and pans, held between my knees like bongos. I finally talked my folks into buying a *real drum set* (secondhand, from a guy up the street, for about fifty dollars). I didn't take delivery on the drum set until a week before our first gig. Since I had never learned to coordinate my hands and feet, I was not very good at keeping time with the kick-drum pedal.

The bandleader, Elwood "Junior" Madeo, had gotten us a job at a place called the Uptown Hall, at 40th and Mead in the Hillcrest district of San Diego. Our fee: *seven dollars—for the whole band*.

On the way to the gig, I realized that I had forgotten my drumsticks (my only pair), and we had to drive back across town to get them. Eventually I was fired because they said I played the cymbals too much.

It's hard to be a drummer-in-training, because there are very few apartments that are soundproof enough to practice in. (Where do good drummers *really* come from?)

## Varèse

**December 22,1883–November 6, 1965**

Rock and roll albums didn't appear in the marketplace until several years after rock itself was invented. In the early fifties, teenagers bought 78s or 45s.

The first rock and roll album I ever saw was around 1957— *Teenage Dance Party*. The cover showed a group of VERY WHITE TEENS, dancing, with confetti dangling all over the place near some soda bottles. Inside was a collection of songs by black doo-wop groups.

Back then, my record collection consisted of five or six rhythm-and-blues 78-RPM singles. Since I was a lower-middle-class teenager, the retail price of any kind of slowly rotating hi-fi vinyl seemed entirely out of the question.

One day I happened across an article about Sam Goody's record store in *Look* magazine which raved about what a wonderful merchandiser he was. The writer said that Mr. Goody could sell **anything**—and as an example he mentioned that he had even managed to sell an album called *Ionisation*.

The article went on to say something like: *"This album is nothing but drums—it's dissonant and terrible; the worst music in the world."* Ahh! Yes! That's for me!

I wondered where I could get my hands on a record like that, because I was living in El Cajon, California—a little cowboy kind of town near San Diego.

There was another town just over the hill called La Mesa— a bit more upscale (they had a 'hi-fi store'). Some time later, I was staying overnight with Dave Franken, a friend who lived in La Mesa, and we wound up going to the hi-fi place—they were having a sale on R&B singles.

After shuffling through the rack and finding a couple of Joe Huston records, I made my way toward the cash register and happened to glance at the LP bin. I noticed a strange-looking black-and-white album cover with a guy on it who had frizzy gray hair and looked like a mad scientist. I thought it was great that a mad scientist had finally made a record, so I picked it up —and there it was, the record with "Ionisation" on it.

The author of the *Look* article had gotten it slightly wrong —the correct title was *The Complete Works of Edgard Varèse, Volume I,* including "Ionisation," among other pieces, on an obscure label called **EMS** *(Elaine Music Store)*. The record number was **401.**

I returned the Joe Huston records and checked my pockets to see how much money I had—I think it came to about $3.75. I'd never bought an album before, but I knew they must be expensive because mostly old people bought them. I asked the man at the cash register how much EMS 401 cost.

*"That gray one in the box?"* he said. *"$5.95."*

I'd been searching for that record for over a year and I wasn't about to give up. I told him I had $3.75. He thought about it for a minute, and said, *"We've been using that record to demonstrate hi-fi's with—but nobody ever buys one when we use it. I guess if you want it* **that bad** *you can have it for $3.75."*

I couldn't wait to hear it. My family had a genuine *lo-fi* record player: a **Decca.** It was a little box about four inches deep, sitting on short metal legs (because the speaker was on the bottom), and it had one of those clunky tonearms that you had to put a quarter on top of to hold it down. It played all three speeds, but it had never been set to 33⅓ before.

The record player was in the corner of the living room where my mother did the ironing. When she bought it, they gave her a free record of "The Little Shoemaker," by some middle-aged white-guy singing group on Mercury. She used to listen to "The Little Shoemaker" while she was ironing, so that was the only place where I could listen to my new Varèse album.

I turned the volume all the way up (in order to get the maximum amount of 'fi'), and carefully placed the *all-purpose osmium-tipped needle* on the lead-in spiral to "Ionisation." I have a nice Catholic mother who likes to watch Roller Derby. When she heard what came out of that little speaker on the bottom of the Decca, she looked at me like I was *out of my fucking mind*.

It had sirens and snare drums and bass drums and a lion's roar and all kinds of strange sounds on it. She forbade me to play it in the living room ever again. I told her that **I** thought it was really great, and I wanted to listen to it **all the way through.** She told me to take the record player into my bedroom.

My mother never got to hear "The Little Shoemaker" again.

The record player stayed in my room, and I listened to EMS 401 over and over and over, poring through the liner notes for every bit of information I could glean. I couldn't understand all the musical terms, but I memorized them anyway.

All through high school, whenever people came over, I

would force them to listen to Varèse—because I thought it was *the ultimate test of their intelligence.* They also thought I was out of my fucking mind.

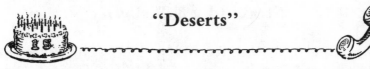

## "Deserts"

On my fifteenth birthday, my mother said she would spend five dollars on me (a lot of money for us then), and asked me what I wanted. I said, *"Well, instead of buying me something, why don't you just let me make a long-distance phone call?"* (Nobody in our house had ever made a long-distance phone call.)

I decided that I would call Edgard Varèse. I deduced that a person who looked like a mad scientist could only live in a place called Greenwich Village. So I called New York information and asked if they had a listing for Edgard Varèse. Sure enough, they did. They even gave me the address: 188 Sullivan Street.

His wife, Louise, answered the phone. She was very sweet, and told me he wasn't there—he was in Brussels working on a composition for the World's Fair ("Poème électronique")—and suggested I call back in a few weeks. I don't remember exactly what I said when I finally spoke to him—probably something articulate like *"Gee—I really dig your music."*

Varèse told me that he was working on a new piece called "Déserts," which thrilled me since Lancaster, California, was in the desert. When you're fifteen and living in the Mojave Desert, and you find out that the World's Greatest Composer (who also looks like a mad scientist) is working in a secret Greenwich Village laboratory on a **'song about your hometown'** (so to speak), you can get pretty *excited.*

I still think "Déserts" is about Lancaster, even if the liner notes on the Columbia LP insist that it is something more *philosophical.*

All through high school I searched for information about Varèse and his music. I found one book that had a photo of him as a young man, and a quote, saying he would be just as happy growing grapes as being a composer. I liked that.

## Stravinsky & Webern

The second 33⅓-RPM record I bought was by Stravinsky. I found a budget-line recording (on Camden) of *The Rite of Spring* by something called 'The World-Wide Symphony Orchestra.' (Sounds pretty official, eh?) The cover was a green-and-black abstract whatchamacallit, and it had a magenta paper label with black lettering. I loved Stravinsky almost as much as Varèse.

The other composer who filled me with awe—I couldn't believe that anybody would write music like that—was Anton Webern. I heard an early recording on the Dial label with a cover by an artist named David Stone Martin—it had one or two of Webern's string quartets, and his Symphony op. 21 on the other side. I loved that record, but it was about as different from Stravinsky and Varèse as you could get.

I didn't know anything about twelve-tone music then, but I liked the way it sounded. Since I didn't have any kind of formal training, it didn't make any difference to me if I was listening to Lightnin' Slim, or a vocal group called the Jewels (who had a song out then called "Angel in My Life"), or Webern, or Varèse, or Stravinsky. To me it was **all good music.**

 ## My All-American Education

There were a few teachers in school who really helped me out. Mr. Kavelman, the band instructor at Mission Bay High, gave me the answer to one of the burning musical questions of my youth. I came to him one day with a copy of "Angel in My Life"—my favorite R&B tune at the time. I couldn't understand why I loved that record so much, but I figured that, since he was *a music teacher,* maybe **he** knew.

*"Listen to this,"* I said, *"and tell me why I like it so much."*
*"Parallel fourths,"* he concluded.

He was the first person to tell me about twelve-tone music. It's not that he was a fan of it, but he did mention the fact that *it existed,* and I am grateful to him for that. I never would have heard Webern if it hadn't been for him.

Mr. Ballard was the high school music instructor at Antelope Valley High. He let me conduct the orchestra a couple of times, let me write music on the blackboard, and had the orchestra play it.

Mr. Ballard also did me a big favor without knowing it. As a drummer, I was obliged to perform the gruesome task of playing in the marching band. Considering my lack of interest in football, I couldn't stand sitting around in a stupid-looking uniform, going *'Da-ta-da-da-ta-ta-taaaah; CHARGE!''* every time somebody kicked a fucking football, freezing my nards off every weekend. Mr. Ballard threw me out of the marching band for **smoking in uniform**—and for that I will be *eternally grateful.*

My English teacher at A.V. was Don Cerveris. He was also a good friend. Don got tired of being a teacher and quit—he wanted to be a screenwriter. In 1959, he wrote the screenplay for a super-cheap cowboy movie called *Run Home Slow,* and helped me get my first film scoring job on it.

## My Other Obsession

While other guys in high school were spending their money on cars, I spent my money on records (I didn't have a car). I went to *used record outlets* to buy jukebox records of rhythm-and-blues songs.

There was a place in San Diego on the ground floor of the Maryland Hotel where you could buy R&B singles unobtainable elsewhere—all those Lightnin' Slim and Slim Harpo sides on the Excello label. (The reason you couldn't order them in the 'white-person record stores' was that Excello had a policy that if a store wanted to carry their R&B line, it also **had** to take their gospel catalog.) The only way I could get a Lightnin' Slim record was to travel a couple hundred miles and buy it second-hand, all scratched up.

 # Homemade Boogie

San Diego had neighborhood gangs, and each neighborhood had its own 'cool band'—the equivalent of the 'home team' in football. These bands competed with each other—who had the best musicianship, wardrobe, choreography.

A 'good band' had to have at *least* three saxophones in it (one of which **had** to be a **baritone**), two guitar players, bass and drums. It was regarded as a *more serious band* if everybody wore a pink flannel, one-button roll sport coat. It was **really** good if they had pants to match—and it was **superb** if all the guys in the front row knew the same *steps,* and if they went *'up and down'* at the same time on the fast songs.

The people who went to see these bands **really** loved them. These weren't 'rock shows' put on by 'promoters'—instead, there were girl gangs who would rent the hall, hire the band, hang the crepe paper, and sell the tickets. (The first gig I ever played—the one where I forgot my drumsticks—was sponsored by one of them, the "BLUE VELVETS.")

 # Life in the Slow Lane

I spent more time with Don (Captain Beefheart) Van Vliet when I was in high school than after he got into 'show business.'

He dropped out during his senior year, because his Dad, who was a Helms Bread truck driver, had a heart attack and 'Vliet' (as he was known then) took over his route for a while—but most of the time he just stayed home from school.

His girlfriend, Laurie, lived in the house with him, along with his Mom (Sue), his Dad (Glen), Aunt Ione and Uncle Alan. Granny Annie lived across the street.

The way Don got his 'stage name' was, Uncle Alan had a habit of *exposing himself* to Laurie. He'd piss with the bathroom door open and, if she was walking by, mumble about his appendage—something along the lines of: *"Ahh, what a beauty! It looks just like a big, fine* **beef heart.***"*

Don was also an R&B fiend, so I'd bring my 45s over and we'd listen for hours on end to obscure hits by the Howlin' Wolf, Muddy Waters, Sonny Boy Williamson, Guitar Slim, Johnny "Guitar" Watson, Clarence "Gatemouth" Brown, Don and Dewey, the Spaniels, the Nutmegs, the Paragons, the Orchids, the etc., etc., etc.

There were piles of sweet rolls in the kitchen, like pineapple buns that didn't sell that day—the place was *crawling* with starch—and we'd eat mounds of them while the records were playing. Every once in a while Don would scream at his mother (always in a blue chenille bathrobe), **"Sue! Get me a Pepsi!"** There was **nothing** else to do in Lancaster.

Our major form of recreation, other than listening to records, was to go for coffee in the middle of the night to the Denny's on the highway.

If Don was short on cash (this was before he took over the bread truck route), he'd open the back door of the truck, pull out one of the long drawers with the dead buns on it and make Laurie crawl through the slot, into the locked cab, where she would sneak a few bucks out of his Dad's change-maker.

After coffee, we'd ride around in his light blue Oldsmobile with the homemade werewolf-head sculpture in the steering wheel, and talk about people who had large ears.

# CHAPTER 3

# An Alternative To COLLEGE

I got married for the first time when I was about twenty years old. I had gone to Antelope Valley Junior College in Lancaster and Chaffey Junior College in Alta Loma for the express purpose of meeting girls. I had no interest in higher education, but after finishing high school it occurred to me that if I wasn't in school, I wasn't going to meet any—so I 'reenlisted.'

At Chaffey, I met Kay Sherman. We dropped out of school,

started living together and got married. I went to work for a company called *Nile Running Greeting Cards.* Their line consisted mostly of silk-screened greetings, designed for elderly women who liked flowers. I worked in the silk-screen department and, after a while, wound up designing a few of the floral horrors myself.

Then came a part-time job writing copy and designing ads for local businesses, including a few *beauties* for the First National Bank of Ontario, California. I also had short stints as a window dresser and a jewelry salesman and—the worst one—I sold *Collier's Encyclopedias,* door to door. That was truly wretched—but at least I got an inside look at how that shit is done.

First, they make you go to school for three or four days to memorize the sales pitch (from which you are **not allowed to deviate,** since they tell you that they paid a lot of money to a psychologist somewhere who figured it all out). The guy who figured out the one I had to memorize should have his license revoked—or do those guys ever *get* a license?

They teach you psychological tricks to convince people who can't even afford a loaf of bread to pay three hundred bucks for a set of books they can't even read. For instance: when you go to pitch the deal, and you have the sales contract on your clipboard, you should hold the pen under your thumb at the top of the board, near the clip. When you hand the clipboard to the person *("Sir, why don't you just take a look at what it says right here—"),* you release your thumb and let the pen roll down the clipboard into the guy's hand—and before he knows what the fuck happened to him, he's got the contract **and** the pen in **his** hands.

Then, the idea was to unfurl a rolled-up piece of oilcloth with a photo on it, showing what this incredible plywood bookcase with the books sticking out of it would look like in **his home.** Then I let him hold an *actual book*—the one that had the plastic overlays of the human body. I lasted a week.

In the world of 'professional entertainment,' I wasn't faring much better. I was working weekends with a four-piece lounge band called Joe Perrino and the Mellotones, at Tommy Sandi's Club Sahara in San Bernardino.

The management *allowed* us to play *one* [1] *'twist number' per night*. The rest of the night we were supposed to play "Happy Birthday," "Anniversary Waltz" and "On Green Dolphin Street." I wore a white dinner jacket and bow tie and black pants and sat on a bar stool and played the electric guitar. I got so sick of it that I quit, put the guitar in the case, stuck it behind the sofa and didn't touch it for eight months.

One of the other great jobs was as a rhythm guitarist in a pickup band at a Christmas dance in a Mormon recreation hall. The room was decorated with wads of cotton hanging on black thread (snowballs, *get it?*). The band consisted of sax, drums and guitar. I borrowed a *fake-book* so I could follow the chord changes, since I didn't know any of the tunes. The sax player was, in civilian life, a Spanish teacher from the local high school. He had no sense of rhythm and couldn't even count the tunes off, but *he* was *the leader* of the band.

I didn't know anything about Mormons at the time, so, during a break when I lit up a cigarette, it was as if The Devil Himself had just made a rare personal appearance. A bunch of guys who looked like they weren't quite ready to shave yet started flailing over to me and, in a brotherly sort of way, escorted my ass out the door. I knew I was going to love show business if I ever got into it.

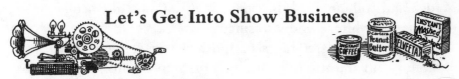

## Let's Get Into Show Business

At that time there was a place called the Pal Recording Studio in (don't laugh) Cucamonga, California. It was established by an amazing gentleman named Paul Buff.

Cucamonga was a blotch on a map, represented by the intersection of Route 66 and Archibald Avenue. On those four corners we had an Italian restaurant, an Irish pub, a malt shop and a gas station.

North, up Archibald, were an electrician's shop, a hardware store and the recording studio. Across the street was a Holy Roller church, and up the block from that was the grammar school.

Buff had lived in Cucamonga before enlisting in the Marines. While serving, he decided to learn electronics, so that when he got out he could apply what he had learned and build his own recording studio. He got out, rented a place at 8040 Archibald Avenue and set out to change the direction of American Popular Music.

He didn't have a mixing console, so he built one—out of an old 1940s vanity. He removed the mirror and, right in the middle, where the cosmetics would have gone, installed a metal plate with Boris Karloff knobs on it.

He built his own homemade, five-track, half-inch tape recorder—at a time when the standard in the industry was mono. (I think only Les Paul had an eight-track then. Buff was able to overdub the same way Les Paul could, but in a more primitive manner.)

He wanted to become a singer-songwriter, so he listened to all the latest hit records, figured out what the hooks were and, through a mysterious process, created his own little hook-laden replicas.

He taught himself how to play the five basic instruments of rock and roll: *drums, bass, guitar, keyboards* and *alto saxophone*—then taught himself how to sing.

He made master tapes of finished songs, then drove into Hollywood and attempted to lease them to Capitol, Del-Fi, Dot and Original Sound.

Some of these tunes actually became 'regional hits.' "Tijuana

Surf" (with Paul multitracking himself) became a long-running number-one record in Mexico. I wrote and played guitar on the B side, an instrumental called "Grunion Run." It was released on Original Sound under the name of the Hollywood Persuaders.

I worked with him for about a year until he got into financial trouble and was in danger of losing his studio.

So, remember the really cheap cowboy movie that my high school English teacher wrote the script for in 1959? After endless delays, *Run Home Slow* (starring Mercedes McCambridge) was completed and scored in 1963. I even got paid for it—not all of it, but most of it. I took part of the money and bought a new guitar, and used the rest to 'buy' Pal Records from Paul. In other words, I agreed to take over his lease and the rest of his debt.

Meanwhile, my marriage fell apart. I filed for divorce, moved out of the house on G Street, and into **'Studio Z,'** beginning a life of obsessive overdubbage—nonstop, twelve hours a day.

I had no food, no shower or bathtub; just an industrial sink where I could wash up. I would have starved in there if it hadn't been for Motorhead Sherwood. I knew him from Lancaster. He came to Cucamonga and didn't have a place to stay, so I invited him to move into the studio with me.

Motorhead had a way with cars and also played the saxophone—a useful combination. When the Mothers were finally formed, he worked for us as a roadie, and later joined the band.

One day Motorhead, by some illicit means, acquired a box of foodstuffs from a mobile blood bank. He got some instant mashed potatoes (I still don't know why a bloodmobile would carry instant mashed potatoes, but that's where he said he got them), some instant coffee and some honey.

By then I had landed a weekend gig at a place called the Village Inn, in Sun Village, eighty miles away. The pay came to fourteen dollars a week (seven bucks per night), minus gas.

With that, I bought peanut butter, bread and cigarettes. One week we splurged and bought a whole brick of Velveeta.

Goin' back home
To the Village of the Sun,
Out in back of Palmdale
Where the turkey farmers run

I done
Made up my mind
And I know I'm gonna go to Sun
Village, good God,
I hope the wind don't blow

It'll take the paint off your car
And wreck your windshield, too
I don't know how the people stand it,
But I guess they all do,
'Cause they're all still there
(Even Johnny Franklin too)
In the Village of the Sun
Village of the Sun
Village of the Sun, son—
Sun Village, to you
What you gone do?

Little Mary, and Teddy, and Thelma, too
Where Palmdale Boulevard cuts on through—
Past the Village Inn & Barbecue
(I heard it ain't there—I hope it ain't true)
Where the stumblers gonna go to watch the lights turn blue?

"Village of the Sun" from the album *Roxy & Elsewhere,* 1974

When I was in high school, in Lancaster, I formed my first band, the Black-Outs. The name derives from when a few of the guys, after drinking peppermint schnapps, purchased illicitly by somebody's older brother, blacked out.

This was the only R&B band in the entire Mojave Desert at that time. Three of the guys (Johnny Franklin, Carter Franklin and Wayne Lyles) were black, the Salazar brothers were Mexican and Terry Wimberly represented the other oppressed peoples of the earth.

Lancaster was a boomtown then. There was a huge influx of technical employees (guys like my Dad) who had dragged their families into this godforsaken place in order to work on the missile projects at Edwards Air Force Base. The original inhabitants, sons and daughters of alfalfa farmers and feed-store owners, held all the newcomers in *low esteem*. We were the people from *"down below"*—a term used to describe anyone who was not from the high desert area where Lancaster was located.

The pecking order at the high school was pretty well laid out: members of the social elite (the lettermen and cheerleaders) were all reproductive by-products of the coots and codgers that ran the local feed & grain business. The lowest rung on the ladder in this 1957 social arrangement was reserved for the sons and daughters of the black families who raised turkeys in an area beyond Palmdale—Sun Village. Only slightly above that rung was a little slot for the Mexicans.

The fact that this was an "integrated" band disturbed a lot of people. This distress was compounded by the fact that, prior to my arrival, someone had put on a rhythm-and-blues show at the fairgrounds, and legend had it that *"colored people brought dope into the valley when they did that damn show, and we're never gonna let that kind of music 'round here again."*

I didn't know about any of this shit when I put the band together. Anyway, my part-time job in high school was work-ing in a record store for a nice lady named Elsie (sorry, I can't remember her last name) who liked R&B. As you can imagine, in a town like that, paying gigs for an "integrated R&B band" were few and far between. One day, I got a great idea: I decided to promote my own gig—a dance—at the local women's club hall, and I asked Elsie to help me. I wanted her to rent the hall for us, and she agreed to do so. Now, I'm pretty sure about this —it was Elsie who had promoted the original "colored-person show with optional chemical commodities"—and I didn't fully grasp the local sociopolitical ramifications of all this when I asked her to book the hall.

So, everything was set—the band rehearsed out in Sun Vil-lage in the Harrises' living room, we had our song list, we were selling tickets, everything was fine. The evening before the dance, while walking through the business district at about six o'clock, I was arrested for vagrancy. I was kept overnight in the jail. They wanted to keep me long enough to cancel the dance —just like in a really bad 1950s teenage movie. It didn't work. Elsie and my folks got me out.

### The Bug

We played the dance. It was a lot of fun. We had an enormous turnout of black students from Sun Village. Motorhead Sherwood was the hit of the evening—he did this weird dance called *"The Bug,"* where he pretended that some creature was tickling the fuck out of him, and he rolled around on the floor, trying to pull it off. When he 'got it off,' he threw it at girls in the audience, hoping that they would flop around on the floor too. A few of them did.

After the dance, as we were packing our stuff into the trunk of Johnny Franklin's wasted blue Studebaker, we found ourselves surrounded by a large contingent of lettermen (The White Horror), eager to cause physical harm to our disgusting little 'integrated band.' This was a mistake because, upon seeing the *Gathering of the Ugly Jackets,* a few dozen 'Villagers' started hauling chains and tire irons out of their trunks, with a look in their eyes that said, *"The night is young."*

The lettermen folded, in total humiliation—God, they're so sensitive about that sort of thing—and went home to their coots & codgers. They remained hostile to me and the other guys in the band all the way through to graduation.

Now, these upstanding young gentlemen were pretty well plugged into the cheerleading squad, and (I know I'm not imagining this) those girls *did not like me very much*—and so it came to pass, during a school assembly to inaugurate the new gymnasium, one of these maidens *(name omitted because I'm a nice guy)* was given the honor of leading the entire student body in a rousing rendition of the school song, a truly nauseating piece of poetry, sung to the the tune of "Too-Ra-Loo-Ra-Loo-Ra (It's an Irish Lullabye)," a song SO SPECIAL that it had to be sung STANDING UP.

In order for her to fulfill her mission, *Ms. Name Omitted* had to get the entire crowd on its feet—even me—which led her to shout sneeringly into the microphone: *"Everybody up! And that means* **YOU TOO, FRANK ZAPPA!"**

I remained seated and, as a hush fell over the audience, without the aid of a PA system, proceeded to spoil her entire afternoon by inquiring: *"Why don't you go fuck yourself,* [name omitted because I'm a nice guy]*!"* This was a word you were not supposed to shout in those days—especially to a girl who jumped up and down on weekends with wads of crepe paper in her hands. She collapsed, sobbing, and had to be helped out the door by the other pom-pom rustlers. It was the worst white female impersonation of the James Brown cape-over-the-shoulder routine ever performed in the Western Hemisphere.

The final wrap-up in the case of *Ms. Name Omitted* took place right around sunrise, after the senior all-night party. I made her laugh while she was eating breakfast at the nicest coffee shop in town, surrounded by her friends, and iced tea came out of her nose.

Anyway, the reason I brought up all this old Lancaster stuff in here is to provide some details concerning the lyrics to "Village of the Sun" (which, by my admittedly peculiar standards, strikes me as a sentimental lyric—and there aren't many of *those* in **my** catalog). We're not going to take it apart line by line, but a few references are worth following up on.

> **It'll take the paint off your car**
> **And wreck your windshield, too**
> **I don't know how the people stand it,**
> **But I guess they all do**

You could always tell if a guy was a 'desert rat' by the windshield on his car. The wind was a constant factor, and so were the microscopic particles of sand it carried, capable of pitting a windshield till you couldn't see out of it anymore, simultaneously reducing the finest custom paint job to garbage in an amazingly short period of time.

(I heard it ain't there—I hope it ain't true)
**Where the stumblers gonna go to watch the lights turn blue?**

I heard that the Village Inn was destroyed by fire in a 'racial incident' in the early 1970s, and that the people in the neighborhood had acquired the habit of shooting each other.

However, while I was working there, it was a great little place. Between sets they'd turn on the jukebox and, as soon as they did, a guy they called *"The Stumbler"* would go over to it, and dance *FOR* it—he'd sort of worship it, as if it was *The Shrine Of Music*. Eventually, he'd be joined by a couple of 'assistant stumblers,' and they'd all bob and weave and grovel in front of it.

I watched this for a few weeks and finally, one night, decided to talk to him. I thought he'd be some kind of space-wino. He wasn't—he was an okay guy. He was drunk, to be sure, but not out of his mind—just happy. He invited me to go to his house. I couldn't turn this offer down—like it says on the *Freak Out!* album: *"Who could imagine . . ."* what kind of a place Mr. Stumbler lived in? I had to find out.

After the gig, I followed him out into the desert a few miles, to a small turkey ranch. There was a handmade sort of house with cinder-block steps. The light was on in the front window. I followed him in. In spite of the shabby exterior, the living room was pleasant, with new furniture and a very large, very new Magnavox stereo. Apparently he'd been listening to some records before his evening romp in front of the jukebox— maybe a pregame warmup. The album on the turntable was Stravinsky's *Firebird Suite*.

## The Soots

After I moved into 'Studio Z,' Don Van Vliet came to visit. I made some recordings with him then which predated the Beefheart Magic Band. The group was called the Soots. Some of the songs were "Metal Man Has Won His Wings," "Cheryl's Canon" and a cover version of the Little Richard song "Slippin' and Slidin' " (as if sung by the Howlin' Wolf). In those days certain record companies would lease the master recordings of independent producers. A producer would bring in a finished piece of product and be given a cash advance against royalties. The producer still owned the master. The releasing company would have the use of it for a few years, after which control of the master would revert to the producer. Through Paul Buff I had met people in Hollywood who worked in those departments, so I went to a guy at Dot Records named Milt Rogers with two of the Soots masters. He listened for a while and said, *"We can't release these—the guitar is distorted."*

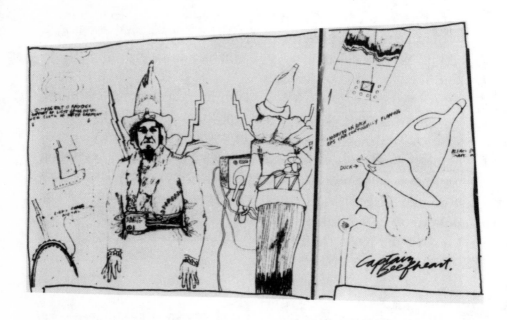

## Bongo Fury

Don eventually formed Captain Beefheart and His Magic Band, released a single through A&M and proceeded to sign an amazing assortment of contracts with just about anybody who had a pen to stick in his hand. He was in contractual bondage all over the place. Companies weren't paying him, but the contracts were written in such a way that he was precluded from recording—they had him tied up for years. When he did the *Bongo Fury* tour with us in 1976, he was just about destitute.

Life on the road with Captain Beefheart was definitely not easy. He carried the bulk of his worldly possessions around in a shopping bag. It held his art and poetry books and a soprano sax. He used to forget it in different places—just walk away and leave it, driving the road manager crazy. Onstage, no matter how loud the monitor system was, he complained that he couldn't hear his voice. (I think that was because he sings so hard he tenses up the muscles in his neck, causing his ears to implode.)

## *Trout Mask Replica*

The high point of our relationship (according to *Rolling Stone* —and aren't they some kind of *authority* on these matters?) was making the *Trout Mask Replica* album together in 1969. Don is not technically oriented, so, first I had to help him figure out what he wanted to do, and then, from a practical standpoint, how to execute his demands.

I wanted to do the album as if it were an *anthropological field recording*—in his house. The whole band was living in a small house in the San Fernando Valley (we could use the word **cult** in here).

I was working with Dick Kunc, the recording engineer on *Uncle Meat* and *Cruising with Ruben & the Jets*. To make remote recordings in those days, Dick had a Shure eight-channel mixer remounted in a briefcase. He could sit in a corner at a live gig with earphones on and adjust the levels, and have the outputs of the briefcase mixer feeding a Uher portable tape recorder.

I had been using that technique with the M.O.I. for road tapes. I thought it would be great to go to Don's house with this portable rig and put the drums in the bedroom, the bass clarinet in the kitchen and the vocals in the bathroom: complete isolation, just like in a studio—except that the band members probably would feel more at home, since they *were* at home.

We taped a few selections that way, and I thought they sounded terrific, but Don got paranoid, accused me of trying to do the album on the cheap, and demanded to go into a **real** recording studio.

So we moved the whole operation to Glendale, into a place called Whitney, the studio I was using at that time—owned by the Mormon church.

The basic tracks were cut—now it was time for Don's vocals. Ordinarily a singer goes in the studio, puts earphones on, listens to the track, tries to sing in time with it and away you go. Don couldn't tolerate the earphones. He wanted to stand in the studio and sing as loud as he could—singing along with the audio leakage coming through the three panes of glass which comprised the control-room window. The chances of him staying in sync were nil—but that's the way the vocals were done.

Usually, when you record a drum set, the cymbals provide part of the 'air' at the top end of the mix. Without a certain amount of this frequency information, mixes tend to sound claustrophobic. Don demanded that the cymbals have pieces of corrugated cardboard mounted on them (like mutes), and that circular pieces of cardboard be laid over the drum heads, so Drumbo wound up flogging stuff that went *"thump! boomph! doof!"* After it was mixed, I did the editing and assembly in my basement. I finished at approximately 6:00 A.M. on Easter Sunday, 1969. I called them up and said, *"Come on over; your album is done.''* They dressed up like they were going to Easter church and came over. They listened to the record and said they loved it.

The last time I saw Don was 1980 or '81. He stopped by one of our rehearsals. He looked pretty beat. He had gone back and forth with some contracts at Warner Bros., and it just hadn't worked out. I suppose he is still living in Northern California, but not recording anymore. He bought some property up there —someplace where he could see whales swim by.

## Let's Make a Movie

Going backwards again . . . shortly after moving into 'Studio Z,' I heard about an auction at the F. K. Rockett Studios in Hollywood. They were going out of business and dumping some scenery. For fifty dollars I bought more scenery than I could fit in the studio, including a two-sided cyclorama—purple on one side for night, blue on the other side for day—a kitchen, a library interior, a building exterior—everything I needed to make a cheap movie. Every piece that would fit through the doors was dragged in, set up and repainted.

I ended up sleeping in the set for *Billy Sweeney's Laboratory*. In the back of the studio, next to the toilet, I built a totally implausible, two-dimensional, cardboard rocket ship.

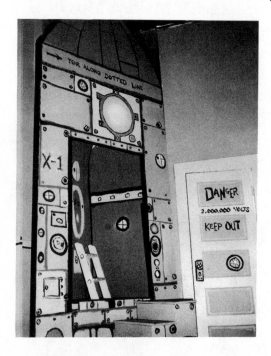

I painted all the sets myself and wrote a script based on the people and facilities available at the time: *Captain Beefheart vs. the Grunt People*. Then came the hard part—trying to raise money to make the movie.

The *Ontario Daily Report* ran a feature story on me and my project in its Sunday centerfold—about how a weird guy in Cucamonga was trying to make a science fiction movie called *Captain Beefheart vs. the Grunt People*. It was probably that story which caused the San Bernardino County vice squad to take an interest in me.

This was in 1962—my hair was short then, but the local folks thought I had *long* hair. The unspoken dress code for a Cucamongan male of that period, for all occasions, was a white, short-sleeved sport shirt with a bow tie (Pee-Wee Herman would have been a fashion plate). T-shirts were considered **avant-garde.**

I put out a casting call for local people to play in the movie. A man came to audition for the role of the asshole: Senator Gurney. I later found out that he was a member of the San Bernardino County vice squad, sent to entrap me.

The vice squad had bored a hole through the studio wall and was spying on me for several weeks. The local political subtext to all this had something to do with an impending real estate development which required the removal of the tenants before Archibald Avenue was widened.

The other part of the subtext had to do with a girl I met in a restaurant in Hollywood. She had a friend—a white girl with a black baby. They needed a place to stay. Next stop, Cucamonga.

She and her girlfriend used to play with the baby on the sidewalk in front of the studio, in plain view of the Holy Rollers lurking in the church across the street. Apparently this caused some psychological stress on the congregation and, shortly thereafter, I was visited by the man who had auditioned. He didn't get the part, but he did turn out to be quite an actor.

A few weeks later he returned, disguised as (don't laugh) a used-car salesman. He told me that some of his friends were having a party the following week. Since I had a sign outside the studio (purchased at the auction) that said *"TV Pictures,"* he wanted to know if I could make him an 'exciting film' for the entertainment of his brethren.

Eager to help (as opportunities to entertain the gentlemen in this fascinating profession do not occur every day), I explained that films cost a lot of money and suggested instead an audio tape.

He gave me a verbal list of all the different sex acts he wished to have included on the tape. I didn't know at the time, but he was broadcasting our conversation to a truck parked outside the studio through his (don't laugh) wristwatch.

wrist
Radio

I told him I could make a tape like that for one hundred dollars, and have it for him the next day. That evening, I manufactured the tape with the help of one of the girls—about half an hour's worth of bogus grunts and squeaky bedsprings. There was no actual sex involved.

I stayed up all night to edit out the laughs and then added some background music—a complete production. The next day the auditionee, whose name was **Detective Willis,** showed up and handed me fifty dollars. I said the deal was for one hundred dollars and refused to hand over the tape—it never changed hands. In spite of that, the door flew open, flashbulbs popped, reporters ran all over the place and handcuffs were slapped on my wrists.

The vice squad arrested me and the girl, and confiscated every tape and every piece of film in the studio. They even took my 8mm projector as 'evidence.'

I was flat broke and couldn't afford a lawyer. I phoned my Dad, who had recently had a heart attack—he couldn't afford a lawyer either. He had to take out a bank loan in order to bail me out.

Once I got out, I went to see Art Laboe. He had released some of my material on his Original Sound label ("Memories of El Monte" and "Grunion Run") and got an advance on a royalty payment, which I used to bail out the girl.

I tried to get the ACLU to take an interest in the case but they wouldn't touch it. They said it wasn't important enough and that, yes, there had been quite a few cases of illegal entrapment in that area. By then my Dad had been able to hire a lawyer, who said my only hope was to plead *nolo contendere* (no contest—or *"I'm so broke I can't even buy justice in Cucamonga, so I'll just give a thousand bucks to this lawyer here and keep my fucking mouth shut, hoping you don't give me the death penalty").*

Before the trial, my white-haired legal expert asked me, *"How could you be such a fool to let this guy con you? I thought* **everybody** *knew Detective Willis. He's the kind of guy who earns his living waiting around in public restrooms to catch queers."*

I answered, *"I don't stand around in toilets—I never heard about guys that get paid to do that."* What was it? My fault that I never dreamed that scum like Willis existed, or that somebody in the government set aside tax dollars to provide guys like him with a salary and a 'research budget'? I was going to have to crank up my imagination a little to compensate for this dreadful revelation.

I was charged with *"conspiracy to commit pornography."* The pornography charge was, under state law, a misdemeanor. The conspiracy charge, on the other hand, was a felony—requiring impressive amounts of penal servitude.

So, how does one engage in *"conspiracy to commit pornography?"* In California, if two or more people discuss the commission of any crime—no matter how small (like jaywalking maybe)—it magically becomes a conspiracy, and the penalties escalate beyond reason. It was presumed that I had discussed the making of the tape with the girl and, therefore, was eligible for ten to twenty years' hard time. Still want to move to California, folks?

At one point in the trial, the judge took me and the girl into his private chambers, along with all the lawyers, listened to the tape and started laughing. It **was** funny—and nowhere near as bizarre as the vocal noises eventually released on side four of the *Freak Out!* album.

The laughter infuriated the twenty-six-year-old assistant DA who prosecuted the case. He demanded, *in the name of justice,* that I be forced to serve time for this heinous offense.

The final verdict: guilty of a misdemeanor. The sentence: **six months in jail, with all but ten days suspended, and three years' probation—during which I could not violate any traffic laws or be in the company of any woman under twenty-one without the presence of a competent adult.**

The sentence also provided for the expungement of my 'criminal record'—after one year there would be nothing on the books saying that I ever went to jail. After the sentence had been pronounced, I was placed in the holding tank in the back of the courthouse, to wait for the sheriff's bus to take me to the county jail. I was reading a long piece of jailhouse poetry scribbled on the wall ("The Ballad of Do-Do Mite") when Detective Willis walked in and said, *"If you'll give me permission to decide which of those tapes we confiscated are* **obscene,** *we'll give you back all the rest of them—***erased.***"*

I said, *"First of all, I do not have the authority to change you from a policeman into a judge, and furthermore, you have no right to do anything to those tapes—the case is closed—and I'm going to come after you to get them back"*—but I never was able to get any of the stuff back, and to this day I don't know what happened to it.

## Let's Go to Jail

The ten days I spent in *Tank C* at the San Bernardino County Jail were very educational. Unless you've been to jail, you can't imagine what it's actually like. This wasn't like the jail in Lancaster where they gave you pancakes in the morning. This was **ugly jail.**

There was an enormous black guy in there called *"Slicks"* (because his lips looked like those big smooth racing tires called *'cheater slicks'*). He was in for stealing copper. **Copper?**

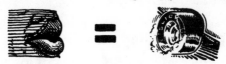

Vagrants used to go to the San Bernardino rail yards and pry the copper brake shoes off boxcars and sell them as scrap metal at a junkyard down the street. Slicks figured that if the junk dealers would pay pretty good for little lumps of copper, they'd pay *real good* for a **really big hunk.** So he planned to break into the local telephone company compound, where huge rolls of telephone cable were stored.

The place had a chain-link fence around it. Slicks planned to climb over the fence, put a pole through one of the rolls—like an axle—throw a rope over the fence, hook it up to the 'axle,' pull on the rope and let the giant roll crush down the fence. Then, he was going to take it out into the desert, burn the insulation off the wire and sell the copper.

He got as far as climbing over the fence and into the compound before the dogs got him. Is this The Crime Of The Century, or what?

There was a Mexican kid in there, about nineteen years old, who had been locked up for three weeks, awaiting *extradition to Beverly Hills* on a *jaywalking ticket.*

The guards left the lights on all night to keep us from sleeping. It was about 104 degrees in there during the day.

We were supplied with one razor blade per day, and one small shower stall at the end of the cell block for forty-four men. The scum on the shower basin was about four inches thick. I didn't shave or take a shower the whole time I was there.

The food was not terrific. One morning I found a giant cockroach in the bottom of my cream o' wheat. I put it in an envelope with a letter to Motorhead's mother. The jail censor found it, and the warden threatened me with solitary if I ever tried anything like that again.

There were two guys they called *the Chow Hounds* who would literally eat **anything.** They would wait until everybody took the first bite of food and found it repulsive, then they would hold their trays out while the other inmates dumped their 'chop suey' onto them, forming miniature haystacks of . . . who the fuck knew what it was.

We were given one half hour to eat before the trays were re-collected. The Chow Hounds's trays were always clean.

This gave me a real good whiff of California law, California lawyers, and an inside look at the California penal industry in action. I haven't seen anything since then to change my opinion of how poorly the system works.


## More Information About What I Eat

After I got out of jail I realized that they were going to tear down the studio and widen the street, and there was nothing I could do about it. It was so sad. I had to get the wire cutters and yank all my equipment out of there and evacuate 'Studio Z.' I had to leave all those sets I had painted, the rocket ship, the mad scientist's lab—everything.

I moved from Cucamonga into a little apartment at 1819 Bellevue Avenue, in the Echo Park section of Los Angeles, and got a job at Wallich's Music City, a record store in downtown L.A. I worked as a salesman in the singles department.

I had just enough money to make bus fare back and forth for the first week, but no money for food. So with my first paycheck I went to a little Filipino market at the bottom of the hill and bought a bag of rice, a bag of red beans, a quart of Miller High Life and some condiments to flavor the rice and beans. I went back to the house and made a big pot of stuff that I planned to live on for the next week.

I ate a big dish of it and drank some beer. My stomach swelled up as if the Alien was going to pop out. I fell off the chair, writhing in agony—cursing the Miller High Life company.

## Let's Meet Jesus

While I was working at the store, a black guy named Welton Featherstone came in, shopping for singles. We got to talking and he asked me if I'd ever been to church. I told him I'd been raised a Catholic, and he said, *"No, I mean have you ever been to a **real** church?"*

He told me about a place called **the World Church,** which happened to be right around the corner from where I lived. It was run by O. L. and Velma Jaggers, a husband-and-wife evangelical team. He said, *"You won't believe it. Tonight's 'Baptism Night'—you gotta go down there and check it out."*

I had actually seen O. L. Jaggers on TV once—he had a local 'religious' program that ran for a short time. During the show I saw, he stood by a blackboard and drew diagrams as part of the 'answer' to a letter he claimed to have received from a deeply troubled viewer. The letter requested a theological explanation of UFOs, and the reverend obliged with this answer:

*"Flying saucers are nothing more than cherubim and seraphim. Because of the great speed at which they travel, their tiny bodies begin to glow when they come in contact with our atmosphere. . . ."*

So, I went to the World Church. It was a large Quonset hut near Temple and Alvarado. Instead of an altar it had a stage with flowers and fake gold knickknacks, displayed between an all-white piano and an all-white organ.

Over the stage was an enormous cardboard cutout of Jesus, posed like Superman in the takeoff position, projecting out, over the audience.

It was illuminated on either side by small clusters of red and blue lights—like the ones they use in the driveways of apartment houses called 'Kon-Tiki.'

The congregation was poor—black, Filipino, Japanese and Mexican. They were subjected to three collections during the hour I was there.

The 'baptism tank' stretched across the rear of the stage. It was a waist-high sort of aquarium-thing, filled with green water. The baptismal contestants wore white robes. Jaggers dunked each victim into the tank, dragging him (sort of by the scruff of the neck), with his head under water, the length of it. One guy couldn't hold his breath and came up gagging. It was pretty disgusting.

As I was about to leave, I heard him announce (into a hand-held Neumann U-87), during the third collection, *"Jesus just told me that you have another thousand dollars in your pockets."* A bunch of people got out of their seats and marched down the aisle, like zombies, dishing up wads of cash. As their reward, he said, *"I'm now going to rain down the fire of the Holy Ghost on you!"* They put their fingertips up and started wiggling them, while Dr. Jaggers shouted: *"Fire! Fire! Fire!"* (into a crowded room).

The people responded by going, *"Ooooo! Woooooo,"* as if it was **really getting all over them.** The organist played scary music and the red and blue lights flashed on the cardboard Jesus.

# CHAPTER 4

# Are We Having A Good Time Yet?

During the early days, when Paul Buff still owned the studio, I met Ray Collins. Ray had sung with a number of R&B groups since the mid-fifties, and had recorded with Little Julian Herrera and the Tigers. In 1964, he was supporting himself by working as a carpenter, and on weekends he sang with a group called the Soul Giants at a bar in Pomona called the Broadside.

Apparently he got into a fight with their guitar player, Ray Hunt, punched him out, and the guitar player quit. They needed a substitute, so I filled in for the weekend.

The Soul Giants were a pretty decent bar band. I especially liked Jimmy Carl Black, the drummer, a Cherokee Indian from Texas with an almost unnatural interest in beer. His style reminded me of the guy with the great backbeat on the old Jimmy Reed records. Roy Estrada, who was Mexican-American and had also been part of the Los Angeles R&B scene since the fifties, was the bass player. Davy Coronado was the leader and saxophone player of the band.

I played the gig for a while, and one night I suggested that we start doing original material so we could get a record contract. Davy didn't like the idea. He was worried that if we played original material we would get fired from all the nice bars we were working in.

The only things club owners wanted bands to play then were "Wooly Bully," "Louie Louie" and "In the Midnight Hour," because if the band played anything original, nobody would dance to it, and when they don't dance, **they don't drink.**

The other guys in the band liked my idea about a record contract and wanted to try the original stuff. Davy departed. It turned out that Davy was absolutely right—we couldn't keep a job anyplace.

One of the places we got fired from was the Tomcat-a-Go-Go in Torrance. During this period in American Musical History, anything with "Go-Go" pasted on the end of it was **really hot.** All you were required to do, if you were a musician desiring steady work, was to grind your way through five sets per night of loud rhythm tracks, while girls with fringed costumes did the twist, as if that particular body movement summed up the aesthetic of the serious beer drinker.

The groups that got the most work were the ones who pretended to be English. Often they were surf bands who wore wigs so that they looked like they had long hair, or added the word **Beatles** somewhere in their band name—you get the drift. Beatle clone groups were all over the place. We didn't have long hair, we didn't have band uniforms and we were ugly as fuck. We were, in the Biblical sense of the word, UNEMPLOYABLE.

A converted shoe store in Norwalk with a beer license also fired us. Of course the gig didn't pay that well: fifteen dollars per night divided by four guys.

There was no bandstand, so we were asked to play in a corner, surrounded by tables upon which three middle-aged women (the pride of Norwalk—perhaps relatives of the owner), wearing dark tan pantyhose to hide what I imagined to be Roquefort cheese molded into the shape of human legs, dangled their putrid fringe in our faces while we played (that's right, you guessed it) "Louie Louie."

# How We Got Our First Manager

While I was living in the bungalow where my stomach almost exploded (1964), I ran into Don Cerveris again. On that occasion, Don introduced me to a friend of his named Mark Cheka, a *'pop artist'* from New York's East Village. Mark was about fifty and wore a beret. He was living in West Hollywood with a waitress from the Ash Grove named Stephanie, who was also sort of beatnik-looking.

The main focus of his work was a group of large paintings that looked like police department pistol targets, designed to be viewed under flashing lights, which gave the illusion that the silhouettes were jumping around. I found this a little baffling—but what the fuck do I know from art? We hung out and had some laughs, in spite of the targets.

I had come to the conclusion that the band needed a manager, and had thought *(Ow! Was I going to regret this one!)* that the person required for this important position needed to be someone with an 'artistic background.' Only then, I reasoned, would our aesthetic be properly understood, and, once we had acquired a manager of such sensitivity, our future success in show business would be assured.

So, I convinced Mark to take the mysterious voyage out to Pomona (fifty miles east), where he might listen to the Mothers, live, at the Broadside. What did I know from managing? I told him that if he wanted to manage the group and could get us some gigs to go ahead.

He didn't really know how to do that. What did he know from managing? He brought in a guy named Herb Cohen, who was managing some folk and folk-rock groups and was looking for another act to pick up. Eventually they became joint managers of our band, with a contract negotiated *'on behalf of the group'* by Herb's brother, an attorney named Martin (Mutt) Cohen.

Suddenly we had a **Real Hollywood Manager**—an industrial professional who had actually been booking groups into **Real Hollywood Nightclubs** *for years,* and would presumably do the same **for us.**

After being forced (at great expense) into the Musicians' Union (local 47), we started to pick up slightly better paychecks; however, our new, highly skilled management team was taking fifteen percent off the top. Almost overnight we had jumped from starvation level to poverty level.

## The Early Freak Scene in L.A.

On Mother's Day, 1964, the name of the band was officially changed to the Mothers. We had begun to build a little constituency on the psychedelic dungeon circuit.

There was a 'scene' evolving in L.A. at that time—something very different from the 'scene' in San Francisco.

San Francisco in the mid-sixties was very chauvinistic, and ethnocentric. To the *Friscoids'* way of thinking, everything that came from THEIR town was **really important Art,** and *anything* from *anyplace* else (especially L.A.) was dogshit. *Rolling Stone* magazine helped to promote this fiction, nationwide.

One of the reasons musicians moved to San Francisco was to be certified as part of **The Real Deal.** The other was the 'Kool-Aid Bonus' at the Grateful Dead concerts.

The scene in Los Angeles was far more bizarre. No matter how 'peace-love' the San Francisco bands might try to make themselves, they eventually had come south to evil ol' Hollywood to get a record deal.

My recollection is that the highest cash advance paid for signing any group during that time was for the Jefferson Airplane—an astounding, staggering, twenty-five thousand dollars, an unheard-of sum of money.

The Byrds were the be-all and end-all of Los Angeles rock then. They were 'It'—and then a group called Love was 'It.' There were a few 'psychedelic' groups that never really got to be 'It,' but they could still find work and get record deals, including the West Coast Pop Art Experimental Band, Sky Saxon and the Seeds, and the Leaves (noted for their cover version of "Hey, Joe").

When we first went to San Francisco, in the early days of the Family Dog, it seemed that everybody was wearing the same costume, a mixture of Barbary Coast and Old West—guys with handlebar mustaches, girls in big bustle dresses with feathers in their hair, etc. By contrast, the L.A. costumery was more random and outlandish.

Musically, the northern bands had a little more country style. In L.A., it was *folk-rock to death*. Everything had that fucking D chord down at the bottom of the neck where you wiggle your finger around—like "Needles and Pins."

The blues was acceptable in San Francisco, but didn't go over in Hollywood at all. I remember the Butterfield Blues Band playing at the Trip. They were hot shit everyplace else in the country, but the people in L.A. would rather have listened to "Mr. Tambourine Man."

## Just Plain Folks

I had seen Lenny Bruce a number of times at Canter's Deli, where he used to sit in a front booth with Phil Spector and eat knockwurst. I didn't really talk with him until we opened for him at the Fillmore West in 1966. I met him in the lobby between sets and asked him to sign my draft card. He said no—he didn't want to touch it.

At that time, Lenny lived with a guy named John Judnich. John earned his living part-time by renting PA systems to local groups. A state-of-the-art system then consisted of two Altec A-7 cabinets powered by a 200-watt amplifier, and **no monitor system** (they hadn't been invented yet—the old-school audio wizards had convinced everyone that it was impossible to put a microphone **that close** to any speaker). Vocalists had no way to hear what they were singing—they could only hear their voices bouncing off the back wall, from the main PA. We used Judnich's system to perform in the Shrine Exposition Hall (about five thousand seats). Anyway, John used to visit every once in a while, and it was on one of these occasions that he introduced us to "Crazy Jerry."

Jerry was about thirty-five or forty, and had been in and out of mental institutions for years. He was addicted to *speed*. When he was a young boy, his mother (who worked for the Probation Department) presented him with a copy of *Gray's Anatomy*. He read it dutifully and noted that in some of the illustrations of muscles it said, *"such and such a muscle, when present—,"* and so it was that Jerry set out to develop the *"when present"* muscles of the human body. He invented 'exercise devices' for those 'special areas' that had not been inhabited by muscle tissue since the book was written.

He didn't look like a bodybuilder, but he was very strong. He could bend re-bars (the steel rods used to reinforce concrete) by placing them on the back of his neck and pulling forward with his arms. As a result of this personal experimentation, he had sprouted weird lumps all over his body—but that was just the beginning.

Somewhere along the line, Jerry discovered that he loved—maybe was even addicted to—**electricity.** He loved getting shocked, and had been arrested a number of times when unsuspecting suburbanites had discovered him in their yards, with his head pressed against the electric meter—because he just wanted to be *near* it.

He and a friend once jumped over the fence of the Nichols Canyon power substation for the same reason. The friend nearly died from electrocution. Jerry escaped.

He lived for a while in Echo Park with a guy called **"Wild Bill the Mannequin-Fucker,"** in a house filled with store mannequins. Wild Bill was a chemist who made speed. Jerry used to carry equipment and ingredients up the steep hill to the lab, in exchange for lodging and free drugs.

Wild Bill had a hobby. The mannequins in the house had been painted and fitted with rubber prosthetic devices so he could fuck them. On festive occasions, he would invite people over to *"fuck his family"*—including a little girl mannequin (named *Caroline Cuntley*).

Jerry wanted to be a musician, so he taught himself to play the piano by using a mirror. He told me that by watching his hands in a mirror, placed *"just so,"* it made the distance between the keys look smaller, and it was a lot easier to learn that way. He also wore a metal hat (an inverted colander) because he was afraid that people were trying to read his mind.

One morning, my wife, Gail, and I woke up to find Crazy Jerry hanging by his knees—like a bat—from the branch of a tree in our backyard, right outside the bedroom window. Later that night, in our basement, I made a recording of his life story.

He didn't have any teeth, so it was hard for him to talk, but in the course of a few hours we learned that, once, when he was in 'The Institution' and they were shooting him full of Thorazine, he was able to jump a twelve-foot fence and get away from the guards.

He went to his mother's house to hide out. The house was locked, so he crawled in under the house and came up in the kitchen through the bread drawer. He got in bed and went to sleep. His mother, the probation officer, came home, found him and turned him in again.

Compared to Jerry and Bill, Lenny Bruce was quite normal. At that time, according to Judnich, Lenny used to stay up all night dressed in a doctor's outfit, listening to Sousa marches and working on his legal briefs. It was sort of colorful in Southern California in those days—but a couple of Republican Administrations and **poof!**

## Duke of What?

In 1965, there were only three clubs in Hollywood that meant anything in terms of being seen by a record company, all of them owned by the same 'ethnic organization.'

One was called the Action, one was called the Trip, and the other was the Whisky-a-Go-Go.

The Action was a place where actors and television personalities went to hang out with hookers; the Whiskey was the permanent residence of Johnny Rivers, who played there for years; and the Trip was the big showplace where all the recording acts played when they came to town—Donovan, the Butterfield Blues Band, Sam the Sham and the Pharoahs; bands like that all played there.

There were a few other clubs in town, but they didn't have the same status as those places. A new group coming to work on the circuit would start at the Action; then, maybe on Johnny Rivers's day off, they could play at the Whisky (but they wouldn't get their name on the marquee, which would still say "Johnny Rivers"), and, if they got a record contract, they got to play in the Trip. We eventually landed a job at the Action.

On Halloween night 1965, during the break before the last set, I was sitting on the steps in front of the place, wearing khaki work pants, no shoes, an 1890s bathing shirt and a black homburg hat with the top pushed up.

John Wayne arrived in a tux with two bodyguards, another guy and two ladies in evening gowns—all very drunk.

Reaching the steps, he grabbed me, picked me up and started slapping me on the back, shouting, **"I saw you in Egypt and you were great . . . and then you blew me!"**

I took an immediate dislike to the guy. Remember, all kinds of show people went to this club, from Warren Beatty to Soupy Sales, so it wasn't unusual for someone like *"the Duke"* to show up.

The place was packed. When I got up on stage to begin the last set, I announced: **"Ladies and gentlemen, as you know, it's Halloween. We were going to have some important guests here tonight—we were expecting George Lincoln Rockwell, head of the American Nazi Party—unfortunately, he couldn't make it—but here's John Wayne."**

As soon as I said that, he got up from his table, stumbled onto the dance floor, and started to make a speech. I leaned the microphone down so everyone could hear it; something along the lines of **"—and if I'm elected, I promise to. . . ."** At that point, one of his bodyguards grabbed him and made him sit down. The other one handed the microphone back to me and told me to cool it or there was going to be BIG TROUBLE.

At the end of the show, the manager of the club came over to me and said, **"Be nice to the Duke, because when he gets like this he starts throwing fifty-dollar bills around."**

I had to pass his table on my way out. As I went by, he got up and smashed my hat down on top of my head. I took it off and popped it back out. This apparently annoyed him, as he shouted, **"You don't like the way I fix hats? I've been fixin' hats for forty years."** I put it back on my head and he smashed it down again. I said, **"I'm not even gonna give you a chance to apologize,"** and walked out.

## How We Got Our First Record Deal

Not long after that, Johnny Rivers went on tour and we were hired as a temporary replacement at the Whisky-a-Go-Go. By chance, Tom Wilson, a staff producer for MGM Records, was in town. He was up the street, at the Trip, watching a 'big group.' Herb Cohen talked him into a quick visit to the Whisky. He walked in while we were playing our 'BIG BOOGIE NUMBER'—the only one we knew, totally unrepresentative of the rest of our material.

He liked it and offered us a record deal (thinking he had acquired the ugliest-looking white blues band in Southern California), and an advance of twenty-five hundred dollars.

The average budget for an LP in those days was six to eight thousand dollars. Most albums consisted of the A and B sides of an artist's hit single, plus seven or eight other "filler tunes" —just enough to satisfy the minimum contractual time per side (fifteen minutes).

The other industrial norm was that most groups didn't really play their own instruments for the basic tracks on their albums. They'd arrive in a Purple-Hazish condition and play the song a few times, after which the producer or A&R man would tweeze it, then the studio musicians who had been standing by would learn the tweezed version and play it—in tune, and with a *"good beat."* There was a whole bunch of 'session specialists' who ghosted for the major acts then (the Monkees were the classic example of one of these acts).

We played all our own basic tracks on *Freak Out!*, with studio musicians added only for orchestrational color.

## Hungry Freaks

Wilson was based in New York, and had gone back there after booking the dates for the sessions. We were broke. MGM didn't give us the advance right away—the money was supposed to come later.

The producer of *Run Home Slow,* Tim Sullivan, still owed me some money for the film score. When I finally located him, he was working out of a building on Seward Street, in Hollywood (Decca's old scoring stage).

He didn't have any cash but, in lieu of payment, he let us use his place to rehearse in. We had the best rehearsal hall any band could ever want, but we were starving. We collected soda bottles and cashed them in, using the proceeds to buy white bread, bologna and mayonnaise.

## Thanks, Jesse

Finally, the day of the first session rolled around—about three in the afternoon at a place called TTG Recorders, Sunset Boulevard at Highland Avenue.

The MGM Records accounting representative was a stingy old guy named Jesse Kaye. Jesse walked around with his hands behind his back, pacing the floor while we were recording, making sure nobody ran up any extra overtime costs by going beyond the three hours allotted for each session.

During a break, I went into the control booth and told him: *"Look, Jesse, we got a little problem here. We would like to stay on schedule. We would like to get this all done in the three hours—these glorious three hours that you've given us to make this record—but we don't have any money and we're all hungry. Could you lend me ten bucks?"*

There was a drive-in restaurant downstairs from the studio, and I figured ten 1965 dollars would be enough to feed the whole band and get us through the session. Well, Jesse's reputation was such that, if anybody had seen him lending money to a *musician,* he would have been **ruined.** He didn't say yes and he didn't say no. I walked away, figuring that was it—I wasn't going to ask him anymore. I went back into the studio and prepared for the next take. Jesse walked in. He had his hands behind his back. He came over, casually, and pretended to shake hands with me. There was a ten-dollar bill rolled up in his palm. He tried to pass it to me, except I didn't realize what was going on, and the money fell on the floor. He made a face like **"Oh, shit!"** and grabbed it up real fast, hoping nobody had seen it, and stuffed it into my hand. Without this act of kindness from Jesse, there might not have been a *Freak Out!* album.

## Who Are the Brain Police?

Tom Wilson had returned to Los Angeles for the sessions. He was in the control booth as we began recording the first tune, "Any Way the Wind Blows." He was tapping his foot and nodding (the way record producers do in the movies). The second tune was "Who Are the Brain Police?" . . .

What will you do if we
Let you go home,
And the plastic's all melted
And so is the chrome—
**WHO ARE THE BRAIN POLICE?**

What will you do when the
Label comes off,
And the plastic's all melted
And the chrome is too soft—
**WHO ARE THE BRAIN POLICE?**

What will you do if the
People you knew
Were the plastic that melted
(And the chromium too?)
**WHO ARE THE BRAIN POLICE?**

"Who Are the Brain Police?" from the album *Freak Out!*, 1966

I could see through the window that he was scrambling toward the phone to call his boss—probably saying: **"Well, uh, not** *exactly* **a 'white blues band,' but . . . sort of."**

*Freak Out!* was a double album, and all the songs on it were **about** something. It wasn't as if we had a hit single and we needed to build some filler around it. Each tune had a function within an overall satirical concept.

You're probably wondering
Why I'm here,
And so am I! So am I!
Just as much as you wonder,
'Bout me bein' in this place,
That's just how much I marvel
At the lameness on your face—
You rise each day the same old way,
And join your friends out on the street,
Spray your hair
And think you're neat,
I think your life is incomplete,
But maybe that's not for me to say—
They only pay me here to play.

"You're Probably Wondering Why I'm Here" from the album *Freak Out!*, 1966

As the sessions continued, the more enthusiastic Wilson became. About the middle of the week I told him, *"I would like to rent five hundred [1965] dollars' worth of percussion equipment for a session that starts at midnight on Friday, and I want to bring all the freaks from Sunset Boulevard into the studio to do something special."* He agreed.

We got the equipment and the freaks and, starting at midnight, recorded what turned out to be side four of the album. Wilson was on acid that night. I didn't know he had taken it— he told me later. I've tried to imagine what he must have been thinking, sitting in that control room, listening to all that weird shit coming out of the speakers, and being responsible for telling the engineer, Ami Hadani (who was not on acid), what to do.

## What's in a Name?

By the time *Freak Out!* was edited and shaped into an album, Wilson had spent twenty-five or thirty thousand dollars of MGM's money—a ridiculous sum in those days, even for a double LP. (In fact, I believe *Freak Out!* was **the first** rock double LP.)

We were then informed that they couldn't release the record —MGM executives had convinced themselves that no DJ would ever play a record on the air by a group called **"The Mothers"** (as if our name was going to be *The Big Problem*).

They insisted that we change it, and so the stock line is:

**"Out of necessity, we became the Mothers of Invention."**

*Freak Out!* by *"The Mothers of Invention"* finally hit the street. Listeners at the time were convinced that I was up to my eyebrows in chemical refreshment. No way. As a matter of fact, I had several arguments with the guys in the band who **were** into *'consciousness-altering entertainment products.'* The whole thing blew up at a band meeting when Herb Cohen wanted to get rid of Mark Cheka. Cohen said we could continue to give Mark a percentage, but he wanted to take over since, basically, Mark didn't know squat about the management business.

*"Well, as long as we're cleaning house here,"* some of the guys thought, *"let's get rid of that Zappa asshole too."* Yes, folks, some members of the band wanted me to **go away and leave them alone** because (don't laugh) **I wasn't using drugs.**

The classic line of the meeting was delivered by Ray Collins: *"You need to go to Big Sur and* **take acid** *with someone who believes in* **God.***"* Pheeeeeuuuuuuw.

## Our First Tour

Undaunted by this fascinating suggestion, I continued my duties as the *'resident asshole.'*

The very first Mothers of Invention tour took place in 1966, at a time when hardly anybody outside of L.A. and San Francisco had long hair. We were all ugly guys with weird clothes and long hair: just what the entertainment world needed. Fuck all those beautiful groups.

It was a low-budget promo tour, set up by MGM, taking us first to Washington, D.C., for a television show called *Swingin' Time* on channel 20—a TV dance show for the sons and daughters of our nation's leaders.

The show had put together a *"Freak Out Dance Contest,"* and invited the contestants to dress *"freakishly"* for the event. How **freakish** were they? The weirdest guy in the room was wearing two different-colored socks.

In Detroit, we did a television show where we were asked to do something **perverted**: *"lip-sync our hit."* We didn't have a 'hit,' but the producer said, *"Lip-sync your hit—or else."* So I asked, *"Do you have a prop department here?"* Fortunately, there was one.

From it, I gathered an assortment of random objects and built a set. We had been asked to pretend to play either "How Could I Be Such a Fool?" or "Who Are the Brain Police?" so I suggested that each member of the group choose a *repeatable physical action,* not necessarily in sync with (or even related to) the lyrics, and do it over and over until our spot on the show was concluded—Detroit's first whiff of homemade prime-time Dada.

Next stop: Dallas. We flew into Love Field and found ourselves walking down a long hall, full of soldiers and sailors—stopped dead in their tracks, staring in *utter disbelief.* They didn't say anything. They didn't throw anything at us. They didn't shoot us like *Easy Rider*—they just **stood** there.

We were then whisked off to a shopping mall, to some downstairs place where yet another TV teenage dance show was in progress. We played live on that one.

The high point of the performance was Carl Franzoni, our 'go-go boy.' He was wearing ballet tights, *frugging violently.* Carl has testicles which are bigger than a breadbox. **Much** bigger than a breadbox. The looks on the faces of the Baptist teens experiencing *their grandeur* is a treasured memory.

## My Fabulous Wife

At the end of this grueling three-city tour, I was introduced to a fascinating little vixen, employed as a secretary at the Whisky-a-Go-Go: **Adelaide Gail Sloatman.** It took a couple of minutes, but I fell (don't laugh) in love, and we started living together—eventually memorializing the union in a severely ridiculous civil ceremony in 1967.

We got married a couple of days before I left for the first European tour. She was nine months pregnant, with delivery imminent. We went to the New York City Hall, arriving just before closing time. I didn't have a wedding ring—in fact, Gail **still** doesn't have a wedding ring.

There was a vending machine on the counter where you picked up the license that sold ballpoint pens with *"Congratulations from Mayor Lindsay"* printed on them: ten cents apiece. I had to buy one in order to fill out the form.

We then rushed over to one of the little *'marrying cubicles.'* It was green inside, and reminded me of a pool table. In the middle of the room was a cheesoid Formica *replica-pulpit.* On it was a time clock, the kind you would punch in on when you went to work. The *Man In Charge* punched our card, recited **The Formula,** and asked for **The Ring.** I told him I had a ballpoint pen, and pinned it on Gail's bulging maternity dress.

Yes, folks, I do have a little bit of **something** in common with my 'brother-in-Christ,' Pat Robertson—except I never lied about it.

## Brown Shoes Don't Make It

In its initial release, MGM reported to us that the sales of *Freak Out!* amounted to a paltry thirty thousand units—not exactly a hit. Our royalty was sixty or seventy cents per double LP, which wasn't so bitchen either. On paper, at least, we had a flop. The accounting statements indicated that **WE owed MGM money.**

When it came time for us to do our second album, *Absolutely Free,* MGM proclaimed that we couldn't spend more than eleven thousand dollars on it.

A world of secret hungers,
Perverting the men who make your laws
Every desire is hidden away,
In a drawer, in a desk,
By a Naugahyde chair,
On a rug where they walk and drool,
Past the girls in the office.

"Brown Shoes Don't Make It" from the album *Absolutely Free,* 1967

## How They Used to Screw You

The recording schedules were ridiculous, making it impossible to perfect *anything* on the album. It was typical of the kind of bullshit we had to put up with until I got my own studio.

When you record for **'a label,'** you're always working on *their* budget—on *their* schedule. When the budget runs out, **that's it.** If the master doesn't sound right, what the fuck do they care? It goes out anyway—it's only 'product' to them.

During this period, I began to hear rumors about problems within MGM. They had one of the best-selling records of all time: the soundtrack to *Dr. Zhivago*—but it turned out that at least a quarter of a million units had disappeared out the back door of the pressing plant, and the same seemed to be true of other MGM artists' albums, including ours.

This trick was called *"The Pressing Plant Overrun."* It was pretty simple: the pressing plant would get an order to press, say, *two thousand units* of *Dr. Zhivago*. The guy operating the press would then be instructed (by whom? we still don't know—) to run off **four thousand units,** then some other guy would pull up in the middle of the night, open the back of his station wagon (or truck or whatever), the boxes of records would get dumped in, then he'd drive to another state and either sell the records to 'friendly dealers' or trade them for rooms full of furniture—and the artists involved would get an accounting statement that showed their sales to be **half** of what they actually were. Everybody was having such a good time in **'flower-power-land'** they didn't realize what kind of hose job they were getting.

That was only the beginning of my problems with multinational record companies. By 1984 I had sued the two industry giants, CBS and Warners, and had learned a lot more about 'creative accounting practices.'

We went through a major legal struggle with MGM over royalties on those first LPs. It took about eight years to resolve. Part of their defense in the case was based on a claim that they had had a (don't laugh) FIRE **AND** A FLOOD in the part of the building where the records pertaining to royalties were stored.

# One Sick Motherfucker with a Razor Blade

I usually don't listen to my records once they are finished and released, but in 1968, during the second European tour, *We're Only In It for the Money* won the Dutch equivalent of a Grammy.

There was an award ceremony, during which I was handed a little statue—with the album playing in the background. I noticed that whole chunks of songs were missing. Someone at MGM had been offended by the lyrics and had arbitrarily chopped portions of them out—in one instance, about eight bars of music—just enough to fuck up the song on the way to the bridge.

**The Big Offender** was a line from the song "Let's Make the Water Turn Black":

> **And I still remember Mama,**
> **With her apron and her pad,**
> **Feeding all the boys at Ed's Cafe—**

I couldn't understand why anyone would chop that out. Years later I learned that an MGM executive was **convinced** that the word *"pad"* referred to a **sanitary napkin.** He became obsessed with the idea that a waitress somewhere was **feeding sanitary napkins to people in a restaurant,** and demanded (in violation of our contract) that it be removed. That guy needs to see a doctor.

When I realized that the record had been censored, I told the people at the ceremony: *"I can't accept this statue. I prefer that the award be presented to the guy who modified the record, because what you're hearing is more reflective of HIS work than mine."* I handed the prize to some people from a 'countercultural' rock publication, who desecrated it nicely and put it on display in their office.

# Boogers from Hell

"Let's Make the Water Turn Black" was a true story about two brothers, Ronnie and Kenny Williams—a couple of musicians I knew in 1962 during the early Paul Buff/Pal Records era (it was Ronnie who introduced me to Paul).

It is difficult to describe these guys, their family and their 'hobbies'—so much of it will sound like fiction—however, let me assure you that this has all been documented on tape, in their own words.

The family was from Arkansas. The Dad (Dink) was a furniture salesman in San Bernardino, but, back in the way-back-when, he used to play 'bones' or 'spoons' in a minstrel show. To relive the golden days of yesteryear he would, from time to time, force his children to accompany him (Ronnie on guitar, Kenny on trombone) in a living room replay of a minstrel routine called *"Lazy Bones."*

The kids often found this to be an inconvenience, as they were fascinated by, and constantly perfecting new techniques for, The Manly Art Of Fart-Burning. Kenny explained to me that it was scientific—that it demonstrated (this is a real quote) *"Compression, ignition, combustion and exhaust."*

I can't remember the Mom's name, but she was a pleasant, hardworking lady who helped pay the rent by waitressing at a place called Ed's Cafe, in Ontario.

Ronnie attended high school in Chula Vista, a San Diego suburb, dropping out in his sophomore year. While in school, he made pocket change by selling homemade *'raisin wine'* to kids in his class.

It was an evil confection, made out of raisins, yeast, sugar and water—then sun-fermented (for at least a couple of days) in mason jars on the roof of the old homestead. (If you care to try this yourself, remember, as Ronnie once explained: *"You wait for the raisins to swell up to about the size of deer turds. . . ."*)

This eventually led to trouble when, in an attempt to raise his product's octane level, he built a still in the backyard, and it exploded.

Ever the professional, he maintained a thick book of 'recipes' for new and exciting beverages. He called it *THE MACHA*. When he finally trusted me enough to display this masterpiece, I asked him, *"Why do you call it 'THE MACHA'?"*

He swallowed some sinus phlegm and said, *"Cuz it reminds me of 'the Mafia'—hyulk, hyulk. . . ."*

After the explosion, the family moved to Ontario, California. Kenny got arrested for something (I don't know what) and went to 'reform school.' In taped interviews he refers to this experience by saying: *"While I was away at boarding school—"*

So, while Kenny was away at 'boarding school,' Ronnie and his pal Dwight Bement (eventually the tenor sax player for Gary Puckett and the Union Gap) had the house pretty much to themselves. Both parents were working, so the guys were in *Dropout Heaven,* spending their days playing poker in Ronnie's bedroom.

During the games (we can't be sure how this part got started), they began a competition of *'booger-smearage'*—on the window by the bed. This window eventually became opaque. One day, the Mom stuck her head into the room and got hysterical, demanding immediate removal of the frosting. According to Ronnie: *"We had to use Ajax and a putty knife to get the damn things off."*

Eventually, Kenny came back from 'boarding school.' For some reason he didn't want to stay in the house, and so he took up residence in the garage—with Motorhead (this was before Motorhead moved in with me).

It was winter when they lived out there and, since there was no toilet in the garage—and not wishing to brave the elements —the lads relieved themselves nightly into some of the Mom's mason jars, lined up along the garage wall, awaiting the installation of next season's home-canned fruits.

Now, Ronnie wasn't the only cardplayer in the family—Kenny also liked to play—and on a few of those cold winter nights, Kenny and Motorhead hosted a few games for the other fun guys in the neighborhood. Eventually, the beer took effect, and everybody started reaching for the jars.

The jars weren't dumped—they were saved as 'trophies.'

Many games later, the boys ran out of jars. The solution to this problem came in the form of a large earthenware crock (like the one Ronnie used to watch the raisins puff up in).

In a festive ceremony, all trophy jars were poured into the crock—just to find out how much piss there was around there [*"Wow! Look at that! We're really pissin' a lot! Jesus H. Christ, what a lot of piss we got here! Haw haw haw . . ."*].

Eventually, Kenny moved back into the house, and Motorhead moved in with me. One day, a few months later, Motorhead visited Kenny and, just for old times' sake, took a peek at the crock in the garage. Lifting the board which covered it, they beheld several 'denizens' swimming in the piss—unknown 'things' that looked sort of like tadpoles.

Kenny fished one out and plopped it on the shop bench. It had a tail, and a head which Kenny described as being *"about as big as your little fingernail—white, with a black dot in the middle of it. . . ."*

Motorhead poked it with a nail and *"some clear stuff came out."* Proud of their scientific discovery, they informed Dink. They were then instructed by the bewildered furniture salesman to *"pour that whole damn crock down the toilet!,"* which is what they did—and to this day, friends, somewhere in the depths of the Ontario sewage system, horrible jelly-wigglers gurgle and multiply—waiting for *their moment* of 'heavy rotation' on MTV.

## A Mere Oversight

Eventually, MGM made an 'innocent mistake': **they missed an option pickup.** They forgot to send us the little piece of paper that says, *"We pick up your option—you are still under contract to us—we still want you to make records for us."*

With that as leverage, we negotiated a **'logo deal.'** Bizarre Productions was created: a label within the MGM company structure—a semi-independent entity—and so *Cruising with Ruben & the Jets* and *Mothermania* were released on the Bizarre/Verve label, distributed by MGM.

There was a lot of nonsense in the press when *Cruising with Ruben & the Jets* came out, about how it had 'fooled people.' I heard one story that a DJ in Philly was playing it like crazy until he found out it was the Mothers, at which point he yanked it. The fact is, everybody knew it was the

Mothers of Invention because it said so on the cover: *"Is this the Mothers of Invention recording under a different name in a last ditch attempt to get their cruddy music on the radio?"*

I conceived that album along the same lines as the compositions in Stravinsky's neoclassical period. If he could take the forms and clichés of the classical era and pervert **them,** why not do the same with the rules and regulations that applied to doo-wop in the fifties?

The listener wouldn't *really* think that a song like "Stuff Up the Cracks" was an honest-to-goodness 1950s song. In terms of timbre, it's right on the fringe (because of the vocal parts)—but those chords would never happen in original doo-wop.

The songs of that period were locked into a choice of three *formula/flavors:* **I-VI-IV-V** ("Earth Angel"), or **I-II-I-II** ("Nite Owl"), or **I-IV-V** ("Louie Louie"). Very seldom would you hear a **III** chord or a flat **VII** chord—or hear someone going from **I** to flat **VII.** There were only a few examples of *that* type of harmonic deviation during the fifties—the best one being

"This Paradise" by Donald Woods and the Bel-Aires on Flip—
so our chord progressions were not exactly part of that tradition.

What **was** consistent with tradition on that album was the
approach to the harmony, the type of vocal style and timbre
used in it, and the simplicity of most of the beats. Of course,
some of the lyrics were on a **sub-Mongoloid** level, but that
was just another norm, carried to an extreme.

> **We made a wish and threw in a coin**
> **And since that day**
> **Our hearts have been joined**
> **So all you young lovers,**
> **Wherever you are**
> **The Fountain of Love**
> **Is not very far**

Give me a fucking break! Is this a song about a douche bag,
**or what?** Some people take that kind of lyric **seriously!**

There are some dead giveaways in that album, too. For instance, on the fadeout of "Fountain of Love" you can hear the
opening notes of *Rite of Spring*. One song has the background
chant of "Earth Angel" superimposed on the chant from another song, and so on.

The satire in *Ruben* worked on two or three levels. **I detest
'love lyrics.'** I think one of the causes of bad mental health in
the United States is that people have been raised on 'love lyrics.'

You're a young kid and you hear all those 'love lyrics,' right?
Your parents aren't telling you the truth about love, and you
can't really learn about it in school. You're getting the bulk of
your 'behavior norms' mapped out for you in the lyrics to some
dumb fucking love song. It's a subconscious training that creates
a desire for an imaginary situation which will *never exist for you.*
People who buy into that mythology go through life feeling
that they got cheated out of something.

What I think is **very cynical** about some rock and roll songs —especially today—is the way they say: **"Let's make love."** What the fuck kind of *wussy* says shit like **that** in the real world? You ought to be able to say *"Let's go fuck,"* or at least *"Let's go* **fill-in-the-blank***"*—but you gotta say *"Let's make love"* in order to get on the radio. This creates a semantic corruption, by changing the context in which the word *'love'* is used in the song.

When they get into drooling about *love* as a **'romantic concept'**—especially in the lyrics of sensitive singer/songwriter types—that's another shove in the direction of **bad mental health.**

Fortunately, lyrics over the last five or six years have gotten to be less and less important, with 'art rock groups' and new wavers specializing in 'nonjudgmental' or 'purposely inconsequential' lyrics. People have stopped *listening* to the lyrics—they are now only **'pitched mouth noises.'**

## Headin' for the Last Roundup

In 1966 and '67, the L.A.P.D. and the Sheriff's Department went to war with the freaks in Hollywood. Every weekend people were rounded up (with no warrants presented or charges stated) as they walked on Sunset Boulevard, forced into Sheriff's buses, driven downtown, held hostage for the evening, then let go—all because they had LONG HAIR.

The places where they used to eat (Ben Frank's on Sunset and Canter's Deli on Fairfax) were under constant surveillance. The city government threatened to take away Elmer (Whisky-a-Go-Go) Valentine's liquor license if he didn't stop booking long-haired acts into his club. There was no place left to work in Hollywood.

## Our New Home

Gail and I moved to New York in 1967 to play in the Garrick Theater on Bleecker Street. The first place we stayed, before we could find an apartment, was the Hotel Van Rensselaer on Eleventh Street. We were living in a small room on one of the upper floors. I was working on the album cover illustration for *Absolutely Free* at a desk by the window. I remember the place being so dirty I couldn't keep the soot off the artwork.

We lived on sandwiches and coffee from the Smiler's Deli around the corner. It was cold enough that a container of milk left on the outside windowsill wouldn't go bad for days (but when you brought it back in it was covered with soot). The Fugs, who were also working in the Village then, tried to launch a protest against **Con Ed** (the suspected source of this evil) by urging concerned citizens to **mail their snot** to the head office.

We were amazed at this grubbiness because we had just come from California, where we had a fairly nice house in Laurel Canyon (for two hundred dollars a month) with a fireplace, two bedrooms, a kitchen, a garage and our very own patch of dirt in the backyard. There were trees around. It was sort of pretty, and we had privacy.

Gail went out to look for an apartment near the Garrick and finally found a place at 180 Thompson Street (apartment 3-C), right around the corner from the theater. I took a break from rehearsal and went with her to look at it. When we got to the door, we found that a wino had passed out, pissed himself, and was wedged against it. In 1967, this was what you got in New York City for two hundred dollars a month.

Our New Home had a bedroom, a living room–kitchenette and a bathroom—with a view of a brick wall out the window. We lived there for several months before we found a sublet near Seventh Avenue on Charles Street, the ground floor of a brownstone.

It was our privilege to occupy this space during the garbage strike. The debris was piled up right outside our bedroom window. We listened to the rats at night.

During the time we lived in the Thompson Street cracker-box, my brother visited me from Los Angeles, along with Dick Barber, his friend from high school (who eventually became our road manager) and another friend, Bill Harris (now a prominent film critic). The three of them were sleeping on the living room floor.

About that time I got the idea for the *We're Only In It for the Money* album, and was looking for an artist capable of creating the ultimate parody of the *Sgt. Pepper* cover. I heard about Cal Schenkel, a former boyfriend of the girl who was our opening act at the Garrick. He came up from Philadelphia and showed me his portfolio. The stuff was great, but the only way to hire him was to find a place for him to stay in New York. (And guess where it was?) So it was Bobby, Bill, Calvin and Dick, on the floor, in sleeping bags.

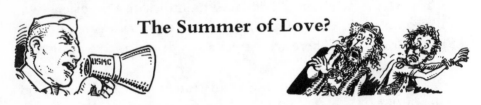

## The Summer of Love?

During that summer, Greenwich Village was absurd. Any rumor, no matter how stupid, could turn out to be true—so, at one point, rumor had it that **a hippie had killed a Marine.**

Stories circulated that the Marines were going to come to the Village and kill all the hippies. Everybody who was hippie-looking had their eyes peeled for people who looked like Marines. Everyone figured they wouldn't *really* come in dressed like Marines, so they were also on the lookout for anyone with hair that was too short, or who had clean fingernails.

In the midst of this, we were working the Garrick, six nights a week, two shows a night, and rehearsing in the afternoon.

New York weather in the summertime is pretty disgusting. Sometime around the first of June, the air conditioner died and the owner of the theater *(David Lee Roth's Dad, I'm told)* decided that it would be too expensive to fix it.

Picture a room like a long, narrow tunnel (actually, a former 'art movie' theater) that holds three hundred people; easily 102 degrees at all times, totally humid, and no air circulating.

The floor of that stage had a green rug on it. When we filmed the "Mr. Green Genes" video, the people on stage had stomped a bunch of vegetables and whipped cream into it, and it never got cleaned.

The stuffed giraffe and the other toys we used in the show lived in a box on the side of the stage, along with chunks of dead vegetables. All organic matter in the theater had begun to reproduce itself, and was producing 'a bad smell.'

## Where's the Beef?

The rotten vegetables were only part of the early M.O.I. 'entertainment statement.' I once proposed the construction of an apparatus which would have been a cross between a gallows and an old-fashioned shower stall. The shower curtain was to have been an American flag, and behind it, hanging from the gallows, was to be a side of beef (at room temperature). I proposed to roll this out at the end of each show, play a fanfare and open the curtain, releasing flies into the audience.

## Our Boys in Uniform

Anyway, we were in there every afternoon, rehearsing. One day, three Marines, in full dress uniform, came through the door, sat down in the front row—and **didn't say anything.** I asked them how they were doing and, of course, did they want to sit in?

I asked them if they knew any songs. One of the guys said that, yeah, they knew "House of the Rising Sun" and "Everybody Must Get Stoned." I said, *"That's great. Would you guys like to sing with us tonight? We'd just LOVE to have Marines singing on stage with us."* They said, yeah, they would.

I said, *"Go across the street to the Tin Angel, have a few drinks, and come back when the show is on."*

When they came back, I brought them up on stage—although it **must** have been against regulations for them to do this kind of thing in full dress—and had them sing "Everybody Must Get Stoned." By that time they were pretty well wrecked, so I suggested, **"Why don't you show the folks in the audience what you guys do for a living."**

I handed them a big baby doll and said, **"Suppose you just pretend that this is a 'gook baby.' "** They proceeded to rip and mutilate the doll while we played. It was *truly horrible.* After it was over, I thanked them and, with a quiet musical accompaniment, showed the ruined parts of the doll to the audience. Nobody was laughing.

## Jimi's New Tailor

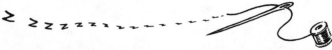

On another occasion, Jimi Hendrix sat in with us. I didn't know him before then, and I can't remember how I was introduced to him—probably met him at the Tin Angel. A few days later he came to visit our cubicle on Charles Street with his friend, drummer Buddy Miles. Jimi was wearing green velvet pants—all decked out—on his way to a party with Buddy. (The only thing that Buddy said was **"Hi, Frank,"** after which he sat on the couch, leaned back and passed out, snoring.) They were there for about an hour and a half. Buddy had a nice nap, and Hendrix ripped his pants at the crotch while demonstrating a dance step. Gail sewed them up for him. When it was time to leave he said, **"Come on, Buddy."** The snoring stopped, and they left.

## Sal Lombardo

One day, on my way to lunch at the T.A., a guy wearing a buckskin suit—*in July*—with a black scraggly beard and hair sticking out all over the place, came up to me and said, *"I want to be in your band."*

*"What do you play?"* I asked. *"Nothing,"* he answered. *"Okay,"* I said, *"you've got the job."* The guy's name was Sal Lombardo.

Later that night, I handed him some maracas and a tambourine—he didn't get paid, but he got to stand onstage and *'be in the band.'*

Part of our show included the concept of nightly *'enforced recreation'*—sort of like audience participation, only **more dangerous.**

We'd be playing something and I'd lean over and say, *"Sal, see that guy over there? Go get him."* Sal would then snatch the guy out of the audience and drag him onstage. It was then my privilege to invent *'recreational activities'* for these hapless individuals, inducing them to *'participate.'* You can see Sal in the video of *Uncle Meat*. He's the guy lying on his back with a corncob in his mouth, having whipped cream squirted in his face during 'Mr. Green Genes." That night his entire buckskin suit was covered with **real** whipped cream. He never had it cleaned. Do you know what **real whipped cream** smells like on BO buckskin at 100-plus degrees? We're talking *bestiality* here.

When we stopped working at the Garrick, Sal went off to

South America to find some Forbidden City. I saw him again about ten or twelve years later, when he showed up at a gig in Sacramento. He was operating a pizza place then. He swore he had found *the Secret City of (fill in the blank with an eleven-syllable word)* in South America—housing untold riches—but he didn't have any way to get the stuff out.

## Loeb & Leopold

There were two suburban Jewish guys who attended the Garrick shows relentlessly. They called themselves '*Loeb & Leopold*' (not the real '*Loeb & Leopold,*' but an incredibly lifelike simulation). They came to at least thirty shows.

At the end of our run they came backstage, opened up their wallets and, with tears in their eyes, showed me all their ticket stubs. They **loved** the Garrick shows.

One of the guys—I'm pretty sure his name was Mark Trottiner—liked to run up the aisle, jump on stage, grab the microphone out of my hand and scream into it as loud as he could. Then he would fall on the stage, roll over like a dog and urge me to spit Pepsi-Cola all over his body. **What a crowd-pleaser.**

Ten years later, I was doing a Halloween show at the Palladium, and I looked out into the audience and thought I saw him. It **had** to be him. I said, *"Aren't you the guy who used to—?"* It **was** him. He grew up to become a record distributor in Queens.

## Louie the Turkey

Another regular was a guy we called *"Louie the Turkey"*—because of his laugh. His real name was Louis Cuneo. He wound up on the *Lumpy Gravy* album as one of the people talking about incomprehensible stuff, inside a piano.

We would always know when Louie was in the theater be-cause we could hear him in the back of the room. I would invite him onstage, give him a stool to sit on, hand him the micro-phone and stop the music. He would sit there and laugh—**at nothing**—and the whole audience would laugh with him for five minutes. Then we thanked him, and he'd leave.

## Custom Entertainment

We opened the Garrick run during Easter vacation 1967. There were lines around the block, in the snow. However, as soon as school reconvened, attendance plummeted. On our worst night we had **three paying customers.** We told them we were going to give them an evening of customized, personal entertainment.

There was a passageway in back of the Garrick that led downstairs to the Cafe au-Go-Go's kitchen. Everybody in the band went down and got hot cider and bunches of little snacks. We put towels over our arms, like waiters, went back, served our audience their refreshments and talked with them for an hour and a half.

On another occasion we had only ten or fifteen people. We asked them whether **they** would like to be the band for the night. They thought it was a good idea, so we gave them our instruments, sat in the audience for an hour and a half and listened to **them** play the show.

# Tom & Jerry

I was in Manny's Musical Instruments in New York sometime in 1967, and it was raining outside. A little guy came walking in, kind of wet, and introduced himself as Paul Simon. He said he wanted me to come to dinner at his house that night, and gave me the address. I said okay and went there.

As I walked in the door, Paul was on his hands and knees in front of what appeared to be a Magnavox stereo—the same model preferred by "the Stumbler" from Sun Village. He had his ear right up to the speaker, listening to a Django Reinhardt record.

Within moments—for no apparent reason—he announced that he was upset because he had to pay six hundred thousand dollars in income tax that year. This was completely unsolicited information, and I thought to myself, If only I could **earn** six hundred thousand dollars. What did you have to earn in order to have to pay that much tax? Then Art Garfunkel came in, and we talked and talked.

They hadn't been on the road in a long time, and were reminiscing about the 'good old days.' I didn't realize that they used to be called Tom & Jerry, and that they once had a hit song called "Hey, Schoolgirl in the Second Row."

I said, *"Well, I can understand your desire to experience the joys of touring once again, and so I'll make you this offer . . . we're playing in Buffalo tomorrow night. Why don't you guys come up there and open for us as Tom & Jerry? I won't tell anybody. Just get your stuff and go out there and sing 'Hey, Schoolgirl in the Second Row'—just play only your old stuff, no Simon & Garfunkel tunes."* They loved the idea and said they would do it.

They did the opener as Tom & Jerry; we played our show, and at the encore I told the audience, *"I'd like to bring back our friends to do another number."* They came out and played "Sounds of Silence." At that point it dawned on everybody that this was the one, and only, the magnificent SIMON & GARFUNKEL. On the way out, after the show, a college-educated woman walked over to me and said, *"Why did you do that? Why did you make fun of Simon & Garfunkel?"*—as if I had pulled some kind of cruel joke on them. What the fuck did she think had just happened? That these two SUPERSTARS had dropped in out of nowhere and we had FORCED them to sing **"OOO-boppa-loochy-bah, she's mine!"**?

# CHAPTER 5

# The Log Cabin

When we returned to California in 1968, we moved into a large log cabin, once owned by old-time cowboy star Tom Mix, at the corner of Laurel Canyon Boulevard and Lookout Mountain Drive.

The living room was seventy-five by thirty feet, with a huge fireplace. Close to a dozen people, mostly employees, lived there. The rent was seven hundred dollars a month.

Cal Schenkel had his own little art department in one wing of the house. In the basement was a one-lane bowling alley and enough space for the band to rehearse. It had two walk-in safes —like bank vaults—and a subbasement which had probably been a wine cellar. It was rustic and decrepit; it really *looked* like an old-time log cabin, with rough-hewn wood, bristling with splinters.

On the day Mick Jagger stopped by for his first visit, one of the above-mentioned splinters crammed itself into the end of the big toe on my right foot, just as I was making my way to the door.

I greeted Mr. Jagger, hopping on one foot. He asked why I was behaving in this manner. I told him about the splinter and hobbled over to a chair. He followed, got on the floor in front of me, located the little wooden tormentor and removed it. We spent about an hour after that discussing European history.

## An Unwanted Visitor

Alongside the house on the grounds was a big concrete fish pond full of weeds. Next to that was a hole in the ground surrounded by a concrete block filled with stagnant water. (I was told that it was a *secret passageway* that went under the street to Harry Houdini's old house on the other side of Laurel Canyon Boulevard. I never found out if that was true.) Running up the hillside, behind the house, was a collection of man-made caves built out of stucco, with electric wiring and light bulbs inside.

The residents at that time included my wife, Gail; my secretary, Pauline Butcher; our road manager, Dick Barber; Pamela Zarubica; Ian Underwood; Motorhead Sherwood; and a girl named Christine Frka—the woman on the cover of the *Hot Rats* album crawling out of the crypt.

Christine Frka was our baby-sitter, along with Pamela Des Barres. Moon was about eight months old, and Dweezil hadn't been born yet. That's the cast of characters and the setting.

One of the reasons we finally moved out was that everybody in Hollywood knew where it was, and they were knocking on the door at all hours of the day and night wanting to have a party.

One summer afternoon I was sitting in the living room with Wild Man Fischer and a few of the GTO's (Girls Together Outrageously). The front door was open. A guy walked in off the street and introduced himself as *"The Raven,"* and said that he *had something for me.*

First he handed me a bottle of fake blood with a rag in it, said, *"I have isolated The Specimen!"* and pulled out an Army .45.

Wild Man Fischer turned white—he knew the guy was crazy. My eyebrows went up and down. He obviously wasn't from Southern California, so I said, *"Have you been in Los Angeles very long?"* *"No,"* he said, *"I just got here."* Trying to be as 'helpful' as possible, I said, *"You know what? If the police see you with that gun around here, you're going to be in a lot of trouble."*

*"Yeah?"* he said.

*"Yeah,"* I said, *"—and I know a place where you can hide it."* Everybody who was in the room got up to perform the mystical ceremony designed to *'Help The Raven Hide His Gun.'*

We went out the front door, around the side, past the fish tank to that hole with the stagnant water in it. I said, *"Look, if you put it in there, they'll NEVER find it."*

Everybody had to throw *something* in the hole. Gail and the rest of the household gathered little objects to toss in. Then we got our visitor to drop his gun in, and I sprinkled some leaves on top of it, saying, *"It's taken care of now."*

We told him we were very busy then, and urged him to leave—and started looking for another house to live in.

## Girls Together Outrageously

The overall stylistic concept of the GTO's had a lot to do with Christine Frka. Unfortunately, she OD'd sometime during the 1970s—I don't know exactly when.

Christine was the one who recommended that I record Alice Cooper, and later provided them with the ideas for their costumes. (When I first saw them, they looked pretty much like a bunch of guys from Arizona.)

Christine used to hang out with Miss Sparkie, Miss Mercy, Miss Pamela, Miss Lucy, Miss Sandra and Miss Cynderella. They were totally dedicated and devoted to **every aspect** of rock and roll—especially the part about **guys in bands who had Big Weenies.**

Miss Mercy's claim to fame at that time was an unusual interest: *butter*. She used to open the refrigerator, remove a quarter-pound stick, and swallow it whole. Miss Sandra always carried a small can of Crisco for personal lubrication.

The only other thing that mattered to them was the concept of *raw, unbridled costumery*. There was strong competition between the ladies as to which one was dressing in the most 'unique' way. (If you can still find it, *Permanent Damage,* the album of the GTO's, manages to give a pretty good flavor of their lifestyle.)

Included in it is a tape of Cynthia Plaster-Caster talking on the phone to Miss Pamela (now known as Pamela *'I'm With the Band'* Des Barres), comparing notes. They both kept diaries, so they had cross-references to the same guys. Noel Redding, bassist from the Jimi Hendrix group, also kept diaries, intertwined with the other two. It would have been great to see them all in one book.

It's unfortunate that the only diaries published so far have been Pamela's. Good as they are, they're not nearly as well written or insightful as Cynthia's.

I met Cynthia Plaster-Caster when the Mothers were working as the opening act for Cream at the International Amphitheatre in Chicago in 1968. This was toward the end of Cream's existence, when all the guys in the band hated each other. Each guy had his own road manager, his own limousine, his own etc., etc., etc.

During a conversation backstage, Eric Clapton asked if I had ever heard of the Plaster-Casters. I said I hadn't. He said *"Well, after the show, come with me. You won't believe this."* So, we went to his hotel.

Upon arrival we found, sitting in the lobby, two girls. One of them had a small suitcase with an oval cardboard emblem glued to the side that said *"THE PLASTER-CASTERS OF CHICAGO."* The other one had a brown paper bag.

They didn't say a word—just stood up and followed us into the elevator, and into the room. The *suitcase girl* opened the suitcase. The other one opened the bag. They took out some 'statuettes': *"Here's Jimi Hendrix, and here's Noel Redding, and here's the roadie from. . . ."*

They put them on the coffee table and took out the rest of their gear—everything a person might need to make a plaster replica of *the human weenus.*

We spent two or three hours talking with them. Neither of us volunteered to be 'immortalized.'

The Plaster-Casters were written up in various publications at that time. Probably as a result of this, our office received a portfolio from a guy who claimed to be doing something similar with *female organs,* casting them in silver. Very nice.

The material used for the molds in each case was the same stuff the dentist puts in your mouth for taking impressions of your teeth. It's a powder called alginate, which, when mixed with water, gets rubbery, and eventually hardens so that plaster can be poured into it.

The way the Plaster-Casters worked was, one of them would mix the goo while the other one gave the guy a blow job. As you can imagine, this sort of thing requires a scientific sense of timing.

The blow-job girl had to take her mouth off the guy's dick at the precise moment the other one slammed the container full of glop onto the end of it, holding it there until it hardened enough to make a good mold. Cynthia wouldn't blow the guys; that was the other girl's assignment. Cynthia mixed the goo.

Meanwhile, the 'subject' had to concentrate on maintaining an erection, otherwise he wouldn't *make a good impression*.

When Hendrix was cast, Cynthia told me, he liked the glop so well, he *fucked the mold*.

## Jazz: The Music of Unemployment

The first time we played with Rahsaan Roland Kirk was at the 1968 *Boston Globe* Jazz Festival. After his performance, when introduced to him backstage, I said I really liked what he was doing, and said that if he felt like joining us onstage during our set, he was more than welcome. In spite of his blindness, I believed we could accommodate whatever he wanted to do.

We began our set, wending our atonal way toward a medley of 1950s-style honking saxophone numbers. During this fairly complicated, choreographed routine, Rahsaan, assisted by his helper (can't remember his name), decided to join in.

In 1969, George Wein, impresario of the Newport Jazz Festival, decided it would be a tremendous idea to put the Mothers of Invention on a jazz tour of the East Coast. We wound up working in a package with Kirk, Duke Ellington and Gary Burton in Miami at the Jai Alai Fronton, and at another gig in South Carolina.

The touring package did not carry its own PA—we had to use whatever speakers existed in each of the venues we were booked into. The hall in South Carolina was rigged with small jukebox speakers, set in a ring around the building. Useless, but there we were—we had to play the show.

Before we went on, I saw Duke Ellington begging—pleading—for a ten-dollar advance. It was really depressing. After that show, I told the guys: *"That's it—we're breaking the band up."*

We'd been together in one configuration or another for about five years at that point, and suddenly EVERYTHING looked utterly hopeless to me. If Duke Ellington had to beg some George Wein assistant backstage for *ten bucks,* what the fuck was I doing with a ten-piece band, trying to play rock and roll—or something that was *almost* rock and roll?

I was paying everybody in the band a weekly salary of two hundred dollars—all year round, whether we were working or not, along with all hotel and travel expenses **when we did get work.** The guys in the band were pissed off—as if their welfare had been canceled—but at that point I was ten thousand dollars in the red.

# CHAPTER 6

# Send In the Clowns

I spent part of 1969 working in the studio on the *Hot Rats* album, and did a few local gigs with Ian Underwood and Sugarcane Harris. It was going nowhere. The album, which I happened to like a lot, sneaked onto the *Billboard* charts somewhere around 99 and vanished immediately. In the United States, at least, I had produced another flop.

(The very idea! An all-instrumental album, except for one vocal cut—and that had to feature *Captain Beefheart!* He's no singer! Why are you wasting America's precious time with this, you asshole!)

As it has turned out, that album, as a catalog item, has outlived just about everything else released in 1970, and, for our beloved friends in the British Isles, stands out as *the only 'good' Zappa album ever released*—more about those guys later.

Sometime in 1970, I had an offer for a major concert performance of the orchestral music accumulating in my closet. During the M.O.I.'s first five years, I had carried with me, on the road, masses of manuscript paper, and, whenever there was an opportunity, scribbled stuff on it. This material eventually became the score for *200 Motels (based on an estimate of the number of gigs we played in the first five years—forty jobs per year?)*.

The performance was to be held at UCLA's Pauley Pavilion (a basketball arena seating about fourteen thousand people), with Zubin Mehta conducting the Los Angeles Philharmonic Orchestra. A pretty big deal.

There was a 'catch,' though—the orchestra didn't really want to play the stuff—they wanted AN EVENT; something 'unique'—like—*uhh,* maybe a **ROCK GROUP** and—*uhhhhh* —a **REAL ORCHESTRA** sort of—*uhhh*—well, you know— **'rocking out together.'** It didn't matter *what* the music was.

This eventually led to a few problems. First of all, I didn't have a 'ROCK GROUP'—the M.O.I. had been disbanded for about a year. Second, there were **no parts copied** for the scores, and I was being asked to pay for this enormous job (seven thousand 1970 dollars). The third problem was that I wanted some kind of tape of the show, and the Musicians' Union wouldn't allow it. (They didn't do anything when some asshole in the audience ran a cassette and made a bootleg album out of it, but they were promising stern action if I made one for my own use—just to find out what my pieces sounded like . . . but let me slow down here.)

We solved problem number one by putting together an interim one-shot *'Mothers-Of-Invention-Sort-Of-Group.'* It did a short tour to warm up, maybe half a dozen dates, and returned to L.A. for the show.

The second problem was solved by me spending the seven thousand bucks on a team of copyists.

The third problem never got solved, and I never got a tape of the show.

It was the most successful indoor concert of the L.A. Phil's season that year—sold out. Somewhere in that mass of spectators were Mark Volman and Howard Kaylan, a.k.a. Flo & Eddie.

They came backstage after the show, said they liked it, and told me that the Turtles had split up and they were looking for something to do. The rest is history.

We worked together for about two years after that on several albums and tours as well as the film *200 Motels*. (For those of you wishing for a whiff of that particular nostalgia, I recommend the acquisition of the film itself, along with the documentary I prepared called *The True Story of "200 Motels,"* available in most outlets through Honker Home Video. That story is best told in pictures.)

## Oh, My Aching Back

People who have never been in a rock band maintain the most ridiculous fantasies about how *glamorous* and *exciting* and *endlessly gratifying* Life On The Road must be. It's not that I haven't had a few laughs out there—but let's just say the ratio isn't that terrific.

Some moments are unique, though. It was the middle of winter in Stockholm, 1971. We had just finished two shows at the Konserthuset. I was walking out of the hall when two kids came up to me and said that they had been to both shows that night, that they had a great idea, and wondered if I'd go along with it.

*"We have a younger brother named Hannes,"* they said, *"who came to the first show with us, and then went home. He has school tomorrow."* The family lived in an area called Tulinge, which is about twenty minutes outside the city. They wanted me to go with them to their house in the middle of the night, sneak into Hannes's room, wake him up and say, *"Hannes! Hannes! Wake up! It's me, Frank Zappa."*

I said, *"Okay, I'll do it."*

I was taken into a typical kid's room filled with the little models he had built. Hannes was asleep in his little bed. It was freezing cold. I woke him up. As expected, he was very surprised.

The mother and father got up, wearing long nightgowns. They were very nice people. We sat in the kitchen until 5:30 A.M. talking politics.

Except for that incident, the 1971 European winter tour gets the award for being the most disastrous. On December 4, we were working at the Casino de Montreux in Geneva, Switzerland, right on the edge of the lake—just in front of *Igor Stravinsky Street*—a venue noted for its jazz festivals.

In the middle of Don Preston's synthesizer solo on "King Kong," the place suddenly caught fire. Somebody in the audience had a bottle rocket or a Roman candle and fired it into the ceiling, at which point the rattan covering started to burn (other versions of the story claim the blaze was the result of faulty wiring). There were between twenty-five hundred and three thousand kids packed into the room—well over capacity.

Since more kids were outside, trying to get in, the organizers had cleverly chained the exit doors shut. When the fire began, the audience was left with two ways out: through the front door, which was pretty small, or through a plate-glass window off to the side of the stage.

I made an announcement—something like: *"Please be calm. We have to leave here. There is a fire and why don't we get out?"* You'd be surprised how well people who speak only French can understand you when it's a matter of life and death. They began filing out through the front door.

As the room was filling with smoke, one of our roadies took an equipment case and smashed the big window. The crew then began helping people to escape through it into some kind of garden place below. The band escaped through an underground tunnel that led from behind the stage through the parking garage.

A few minutes later the heating system in the building exploded, and some people were blown through the window. Fortunately, nobody was killed and there were only a few minor injuries—however, the entire building, about thirteen million dollars' worth, burned to the ground, and we lost all our equipment.

We were in the middle of a sold-out tour with ten more dates to go. Back at the hotel, most of the band voted for finishing the tour—or at least trying. The problem was that, even though we didn't have the greatest equipment in the world, we had been using a few special instruments, including a customized Fender Rhodes piano, and other specialized synthesizer gear we couldn't buy off a shelf in Switzerland. My guitar was gone. All of the stage lights were gone. The PA was gone.

We canceled a week's worth of jobs, during which we scrounged for new equipment. The plan was to get to England two days in advance of **The Big Gig** at the Rainbow, and rehearse with the new gear. We had two nights of double shows coming up and we had to make sure everybody was comfortable with the new stuff.

We had some problems—mikes were feeding back and all kinds of weird shit was happening, but still we managed to make it through the first show. At the end of the first show, we went offstage and came back to do an encore. I think we played "I Want to Hold Your Hand." All I remember after that is waking up in the orchestra pit in pain. I didn't know what had happened to me. In the weeks following the attack, I was able to piece it together, but at the time I had no idea.

The band thought I was dead. I had fallen fifteen feet down into a concrete-floored orchestra pit, my head was over on my shoulder, and my neck was bent like it was broken. I had a gash in my chin, a hole in the back of my head, a broken rib and a fractured leg. One arm was paralyzed.

In those days, I didn't carry a bodyguard; 'security' was supplied by the local promoters. In the case of this concert, the security consisted of two big West Indian guys, at either side of the stage. During the encore, they were off smoking reefer someplace.

In their absence, a guy by the name of Trevor Howell had run up onto the stage, punched me and knocked me over into the pit.

He gave two stories to the press. One of them was that I had been *"making eyes at his girlfriend."* That wasn't true, since the orchestra pit was not only fifteen feet deep but twice as wide, and the spotlight was in my face. I can't even see the audience in those situations—it's like looking into a black hole. I never even saw the guy coming at me.

He told another newspaper that he was pissed off because he felt we hadn't given him *"value for his money."* Choose your favorite story.

After he punched me, he tried to escape into the audience, but a couple of guys in the road crew caught him and took him backstage to hold him for the police. He wound up spending a year in jail for inflicting *"grievous bodily harm"* on me.

The British press found it amusing.

I was taken to a public hospital. I remember being in the

emergency room which, like the rest of London at that time of year, was freezing cold. They were clearly understaffed—a guy two beds down from me had his balls smashed in a brawl someplace, and was howling, unattended.

They couldn't give me any anesthetic because I had a head injury, so after a while I just passed out, and woke up later in a bad-smelling room with beds all around, in a circle, with curtains hung between them. I remember the curtains parting in front of me and a black nurse coming in and seeing my face; like she had just seen a monster. I was pretty mashed up.

I was later transferred to the Harley Street Clinic where I stayed for the next month. I had a twenty-four-hour bodyguard because the asshole who had hit me was out on bail, and we didn't know how insane he was.

When my head had gone over onto my shoulder, it had crushed my larynx, so I couldn't talk. As a result of that, the pitch of my voice dropped a third and has stayed that way ever since (having a low voice is nice, but I would have preferred some other means of acquiring it).

After a month, I learned how to walk on crutches. I was in a cast all the way up to my hip, but my leg refused to heal. They wanted to break my leg again and reset it. I said, *"No, thanks— just leave the fucking cast on."*

I stayed in the cast and in a wheelchair for the better part of a year. Eventually the cast came off and I was fitted with a prosthetic device—one of those things with metal joints and straps and a special shoe. Eventually my leg healed—but it came out a little crooked. One leg is slightly shorter than the other, the cause of many years of chronic back pain.

During my season in the wheelchair, I refused to do any interviews or have photos taken. I still wanted to make music, and managed somehow to produce three albums (*Just Another Band from L.A., Waka/Jawaka,* and *The Grand Wazoo*). I also wrote a science-fiction musical called *Hunchentoot,* and a twisted sort of musical fairy tale called *The Adventures of Greggery Peccary*.

Once I had regained mobility, I decided to go back on the road—with a new band. The band with Mark and Howard didn't exist anymore—they all had to go out and get other jobs during the year I couldn't work.

The first post-wheelchair appearance was as a **reciter,** in a performance of Stravinsky's *L'Histoire du soldat* at the Hollywood Bowl, conducted by Lukas Foss.

Prior to that, I had recorded with a twenty-piece band on the *Grand Wazoo* album, and I decided I wanted to tour with it —just six or eight dates, not really a money-making proposition.

So we did a short tour—the Hollywood Bowl, the Deutschlandhalle in Berlin, the Music Hall in Boston, a couple of shows at the Felt Forum in New York City, someplace I can't remember in Holland, and the Oval Cricket Ground in London.

At the press conference arranged by the promoter of the London date, I discovered the depths to which the British will sink in order to sell a concert ticket. During an interview, a young girl entered the room, handed me a bouquet of flowers and walked away. This resulted in quiet questioning by the other reporters who were waiting in the back of the room to talk with me. She told them she was the girlfriend of the guy who had knocked me off the stage, and that she had brought the flowers as a gesture of remorse. I found out later that the promoter had hired her as a publicity stunt.

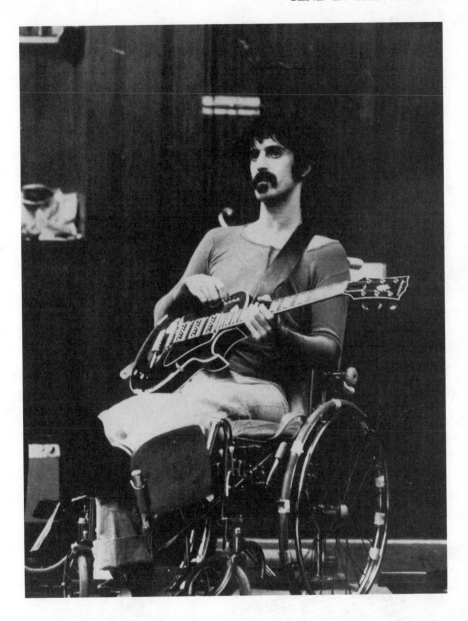

# CHAPTER 7

# Drool, Britannia

As a result of all that, the British have earned a special place in my heart. In 1975, they came through for me once again when I was forced to sue the Crown for breach of contract.

My claim arose as a result of a canceled performance by the Royal Philharmonic Orchestra and the Mothers of Invention, scheduled to coincide with the conclusion of principal photography on the *200 Motels* film.

The Royal Family's attorneys opted to defend their breach by attempting to convert what would have been an arbitratable civil matter into a bogus *obscenity trial,* in the Old Bailey.

The matter was complicated by a catch-22 sort of musicians' union rule governing *rehearsal for a recording session.* According to the rule book, **there is no scale payment rate for rehearsing for a recording session.**

This means that a person hiring an orchestra, for example, either is *prohibited from rehearsal altogether* or has to pay *full recording scale* while the orchestra makes all the mistakes you'd never want to release on a record. The union does, however, permit (and posts a scale rate for) *rehearsal for a* **live concert.**

To navigate this mysterious policy, making it possible for the Royal Philharmonic to rehearse the music for *200 Motels* before recording it, we booked a concert at the Royal Albert Hall, listing the initial rehearsals as **rehearsals for the concert** —all completely legal. If, however, the concert *were not to occur,* the production company (my company) would then have been liable for a massive payment to the union for *"extra recording sessions."*

A *spinster* (her descriptive title in the court documents) named *Marion Herrod* took it upon herself to cancel this sold-out concert at the last minute, after hearing from a trumpet-player friend in the orchestra that the song lyrics were "obscene." (One of the objectionable words was *brassiere*.)

Her action, on behalf of the Crown (her employer), caused substantial and demonstrable financial damages from the concert (as the ticket money had to be refunded, along with the concert preparation costs) and from the potential balloon payment to the musicians' union.

Okay, let me set the scene for you here—the Old Bailey is just like you've seen it in all those British courtroom dramas: dark wood paneling; musty smell; robes; wigs (they're made of horsehair); pompous assholes scorning each other—you get the picture. Here's some stuff you don't know: everybody involved in the proceedings (the judge and both sets of counsels) has to write **everything** down—**in longhand**—on *foolscap* (the long legal paper). There's no 'court stenographer' throttling a plastic machine in the corner, and so everyone is instructed to <u>speak slowly</u>—so, as you read this transcript, *remember,* everybody is talking in <u>slow motion</u>.

Now, the judge: this guy was maybe eighty years old. He looked like a cartoon of a judge—perfect, except he didn't have an *ear trumpet*. During the proceedings, one of the lawyers attempted to introduce the *200 Motels* record album into evidence. Upon seeing it, Justice Mocatta asked, *"What is that?"* The reply: *"It is a phonograph record, your lordship."*

(**MR. CAMPBELL** *appeared as counsel for defense* [*ALBERT HALL*], **MR. OGDEN** *appeared on behalf of the plaintiff* [*ZAPPA*], *before* **MR. JUSTICE MOCATTA.**)
    *"A:"* *indicates the answers of the plaintiff, Frank Zappa.*
    The interrogation took place in the **HIGH COURT OF JUSTICE, QUEEN'S BENCH DIVISION,** on 15th and 16th April, 1975. A series of excerpts follows.

MR. CAMPBELL: Had you played the Albert Hall before?

THE WITNESS: Twice.

MR. JUSTICE MOCATTA: You mean the group had?

A: The group had played at the Albert Hall twice.

MR. CAMPBELL: Can you remember what sort of things you played, the titles? Can you explain it?

A: The first time we played in the Albert Hall was in September of 1967. During that concert some of the song titles were "Call Any Vegetable." The subject matter of that song deals with the concept of apathy between a member of the audience and any form of inert material. Another selection performed in that first concert was a song entitled, "You Didn't Try to Call Me."

Q: Has the thing about *"vegetable"* anything to do with sex?

A: No.

Q: Has the second one you mentioned anything to do with sex?

A: Well, it is a boy-girl situation song but it involves no 'reproductive references.' It deals mainly with the subject of heartbreak, resulting from lack of telephonic communication. . . .

They then proceed to discuss several songs that were to have been performed at the concert.

MR. CAMPBELL: What was the concept of the song **"Would You Go All the Way?"**

A: This song makes reference to the kind of people that you might find in the armed services, and the way in which they attempt to treat girls which they procure for their amusement. It makes reference to the monster from the U.S.O.

Q: That is not an unidentified flying object?

A: No.

Q: What is a *"U.S.O.?"*

A: It is an abbreviation for United States Overseas.

Q: Then, **"She Painted Up Her Face,"** to which objection has been taken. What do you say about that?

A: Well, I think that this is an important piece of material, lyrically.

Q: What is the concept about it?

A: To my knowledge, it is the only song in the repertoire that deals with the subject of a girl who is a groupie.

Q: What is a *"groupie?"*

A: A *"groupie"* is a girl who likes people in a rock-and-roll band. She likes them *very much.*

MR. JUSTICE MOCATTA: She likes what very much?

A: She likes **"the members"** of the band very much.

MR. CAMPBELL: A sort of fan, like a football fan?

A: Only of **"the members."**

Q: Like film stars have fan mails?

A: Yes.

MR. JUSTICE MOCATTA: I did not gather that. I thought you said that this dealt with a girl who in fact was a member of a rock-and-roll band.

MR. CAMPBELL: No, my Lord.

THE WITNESS: I am sorry: girls who "follow **members**."

MR. JUSTICE MOCATTA: I.e., a follower?

A: Yes.

MR. CAMPBELL: A sort of fan?

A: Yes. Shall I continue with an analysis of this song?

Q: Please do so.

A: It is the only piece of material that deals with a look at the *motivations* of the girl. Many groups have done songs about groupies, but coverage of that subject has been superficial and the lyrics to this song represent some kind of landmark in the way in which the subject has been dealt with.

Q: Is it intended as a serious song?

A: Well, I would say it is as serious as anything else I do.

Q: Now we come to **"Bunna Dik"** [sic]. What is the concept of **"Bunna Dik"?**

A: I would like to point out at this time that those lyrics contained in this version of "Bwana Dik" are of a very early draft. The song "Bwana Dik" did not occur in *200 Motels*. It was not included in the film. It is not part of the album.

MR. CAMPBELL: It was, I think, on another record?

A: Yes, but not in this form. The title "Bwana Dik" is in an album called *Live at Fillmore East* but it has nothing to do with the text that you are asking me to analyze here. It was a totally different set of lyrics.

MR. JUSTICE MOCATTA: **"Bunna"** is apparently a West African term, or an African term, for "boss," is it? Is that right?

A: It is the kind of word that you have in a jungle movie. I do not know what it means in reality. It is a *jungle-movie word*.

Q: What does it mean in a jungle movie?

A: You never know **what** it means in a jungle movie, you know, unless somebody can explain to me that that word exists in some special African language. My understanding of *"Bwana"* has always been that it's something

123

that *the guy with the box on his shoulder* says.

MR. CAMPBELL: What do you mean by *"the guy with the box on his shoulder?"*

A: Well, natives walk behind the guy with the helmet, and they have the box on their shoulder.

MR. CAMPBELL: My Lord, he means the bearers in the jungle.

MR. JUSTICE MOCATTA: A sort of porter, or bearer, in a jungle?

MR. CAMPBELL: Yes.

THE WITNESS: Yes.

MR. OGDEN: I am not interested in what my learned friend thinks it is; I am interested in what the witness thinks it is.

MR. JUSTICE MOCATTA: What does **"Bunna Dik"** mean?

A: *"Bwana"* with the *"Dik"* after it would mean a person who, at some time, could wear *one of those helmets,* and could have people treating him in some sort of respected way, and who was also in possession of a *"Dik."*

Q: And what is a **"Dik?"**

A: Well, in this context, it would be a rock-and-roll person's penis.

MR. CAMPBELL: And what is the concept of **"Bunna Dik?"**

A: O.K. I will explain the concept of "Bwana Dik" to you. In every band there is some member of the band who, during the course of touring, gets the opportunity to entertain more girls than the other members of the band. It is like winning a contest. If we carry this concept to a ridiculous extreme, this person could be awarded the *title* of **"Bwana Dik."** The song deals with the fact that each in his own way, each member of the group, secretly believes that he is **"Bwana Dik."**

Q: Oh, I see.

A: And the song attempts to show how foolish this concept is.

Q: Quite, satirically?

A: That is right, it is a satire. . . .

*[Cross examination]*

MR. OGDEN: Let us turn to **"Lonesome Cowboy Burt,"** and if you would look at page 48, please, this song is of Cowboy Burt saying he wants sexual intercourse with a waitress, is it not?

A: No, this song is not *specifically* about Cowboy Burt seeking sexual intercourse with a waitress.

My name is Burtram
I am a redneck
All my friends,
They call me 'Burt'
All my family,
From down in Texas
Make their livin'
Diggin' dirt

Come out here to Californy,
Just to find me
Some pretty girls
The ones I seen
Gets me so horny;
Ruby lips,
'N teeth like pearls!

Wanna love 'em all!
Wanna love 'em dearly!
Wanna pretty girl—

125

I'll even pay!
I'll buy 'em furs!
I'll buy 'em jewelry!
I know they like me;
Here's what I say:


*"I'm lonesome Cowboy Burt!*
*Don'tcha get my feelin's hurt!*
*Come on in this place,*
*'N I'll buy you a taste,*
*'N you can sit on my face—*
*Where's my waitress?"*


I'm an awful nice guy!
I sweat all day in the sun!
I'm a roofer by trade,
Quite a bundle I've made,
I'm a unionized roofin' old
Son-of-a-gun!


When I get off, I get plastered
I drink till I fall onna floor,
Then I find me some *Communist bastard,*
'N stomp on his face till he don't
Move no more!


I fuss, an' I cuss, an' I keep on drinkin',
Till my eyes puff up an' turn red!
I drool on m'shirt,
I see if he's hurt,
Then I kick him again in the head, yes!
Kick him again in the head, now!
Kick him again in the head, boys!
KICK HIM AGAIN IN THE HEAD!

I'M LONESOME COWBOY BURT,
Don'tcha get my feelin's hurt
Come on in this place,
An' I'll buy you a taste,
'N you can sit on my face—
Where's my waitress?
*OPAL, YOU HOT LITTLE BITCH!*

"Lonesome Cowboy Burt" from the album *200 Motels*, 1972

Q: And by your use of the word *"specifically"* you lead one to understand that in part it is about that?

MR. JUSTICE MOCATTA: Well, the implication is that it is about **that?**

A: When you say, *"It is about that,"* **that** is not what the function of the song is. I am trying to understand your terminology. You see, if you can give me some guidelines as to how to understand what is going on here, I can function better.

MR. OGDEN: Mr. Zappa, if I may say so, I do not think you are a stupid man by any means. I think you understand what I am trying to get at. At least in part this song implies that Burt wants sexual intercourse with a waitress, does it not?

A: At least in part this song does imply that a character named Lonesome Cowboy Burt seeks to have some sort of sexual relationship with a waitress.

Q: Thank you. And on page 22, the unamended version, I would be grateful if you would tell us what this phrase means: "and I will buy you a taste, and you can sit on my face"?

A: **"I will buy you a taste"** is a reference to purchasing an alcoholic beverage on behalf of the waitress, and sitting on his face is a reference to the girl sitting on his face.

Q: That being a sensual reference?

A: Not necessarily. It could indicate a piggyback ride in an unusual position.

Q: Are you being serious?

A: Certainly.

Q: **"I will buy you an alcoholic drink and you can have a pick-a-back ride sitting on my face?"**

A: That is not what it says.

Q: I understood you to be indicating that that was what it meant. Have I got you wrong?

A: No, it is open to that interpretation as well as any other.

Q: You wrote it. You must have had something in mind.

MR. JUSTICE MOCATTA: What does it mean, **"You can sit on my face"**?

A: Somebody can sit on your face.

Q: A very unpleasant occupation for the person whose face is being sat upon, is it not?

A: Well, this is an unusual character, this Cowboy Burt.

MR. OGDEN: Mr. Zappa, you are the author of this?

A: Yes.

Q: What did you mean when you wrote it?

A: Well, I pictured a situation where there was a cowboy, whose name is Burt, and his family history has been given in the first part of the song. He is making himself obnoxious in a bar, and that particular line is a line that was extracted from some actual graffiti which I saw in a bar, which was characteristic of the lifestyle and area in which **Burt** functions, and it is something that is meant to help portray the character in his normal speaking style, in the same way as if the song was about a pirate, I would have him saying "Avast ye lubbers" or something like that, and it is the type of thing that this character would say to a waitress.

MR. JUSTICE MOCATTA: But do you say it does have some sexual connotation?

A: It could, by some stretch of the imagination, certainly —the picture of the lower region of the person who was doing the sitting coming in contact with the upper region of the person who was supporting the sitter.

MR. OGDEN: Well, that is all very fine, but let us put it into cruder terms: You mean the naked buttocks of the girl sitting on the man's face?

A: There is no reference in here to naked buttocks.

Q: No, but is that what you meant?

A: No.

Q: And you are unable to tell us what in fact that phrase was meant by you to mean?

A: In fact I have just explained it to you.

MR. JUSTICE MOCATTA: You heard it used by somebody?

A: I saw this graffiti. It was written in graphite on the wall of a toilet in a bar that people like Cowboy Burt go to.

MR. OGDEN: I think I can leave that point.

MR. JUSTICE MOCATTA: What does **"Come smell my fringy shirt"** mean? Is there any particular meaning in that?

A: Certainly.

Q: What does it mean?

A: Have you ever seen a cowboy's shirt?

Q: I am not sure that I have, but tell me what it means.

A: You have to understand what a cowboy's shirt looks like. There are different styles and some of them have fringe across the chest and along the arms, fringe that hangs down. It is a decoration.

Q: I know what you mean.

A: And this song is trying to establish Burt's character. This is a person who dresses like a cowboy, behaves like a cowboy, and smells like a cowboy. He is a hundred percent cowboy, all the way through.

Remember Freddie and Jo?
The night you went to a show?
*(A monster movie)*;
Clutchin' at yer hand
*(Wait ten seconds)*
Clutchin' at yer arm
*(Wait ten seconds)*
Clutchin' at yer elbow—
Where did your brassiere go?
Then the monster came out,
'N everybody shout!
People all around you,
Screamin' at the monster; **The Monster From The U.S.O.**

Who's this dude with his hair straight back?
His new white socks, 'n his pants all black;
His T-shirts rolled—
His watch is gold—
A '55 Chevy that his brother just stoled,
An' his arm's around yer waist—
An' his hand is in yer pants—
An' he asks you for a date
To the servicemen's dance!

Suppose you don't wanna?
What can you do?
When a joker like that
Got his hands on you—
*Oh, baby!*
*T-T-T-Tell me baby,*
Would you go **all the way**
For the U.S.A.?
Would you go **all the way**
For the U.S.O.?
Would you go **all the way**
For the U.S.A.?
Lift up your dress, if the answer is **"no"** . . .

"Would You Go All the Way?" from the album *Chunga's Revenge,* 1970

MR. OGDEN: My Lord, I was leaving that, now, and turning to **"Would You Go All the Way?"** *(To the witness):* Going all the way means having sexual intercourse, does it not?

A: It is an expression that was used in the 1950s to indicate having sexual intercourse. It is an archaic expression which is used to generate laughter.

Q: Well, whatever it is used to generate, that is its meaning?

A: In the 1950s, yes.

Q: And as I understood what you were saying yesterday this was a reference to the American armed forces overseas and the way they treated girls they procured for their amusement?

A: Yes.

Q: And, of course, it is quite plain, if one looks at the unamended version, which is on page 30, that this is a song about sex?

*131*

A: I would say that this song is not specifically about sex.

Q: Well, we have agreed that the title "Would You Go All the Way?" means "Would you have sexual intercourse?" Now let us go on and see how it looks, if one looks at page 30. First of all they go to a movie, then *"clutching at your hand"* . . . *"wait ten seconds"* . . . *"clutching at your elbow"*—then *"Where did your* brassiere *go?"*—which means the man has got his hand on the girl's breast, does it not?

A: No.

Q: Does it not?

A: It means that the brassiere has disappeared mysteriously in the dark of the theater.

Q: I see, and the bit that is crossed out—*"Preston, who reaches for Ruth's breast, and her breast falls out,"* then *"The monster came out."* What would *"The monster came out"* with <u>that</u> mean?

A: The monster is the character that they are watching on the screen at that time.

Q: I see. Was that symbolic of something?

A: Well, in the 1950s monsters played a very important part in the culture of our country, and a lot of my humor revolves around that sort of thing.

Q: I see. In any event, if one reads that, it is quite obviously a seduction scene, is it not, in a cinema?

A: No. To me it would indicate to me that this scene was describing **ineptitude.**

Q: Ineptitude?

A: Yes.

Q: In what sense?

A: Fumbling with each other in the dark.

Q: Yes, but in a sensual context?

A: Not necessarily.

Q: Well, come, Mr. Zappa, just look at it. There is a song entitled "Would you have sexual intercourse"—in effect —then describing how the man clutches the woman's hands, then her arm, then her elbow, then he finds her **brassiere** has gone and her **breast** falls out. This is what the whole song is, *is it not?*

A: No, it is not. It has another page.

MR. JUSTICE MOCATTA: You say *"the monster"* is the breast, do you, or not?

MR. OGDEN: My Lord, I do not know, but your Lordship will have seen that earlier, further up the page, it says, *"Preston, a monster."*

MR. JUSTICE MOCATTA: I am sorry, I had not seen that.

> She painted up her face
> She sat before her mirror
> She painted up her face
> She drew the mirror nearer
>
> *Practisissing, Practiss,* **Practicing!**
>
> The STARE!
> The STARE!
>
> (The 'secret stare' she would use
> If a worthy-looking victim should appear)
> The clock upon the wall
> Has struck the midnight hour!
> She finishes her call;
> Her girlfriend's in the shower

*Practisissing, Practiss,* **Practicing!**
Half a dozen provocative squats!
Out of the shower, she squeezes her spots;
Brushes her teeth;
Shoots a deodorant spray up her twat . . .
(It's getting her, getting her
Hot—*Oh-woh-woh-woh-woh-woh*)
She's just twenty-four
And she can't get off,
A sad but typical case
Last dude to do her
Got in and got soft;
She blew it,
And laughed in his face, yeah!

She chooses all the clothes
She'll wear tonight to dance in!
The places that she goes
Are filled with guys from groups,
Waiting for a chance to break her pants in

PROVOCATIVE SQUATS!
(*gum-me-on-m'lung-a*)
PROVOCATIVE SQUATS!
(*gum-me-on-m'lung-a*)
PROVOCATIVE SQUATS!
(*gum-me-on-m'lung-a*)
PROVOCATIVE SQUATS!
(*gum-me-on-m'lung-a*)

Well, at least there's sort of a choice there;
Twenty or thirty at times there have been—
Somewhat desirable boys there—
Dressed really spiffy, with long hair—
Waiting for girls they could shove it right in
THAT'S IT! SHOVE IT RIGHT IN!
(*eeeeeeuuuuuuueeeep*)

# AND PULL IT RIGHT OUT!
## (*eeeeuuuuuuuuuup*)
# AND SHOVE IT IN AGAIN!
## (unnngh!)

"Shove It Right In" from the album *200 Motels*, 1972

MR. OGDEN: Now, my Lord, I turn to "She painted up her face," at page 51. *(To the witness):* So far as the first page is concerned I need not ask you anything, but turn over to page 52, please. This is the groupies' room, it says, does it not?

A: Yes.

Q: Halfway down, one sees *"Half a dozen provocative squats."* What does that mean?

A: This is a reference to a girl preparing various ways in which she will make herself attractive to the rock and roll musicians that she is going to see at the bar. She is practicing postures which will draw attention to her at the bar.

Q: And what is a **"provocative squat?"**

A: That would be a squat that is a semikneeling position that could be executed during a dance, or, if she was going to the bar, to dance on the dance floor. It is indicating that the girl intends to go to the place where the boys are and dance in such a way that she will attract their attention.

Q: The theme of this song is this, is it not, that this girl has not been able to have completed sexual intercourse?

A: If you just want a general impression of what the song is about, it is about **unhappiness.** That is the real theme of the song.

Q: Yes, unhappiness because the girl has not been able to have complete sexual intercourse, is that right?

A: That is not the only reason she is unhappy.

Q: But that is one of the reasons?

A: Yes.

Q: One sees her sitting before the mirror, painting her face, practicing her stare, a secret stare she would use if a worthy-looking victim should appear. Then we go over to page 34 and one is in the groupies' dressing room, and I see the stage direction says *"Two nude groupies"*—*"She chooses all the clothes she will wear tonight to dance in; the places where she goes are filled with guys from groups, waiting for a chance to break her parts in?"*

A: Her what?

Q: Is it not *"parts"*?

A: *"Pants."*

Q: On it goes. *"At least there is that sort of choice there, twenty or thirty times . . . there have been some desirable boys there—dressed really spiffy, with long hair . . . waiting for girls they can shove it right in"*—that, of course, means sexual intercourse, does it not?

A: Yes, that does, yes, it means shoving it in.

Q: It means the penis going fully into the vagina?

A: Yes, that is true.

Q: And then over the next page there is *"a clock striking midnight and a girlfriend—practicing provocative squats; squeezing her spots, brushing her teeth, shooting a deodorant spray on her body; she is just twenty-four"*—is that a reference to her age?

A: Yes.

Q: *"She can't get off"*—*"getting off"* meaning in this context what?

A: **"Getting off"** in this context indicates that she has trouble achieving an orgasm.

MR. JUSTICE MOCATTA: She has what?

A: She has trouble achieving an orgasm, a sexual climax.

MR. OGDEN: And reciting that the last man who tried to have sexual intercourse with her lost his erection; that is what that means, is it not?

A: That is right, he lost his erection.

MR. OGDEN: My Lord, that is at the bottom of page 35— *"The last dude to do her . . . got in and got soft." (To the witness):* So he lost his erection and therefore could not give her sexual satisfaction and gratification causing her to have an orgasm. Is that right?

A: Yes.

Q: Do you regard that as objectionable, or not, for young boys and girls of, say, fourteen?

A: No.

Q: Or eleven?

A: No.

Q: Or nine?

A: In some instances that might be problematical.

*The final verdict? Justice Mocatta decided that (my paraphrasing)* [1] **THE MATERIAL WAS NOT OBSCENE.** [2] **THE ALBERT HALL HAD, IN FACT, BREACHED ITS CONTRACT.** *But* [3] **AS THE ALBERT HALL IS A ROYAL INSTITUTION, IT WOULD BE IMPROPER FOR AN AMERICAN MUSICIAN TO PREVAIL IN A CASE LIKE THIS, SO—YANKEE, GO HOME.**

# CHAPTER 8

# All About Music

*"Information is not knowledge, knowledge is not wisdom, wisdom is not truth, truth is not beauty, beauty is not love, love is not music. Music is the best."*

Frank Zappa, *Joe's Garage*, 1979

## What Do You Do for a Living, Dad?

If any of my kids ever asked me that question, the answer would have to be: *"What I **do** is composition."* I just happen to use material other than *notes* for the pieces.

Composition is a process of organization, very much like architecture. As long as you can conceptualize what that organizational process is, you can be a 'composer'—**in any medium you want.**

You can be a 'video composer,' a 'film composer,' a 'choreography composer,' a 'social engineering composer'— whatever. Just give me some *stuff,* and I'll organize it for you. That's what I do.

*Project/Object* is a term I have used to describe the overall concept of my work in various mediums. Each project (in whatever realm), or interview connected to it, is part of a larger object, for which there is no 'technical name.'

Think of the connecting material in the Project/Object this way: A novelist invents a character. If the character is a good one, he takes on a life of his own. Why should he get to go to only one party? He could pop up anytime in a future novel.

Or: Rembrandt got his 'look' by mixing just a little brown into every other color—he didn't do 'red' unless it had brown in it. The brown itself wasn't especially fascinating, but the result of its obsessive inclusion was that 'look.'

In the case of the *Project/Object,* you may find a little *poodle* over here, a little *blow job* over there, etc., etc. I am not obsessed by *poodles* **or** *blow jobs,* however; these words (and others of equal insignificance), along with pictorial images and melodic themes, recur throughout the albums, interviews, films, videos (and this book) for no other reason than to unify the 'collection.'

## The Frame

The most important thing in art is **The Frame.** For painting: literally; for other arts: figuratively—because, without this humble appliance, you can't **know** where *The Art* stops and *The Real World* begins.

You have to put a 'box' around it because otherwise, **what is that shit on the wall?**

If John Cage, for instance, says, *"I'm putting a contact micro-phone on my throat, and I'm going to drink carrot juice, and that's my composition,"* then his gurgling qualifies as **his composition** because he put a frame around it and said so. *"Take it or leave it, I now* **will** *this to be* **music.**" After that it's a matter of taste. Without the frame-as-announced, it's a guy swallowing carrot juice.

So, if *music is the best,* what **is** music? Anything **can** be music, but it doesn't **become music** until someone **wills** it to be music, and the audience listening to it decides to **perceive it as music.**

Most people can't deal with that abstraction—or don't want to. They say: *"Gimme* **the tune.** *Do I like this* **tune.** *Does it sound like another* **tune that I like?** *The more* familiar *it is,* **the better I like it.** *Hear those three notes there? Those are the three notes I can sing along with. I like those notes very, very much. Give me a beat. Not a fancy one. Give me a* **GOOD BEAT**—*something I can dance to. It has to go* boom-bap, boom-boom-**BAP.** *If it doesn't, I will* **hate** *it very, very much. Also, I want it* **right away**—*and then, write me some more songs like that—over and over and over again, because I'm* really *into* **music.**"

## Why Bother?

I used to love putting little black dots on music paper. I'd sit for sixteen hours at a time, hunched over in a chair with a bottle of India ink, and draw beams and dots.

No other activity could have enticed me away from the table. I'd maybe get up for coffee or to eat, but, other than that, I was glued to the chair for weeks and months on end, writing music.

I thought it was fun, because I could hear everything in my head, and I kept telling myself how *thoroughly bitchen* it was.

To be able to write a piece of music and hear it in your head is a completely different sensation from the ordinary listening experience.

I don't write 'music on paper' anymore. The incentive to continue was removed by having to deal with symphony orchestras.

## The Anthropology of the Symphony Orchestra

*"I have found, in my varied experience as a conductor, soloist with orchestra, and ordinary listener, that there is a general misuse of power all round, depending in whose hands it happens to repose in any given instance. The orchestra which finds that it has at its mercy a conductor—whom it may dislike for any reason from lack of musicianship to mere unsociability—is frequently as ruthless in its use of power as the conductor who exercises authority merely because he does not fancy a violinist's complexion or the way he sits while playing. Pundits may talk of a conductor's 'authority,' his 'beat' and his 'knowledge of scores,' but actual control of an orchestra is more frequently founded on the less gaudy basis of economics."*

Oscar Levant, *A Smattering of Ignorance* (1942)

Some critics have said that what I do is a perverse form of 'political theater.' Maybe twenty or thirty percent of my lyrics go in that direction—the rest of my activities might be more accurately described as *'amateur anthropology.'*

For example, when a *real* anthropologist studies a tribe, he has to eat the bowl of worms, put the grass skirt on and **go for it.** For me, wandering around in *the Mudd Club* was kind of like that—and so was working with a symphony orchestra.

The string players are a tribe; the brass players are a tribe; the woodwind players are a tribe—subdivided into 'tribe-lets.' *(The mind-set of an oboe player is different from the mind-set of a clarinet player, which is different from the mind-set of a flute player, which is different from the mind-set of a bassoon player.)* The percussionists are another tribe altogether.

Within those divisions and subdivisions, I was able to observe *specific preoccupations*—like: string players tend to be more concerned with their pensions than anybody else in the orchestra.

Apparently there are special pressures experienced by violinists which do not apply to cellists. It takes a long time to learn how to play a violin, and, after you whittle your fingers to the bone, what's the big payoff? A chair in the nineteenth row, sawing away on whole notes, while some guy who might be better at politics (or blow jobs) is sitting in chair number one, getting all the *bitchen solos.*

Viola players are often *failed violinists.* Not too many people who play the viola chose it because they *love* the instrument— they get *demoted* to it. This happens in grade school. (The viola can be a clumsy thing to stick under a kid's chin—so maybe your posture gets weird.) People who can't quite cut it in the violin section get banished to *viola-land.*

Flute players and harpists look to me like they have a bad attitude because of all that *cloud and angel music* they have to play. French horn players are arrogant too—they have to play all the shit that sounds like graduation.

Timpanists? Forget it—they regard themselves as 'special'

because **their drums** have **musical pitches.** *(None of the other orchestral percussionists is allowed to* **double** *on timpani—only the timpanist can play the timpani.)*

In high school, I saw trombone players described in a textbook as *"The Clowns of the Orchestra"* (indicating that the author found the image of grown men earning their living by sliding lubricated tubing back and forth, and leaving pools of spit in front of their chairs, pretty amusing).

When Schönberg introduced the *trombone glissando* into modern orchestral writing, critics of the period were outraged, declaring the sound to be *obscene,* and therefore inappropriate for the concert hall.

Players of certain instruments detest being seated near players of certain other instruments, because the other guy's sound *offends* them. During my visit to Orchestra-Land, I looked at these folks, and the instruments they had chosen to play, and tried to imagine what strange forces had produced those choices.

I got the impression that, in the case of the violin, it might have been (as in Italian families where helpless children are forced into *accordionic submission*) the violin was *the family instrument*, and the guy *had* to learn it.

I don't think there are too many cases where parents have *demanded* that their children learn to play percussion. The same thing with the bassoon. Not too many parents dream of the day when little Waldo will enthrall the neighbors by blowing on a brown thing with a metal doodad poking out the side of it.

The bassoon is one of my favorite instruments. It has the *medieval aroma*—like the days when *everything* used to sound like that. Some people crave baseball—I find this unfathomable—but I can easily understand why a person could get excited about playing a bassoon. It's a *great noise*—nothing else makes *that* noise.

I don't think in the beginning musicians worry about *"how am I going to make a living from playing this?"* They get charmed by the sound of an instrument, and mutate, over time, into victims of its 'behavioral traditions.'

## We Hate Your Dots

When a composer sends a score to an orchestra, in most instances, they don't want to see it. You can't understand how horrible it is to have to go through that unless you have manually copied a score—until you have had to sit there for months (for some guys, years) **drawing dots.**

The process of preparing a score is an endless job. After you have written hundreds of pages of dots upon dots and checked them to make sure that you didn't make a mistake, somebody has to **copy the parts.**

Each score page shows the conductor what everybody in the orchestra is supposed to be doing at any given moment during the piece.

One page of full orchestral score that takes forty-five seconds to play can take sixteen hours to draw.

Before an orchestra can play what you wrote, a **copyist** has to put on his green eyeshade, roll up his sleeves and say, *"Okay, the bells."* He looks at the score, and copies out just what *Mr. Bells* is required to do, moment by moment, throughout the piece. Then he copies out the moment-by-moment instructions for *Mr. Chimes,* and so on down the page for **every instrument in the orchestra.**

A copyist gets paid money for that—a *lot* of money. Who pays for it? The composer, of course.

I have a closet in my basement, full of orchestral scores—the result of about five years' work by as many as five full-time copyists. The salaries paid out during that period ran close to three hundred thousand dollars, and then the only way I got to hear any of it was to spend an even larger amount and **hire** an orchestra to play it.

Thanks to songs like *"Dinah Moe Humm," "Titties & Beer"* and *"Don't Eat the Yellow Snow,"* I managed to accumulate enough cash to bribe a group of drones to grind its way through pieces like *"Mo 'n Herb's Vacation," "Bob in Dacron"* and *"Bogus Pomp"* (eventually released on *London Symphony Orchestra, Volumes I and II*)—in performances which come off like high-class 'demos' of what actually resides in the scores. So, how did I wind up using **those** guys? Well, it's a *long story* . . .

### ORCHESTRAL STUPIDITY #1

In 1976, the people who promoted our rock shows in Austria (Stimmung der Welt) approached me with the idea of doing a concert with the Vienna Symphony. I said okay. After two or three years of pooting around with the mechanics of the deal, work began on the final preparations. The concert was to be funded by the city of Vienna, the Austrian radio, the Austrian television and a substantial investment from me (the cost of preparing the scores and parts).

At the point when the official announcement was made that the concert would take place (I think it was in June or July), there was no written contract with any of the governmental agencies listed above. As it turned out, the person from the Austrian TV who pledged $300,000 toward the budget (which was to cover three weeks of rehearsal, shipping our band equipment, air fares and housing for band members and band and crew salaries— I was not getting paid for any of this) did not **really** have the authority to do so, and was informed by his boss that that amount had **already been committed to other TV projects.** This created a situation wherein the remaining sponsors still had their funds available and

146

wished to proceed, but somebody had to round up the missing $300,000 from another source.

At this point my manager got on a plane to Europe and spent the best part of a month thrashing around the continent, trying to raise the missing bucks. No luck. Between his travel, food, hotels and intercontinental phone calls, plus my investment in copyist fees to prepare the music *(not to mention the two or three years I had spent writing it)*, the total amount I had spent **in cash,** at the time the concert was canceled, came to around $125,000.

### ORCHESTRAL STUPIDITY #2

The second one goes like this: in 1980, in Amsterdam, the head of the Holland Festival came to my hotel and said the Festival wanted to do a *"special performance of my orchestral music"* with the Residentie Orchestra (from The Hague), as well as performances of certain other smaller pieces by the Netherlands Wind Ensemble, all of these performances to take place during one whole 'special week' of the festival.

I told him that I had received several offers in the past (including one from the Oslo Philharmonic where they thought they might be able to squeeze in **two days** of rehearsal), and described the whole Vienna business in glowing terms.

I told him that it would be nice to have the music performed but, since there was *a lot of it* and it was *difficult stuff,* there was no way I would discuss it any further without the guarantee of a minimum of three weeks' rehearsal, and in no way was I interested in spending any more of my own money on projects such as this.

He assured me that they were committed to doing the project and that the rehearsal schedule could be arranged, and not only that—they were willing to pay for the WHOLE THING!

The Holland Festival put up the equivalent of $500,000 for the event. Deals were then made with CBS to record and release the music, more copyists were hired, musicians from the U.S. who were going to play the amplified parts of the score were hired, road crew people who would handle the PA equipment (as the concert was to be held in an eight-thousand-seat hall) were hired and a rock tour of Europe was booked (to help pay the cost of shipping the equipment and the salaries of the U.S. people involved—again, I was not getting paid), all in preparation for another summer orchestral concert that was doomed like the other one.

What happened? Well, first let's understand the economics of a project like this. It involves a lot of musicians and they all like to get paid (this is a mild way of putting it). Also, since it was to be an amplified concert, there is the problem of special equipment to make the sound as clear as possible in the hall. (It was called the Ahoy—a charming sort of Dutch indoor bicycle racing arena with a concrete floor and a banked wooden track all around the room.) Also, there was going to be a recording of the music, necessitating the expenditure of even more money for the rental of the equipment, engineer's salary and travel expenses, etc., etc., etc.

The money from the Dutch government would cover the salaries of the Dutch musicians, for rehearsal and live performance, and also the cost of the rehearsal hall. As usual, everything else in the budget was my problem.

I had to find a way to pay for the recording equipment, the engineer, the extra payments to the musicians for sessions (above and beyond their concert pay) and all post-production (mixing, packaging, etc.) on the album. A deal was made with CBS and that problem was solved.

The next problem was how to pay for the rehearsal salaries and travel expenses for the U.S. musicians who were to be involved, as well as their concert performance salaries. This problem was solved by booking a rock tour of about four weeks' duration for the time between the first orchestral rehearsals (the week of April 20) and the rest (a two-week period toward the end of May, just before the actual orchestra concerts).

The band I was bringing over from the States would be doing a total of seventeen weeks' work, all of it rehearsal except for four weeks of rock shows, one week of orchestral concerts and five days of recording. It was to be a nine-piece group and each musician would have earned $15,000 for the seventeen weeks of work plus having all of their travel expenses paid, all of their food paid for, all of their hotels paid for, etc.

Shortly before the start of rehearsals in the U.S., Vinnie Colaiuta and Jeff Berlin called our office and tried to make secret deals to get their individual salaries raised, saying, *"Don't tell the other guys."*

When I heard of this, I canceled using the electric group with the orchestra, saving myself a lot of time and trouble rehearsing them, and a lot of money moving them around. Plans remained in effect for the orchestral concerts to continue as acoustic events in smaller halls. The recording plans remained the same also . . . five days of recording following the live performances.

About a week or so after the attempted hijack by the U.S. musicians, our office received a letter from the head of the Residentie Orchestra. Among other things, it mentioned that the orchestra committee (a group of players that represents the orchestra members in discussions with the orchestra management) had **hired a lawyer** and were ready to **begin negotiations** to determine how much of a royalty **THEY** would get for making a record.

Since I had already raised the funds from CBS to pay them the necessary recording scale for doing this work, such a demand seemed to be totally out of line with reality, as I had never heard of a situation wherein an orchestra demanded that the composer pay **them** royalties for **their** performance of works **he had written,** nor did I feel it would have been advisable to set a dangerous precedent that might affect the livelihood of other composers, by acceding to the wishes of this greedy bunch of mechanics.

A short time after that the orchestra manager and the guy we originally talked to from the Holland Festival flew to Los Angeles for a meeting to go over final details.

They arrived at my house about midnight. By about 1:30 A.M., I had told them that I never wished to see their mercenary little ensemble, and that permission to perform any of my works would not be granted to them under any circumstances. They left soon after that.

It was determined shortly thereafter that the cost of going through all of this intercontinental frolic had brought my 'serious music investment' to about $250,000 and I still hadn't heard a note of it.

There you have it, folks . . . two orchestral stupidities: a conceptual double concerto for inaudible instruments on two continents, perfectly performed by some of the most exceptional musicians of our time.

Frank Zappa, *Musician* magazine #36, September 1981

# But Did I Learn My Lesson? Nooooooo!

For anyone who ever thought I was a schmuck (or worse), this next section **proves** it. After the Holland deal bit the dust, there was **another one** . . . in Poland . . . actually, **two different orchestras in Poland**—and always the same result: NO MUSIC—LARGE EXPENSE. Anyway, finally I said: *"These European orchestras are a pain in the ass."*

Most of the projects were situations in which a governmental agency was involved—the government of the municipality or the country, whatever it was—situations in which 'official guys' had originally suggested the project, and were supposedly going to be responsible for **paying** for it.

That's when I decided to just go ahead, **pay for it all myself** and do it with **A Real American Orchestra.**

We made a deal with the Syracuse Symphony. We booked a concert date (January 30, 1983) at Lincoln Center. The music was going to be played and recorded in the United States.

Well, somehow, **AFTER** the deal was made, somebody in the Syracuse Symphony 'upper echelon' decided to **DOUBLE** the agreed-upon price by whipping out an assortment of semi-obscure 'local union regulations.' Syracuse priced themselves out of the market.

So I said—actually, by this time, I'm screaming—*"Fuck this! I'm not going to get bent over by some deranged American union extortionist!"*—and that's when I decided to rent the BBC Orchestra (or the equivalent) in England. We called the BBC Orchestra. They were booked for the next five years.

They would have been a good orchestra to do it because they specialize in contemporary repertoire, BUT they weren't available. So, we called the LSO—and, at first, THEY weren't available either.

They were just finishing a film score and had planned a two-week vacation for themselves, after which they were going to start on ANOTHER film score.

The way the LSO works is, it's owned by the musicians—it's a 'cooperative.' THEY decide who's going to be their conductor and what work they're going to do. When my project was suggested to them, they voted to do it rather than take a vacation, so I went ahead. We rehearsed thirty hours, did one live concert, and then did the recording.

The first small disaster was the seating plan I had prepared—it didn't work. The place we had originally rented to do the recording in turned out to be smaller than the floor plan sent to me (because of an immovable motion-picture screen, not shown on the plan, that knocked out eight feet of depth from the rear wall of the stage to the front), so we had to find **another** place to record in.

We tried every 'major concert hall'—every one of them was booked with Christmas shit. We tried all the smaller town halls—same deal. We couldn't find a hall anywhere, so we wound up at Twickenham Studios (a film studio where they used to shoot the '007' movies), on an old soundstage, with completely dead acoustics.

It was big enough to hold the 107-piece orchestra, but it sounded diabolical. So, the setup began. **This was going to be the first multitrack digital recording of a symphony orchestra—ever.**

But before we could record, we had to present the obligatory 'live concert' in order to satisfy the union rehearsal requirements (see "Drool, Britannia," Chapter 7).

This was a disaster. The LSO gives its performances in a wretchedly 'modern' concert hall called the Barbican. The stage was too small to hold the full orchestra, so a bunch of musicians who wouldn't fit (mostly viola players) got to go home—and get paid for it.

One unique facility offered by the Barbican is the stand-up

bar backstage—for the use of the orchestra members. It is well stocked and very efficient. They can pour a whole orchestra's worth of booze in nanoseconds. During the break between pieces, the LSO left the stage and availed itself of this convenience. When it returned to play the next piece, many members were roasted—and so was my music.

## Recording the LSO

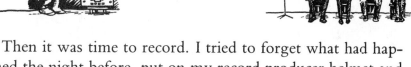

Then it was time to record. I tried to forget what had happened the night before, put on my record producer helmet and set out to confute the laws of physics.

The French horns (eight of them) were one of the early problems. We put several Telefunken U-47s on them, but they were useless.

The problem was the percussion (six individual stations) all around in back of them—we were getting tons of leakage. Even on a tight cardioid pattern, we picked up blobs of low-end **mung** that was wandering around the floor—so I said, *"Although I've never used a PZM [pressure zone microphone] on a French horn before, what have we got to lose?"* We took the large 2½ and put it on the floor behind them and that did it.

We were using a KM-84, flown high over the timpani. We gave up on that and used a 4′ × 4′ Plexiglas sheet to increase *the boundary* on one of the PZM plates, put it on the wall **behind** the timpani and got a great sound.

We were using all the **Prescribed Mikes** for various instruments but, given our acoustic situation in this nasty room, they just didn't work. For example, we tried two AKG 414s, flown above the conductor's podium, for ambience, but all they gave us was an ugly room sound that was like, *"Hey, you want to hear the air conditioner? Let's go. Here it is."*

*Recording musicians want their instruments to sound (at very least)* GLORIOUS—they've been recording for years and they're used to seeing those gray, heavy, **serious-looking** microphones. *["Oooh fuck! Look at this! I'm going to sound BITCHEN in this!"]* THEN somebody comes in and puts a plastic dome with a PZM in it over their heads and they go: *"MY TONE! MY* **PRECIOUS** *TONE! I'm going to sound PLASTIC!"*

The orchestra already had a strange attitude because everything was different from the way they were used to working. They weren't in a concert hall—they were on a dead and dusty soundstage. They didn't have the BIG GRAY MIKE—they had the little plastic bubble over their heads (or they had part of a plastic box on the floor). They had LITTLE TINY WIRES, not BIG SERIOUS WIRES. They could trip over these things (especially since they were so fond of alcohol).

## Mixing the LSO

In ambient recording, there's always some kind of 'LUMP' in the room. Some of them are good and some of them are bad. The more stereo pairs you deal with  in an ambient mix, the more likely you are to experience 'LUMP ACCUMULATION.'

In this recording we had to equalize things to emphasize the natural range that the instrument was playing in and, at the same time, neutralize the lumpage. In this room, the UGLY ZONE was located in two areas: 200 Hz and 63 Hz. Both of those frequencies had to be hauled out.

When we mixed it, as partial compensation for the ugliness of the room, we decided that each section in the music would be treated as a different 'SCENE,' and that each 'SCENE' could occur in any kind of an imaginary ambience that was appropriate to its mood (sort of like stage lighting). At this point, the DEAD ROOM became a blessing in disguise—we could go from scratch, building 'artificial acoustics' with digital impunity.

So, a collection of imaginary environments was created with a Lexicon 224-X digital reverb processor. Each imaginary world had a different set of characteristics. We mixed each section of the music as if it had occurred in its own personalized acoustical space.

Also, because of the way in which the music was mixed, instrumental details came out that you'd never get to hear in the old *'two-mikes-over-the-conductor's-head'* style of recording. In earphones, especially, you get the impression of sitting in the middle of the orchestra, with the apparent room size and surface texture of the walls changing, according to the musical character of each section.

## The 'Human' Element

In 1986 when I released *Jazz from Hell,* an album realized on the Synclavier, a lot of reviewers, especially the British ones, said that it was **cold,** and lacked **the 'human' element**—and so, with great delight, the following year I released *London Symphony Orchestra Vol. II*—because it is *filled* with **'human element artifacts.'**

On the last day of the last session for that album, I was trying to record a piece called "Strictly Genteel." Union rules specified a short break every hour, and during the last hour of the session, the entire trumpet section left the Twickenham Studio grounds and invaded a pub across the street, arriving back to work fifteen minutes late.

Meanwhile the rest of the orchestra had been sitting in the studio waiting for their trumpet buddies to return. Fifteen minutes might not sound like very much time but, in a professional recording session involving 107 players, fifteen minutes is A LONG TIME. In a recording session, every second counts— and is being *paid for* in **Large Dollars.** In spite of the fact that the piece wasn't near being recordable, there was no way I could make the orchestra play overtime; I couldn't regain the fifteen minutes at the end of the session **at any price.**

They made so many mistakes, and played so badly on that piece, that it required forty edits (within seven minutes of music) to try to cover them. We used every mixing trick in the book to hide the out-of-tune notes.

## A Short History of Recording Technology

Audio tools are available now that enable the artist to control timbre to the point where a psychoacoustical or emotional 'spin' can be placed on any given note or passage (just by changing the digital echo program, for instance).

When I started working in the studio, *equalizers* (tone control circuits) were rare. *Compressors* were crude devices that added grotesque amounts of noise to the program material. As these audio tools were refined and made quieter, a new vocabulary of sounds—and new ways to deal with **blocks of sounds**—came into common usage. (One result was that the *overall timbre of commercial broadcasting changed.*)

The 1950s rock and roll record was a mono recording. In most instances, early recordings were made using a single microphone for the band and vocalist(s). The 'mix' was the acoustical result of the distance between the microphone and the singer, the microphone and the drummer, the microphone and the bass player and so on. How far away you were from the microphone determined how 'important' you were in the final mix.

What qualified as an 'acceptable drum sound' on a 1950s recording seems laughable today.

Since they didn't have digital echo then, the 'flavor' and quantity of the reverberation used on a song were determined by the acoustics of the room in which the recording was made. The echo (or absence thereof) described the geography of an 'imaginary landscape' in which a song would be 'photographed' by the microphone. Studios that had good acoustical echo chambers were highly prized. Some became legendary for their 'hit sound.'

The 1960s brought a few more improvements—most notably the fuzz-tone, improvements in the electric bass, improvements in guitar amplifiers and improvements in microphone technology.

Increased sophistication of mixing consoles made it possible for any number of microphones in the room to be combined by the engineer to create new audio illusions, impossible in the acoustical world—a big difference from the mix determined by the distance between the performer and the microphone.

On a multichannel mix you can put a close mike on the kick drum, a close mike on the snare drum, a close mike on the horns and so on—and then combine them. *There is no place in nature where a human being could stand that would allow him to hear all those instruments* **that way** *with his ears.* This artificial acoustical perspective has become the norm.

Eventually, some instruments found their way into the mix without even being 'listened to' by a microphone. These sounds (usually from synthesizers, electric bass and/or guitar) were injected directly into the board through a direct box.

*157*

Digital ambience-creating devices became available. With them, record producers could build 'imaginary rooms' (as I have described) for the mix to reside in.

Using several of those devices, the engineer can create an array of 'imaginary rooms.' This allows individual voices or instruments in the mix to exist in separate and distinct imaginary acoustical environments simultaneously.

## Digital Audio

One of the things I always hated about making records was that no matter what the music sounded like coming through the speakers in the control room, by the time you piled it onto analog tape, you had to live with the buildup of **hiss.**

There are all kinds of artificial ways to **hide the hiss** (Dolby, dbx, C-4D), but it still lives **in the tape.** Some people don't care, because if the program material is always loud, always fuzz-tone, they'll never hear a bit of hiss. But if you're doing soft passages, the minute the music thins out, so that there are spaces between the notes, the hiss creeps in and spoils it.

With digital recording, the only hiss on the tape is the hiss that could come from the mike or the mixing board. The tape itself doesn't generate hiss.

The best way I can think of to explain how digital audio works is to say that it's similar to the way you look at a photograph in a newspaper. The newspaper photo is not a 'continuous-tone photograph'; it's broken up into dots, and your eye resolves the dots, allowing you to believe you've seen an image.

In digital audio you can think of the sounds as dots or slices, but they are actually a string of numbers. A sound from The Real World is sliced up, and stored as complex batches of ones and zeros.

Resolution in digital audio is determined by the sampling

rate. Each string of numbers is one 'sample,' representing a very short slice of time. The number of slices per second is the *sampling rate*. The more slices you take, the better the resolution.

In printing they can use a higher-resolution dot screen for a high-gloss magazine than they can for a newspaper (because of the texture and ink absorption characteristics of the paper they're printing on). You and I know that it's still only a bunch of dots in *National Geographic,* but we can certainly tell the difference in clarity between a photo printed there and one on the front page of *The Daily Bugle.*

## Dance Fever

The most important innovation in recent rock technology is a naughty little appliance, sold in various shapes and sizes, under an assortment of brand names, referred to generically as a *'drum box'* or *'rhythm machine.'* This device is used by people with diagonal zippers on their clothes to provide the inflexible rhythms and obnoxious artificial hand-claps that cause Americans to **'make the dancer face'** (*eyes closed; lips pooched out*— you know the one—as if when you do **that** with your face, it gives you a license to do the other stupid stuff with your buttocks).

Before the emergence of this wondrous tool, record producers worried that the tempo of their hit records would *drift* (maybe a little faster on the chorus when everybody was *banging it out*—maybe a little slower when the *"I love you"* comes in)— **a terrible problem,** which, in the long-long-ago, led to *take* after *take* during the recording session to capture a single performance with **JUST THE RIGHT GROOVE.**

But this is **"The Eighties"** (*phewwww)*—we're modern now, and studio time is more expensive. We can't be waiting around for 'just the right groove.' We need that *sumbitch* in a

**hurry**—science has just proven that Americans (who can barely get their shit together on the assembly line) find it absolutely *UNPOSSIBLE* during their precious off-duty hours to dance to any song unless it's in 4/4 at 120 beats per minute—no fuckin' around now—no 119—no 121—gimme the ol' 120 'n turn up the goddam handclaps! **Ow! Ow! Ow! I'm dancin'! I'm dancin'!**

Other countries have cultures that go back thousands of years. Ours goes back a couple hundred years and it's not even **that bitchen** (since the bulk of what we pound our chests over was abducted from somewhere else), and we go around trying to inflict this 'nonculture' on people all over *The International Elsewhere*—people regarded by many Americans as 'less than human' (of course, this attitude is justified if we're talking about the British—but **seriously,** folks—).

We'd look *a little better,* internationally—perhaps 'more trustable'—if we did a few of the things **they've** been doing for millenia; giving at least *the illusion* that we were almost sort-of like them—*almost sort-of civilized*—so that they could *almost* sort-of talk **to** us, instead of **about** us (as if **We** were **subhuman** . . . or almost *British*).

Believe it or not, there are places in the world where **music** is **important.** There are places in the world where all the arts are a matter of national pride. We come in, making that fucking **'dancer face'** and demand that everybody *respect* us—**do we have any idea how ridiculous that looks?**

## What Is Music?

*"We're coming to the beginning of a new era, wherein the development of the inner self is the most important thing. We have to train ourselves so that we can improvise on anything—a bird, a sock, a fuming beaker! This, too, can be music. Anything can be music."*

Biff Debris in *Uncle Meat*

A person with a feel for rhythm can walk into a factory and hear the machine noise as a composition. If we expand that concept to include light, behavior, weather factors, moon phases, anything (whether it's a rhythm that can be **heard** or a rhythm that is **perceived,** i.e., a color change **over time**—or **a season**), it can be **consumed** as music.

If it can be **conceived as music,** it can be **executed as music,** and **presented to an audience in such a way that they** will **perceive it as music:** *"Look at this. Ever seen one of these before? I built this for you. What do you mean, 'What the fuck is it?' It's a goddam ÉTUDE, asshole."*

When someone writes a piece of music, what he or she puts on the paper is **roughly the equivalent of a recipe**—in the sense that **the recipe is not the food, only instructions for the preparation of the food.** Unless you are very weird, you don't eat the recipe.

If I write someting on a piece of paper, I can't *actually* **'hear'** it. I can conjure up visions of what the symbols on the page **mean,** and imagine a piece of music as it might sound in performance, but **that sensation is nontransferable; it can't be shared or transmitted.**

It doesn't become a 'musical experience' in normal terms until 'the recipe' has been converted into **wiggling air molecules.**

Music, in performance, is a type of sculpture. The air in the performance space is **sculpted into something.** This *'molecule-sculpture-over-time'* is then 'looked at' by the ears of the listeners —or a microphone.

SOUND is 'ear-decoded data.' Things which MAKE SOUND are things which are capable of creating **perturbations.** These perturbations modify (or sculpt) the raw material (the 'static air' in the room—the way it was 'at rest' before the musicians started fucking around with it). If you **purposefully** generate atmospheric perturbations ('air shapes'), you are composing.

# Let's **All** Be Composers!

**A composer is a guy who goes around forcing his will on unsuspecting air molecules, often with the assistance of unsuspecting musicians.**

Want to be a composer? You don't even have to be able to **write it down.** The stuff that gets written down is only a recipe, remember?—like the stuff in Ronnie Williams's *MACHA* book. If you can **think design,** you can **execute design**—it's only a bunch of air molecules, who's gonna check up on you?

### JUST FOLLOW THESE SIMPLE INSTRUCTIONS:

[1] Declare your **intention** to create a 'composition.'

[2] **Start** a piece at **some time.**

[3] Cause **something to happen over a period of time** (it doesn't matter what happens in your 'time hole'—we have critics to tell us whether it's any good or not, so we won't worry about that part).

[4] **End the piece at some time** (or keep it going, telling the audience it is a *'work in progress'*).

[5] Get a part-time job so you can continue to do stuff like this.

# Weights and Measures

In my compositions, I employ a system of weights, balances, measured tensions and releases—in some ways similar to Varèse's aesthetic. The similarities are best illustrated by comparison to a *Calder mobile:* **a multicolored whatchamacallit, dangling in space, that has big blobs of metal connected**

**to pieces of wire, balanced ingeniously against little metal dingleberries on the other end.** Varèse knew Calder, and was fascinated by these creations.

So, in my case, I say: *"A large mass of any material will 'balance' a smaller, denser mass of any material, according to the length of the gizmo it's dangling on, and the 'balance point' chosen to facilitate the danglement."*

The material being 'balanced' includes stuff other than the notes on the paper. If you can conceive of **any material** as a 'weight' and any **idea-over-time** as a 'balance,' you are ready for the next step: the *'entertainment objects'* that derive from those concepts.

## "Anything, Any Time, Anywhere—for No Reason at All"

If a musical point can be made in a more entertaining way by **saying** a word than by **singing** a word, the **spoken word** will win out in the arrangement—unless a *nonword* or a *mouth noise* gets the point across faster.

This frequently occurs when the stage arrangements of old songs get modified to accommodate each new band. The body of the song, the melody line, the words, and the chords remain the same, but all aspects of 'the clothing,' or the orchestration, are up for grabs, based on the musical resources at hand.

With the 1988 band (twelve pieces, including myself), the orchestration was far more luxuriant for some of the older songs than when they were originally recorded, simply because I didn't want to have eleven guys standing around onstage with nothing to do.

Songs written with one idea in mind have been known to mutate into something *completely* different if I hear an 'optional vocal inflection' during rehearsal. I'll hear a 'hint' of something

*163*

(often a mistake) and pursue it to its most absurd extreme.

The 'technical expression' we use in the band to describe this process is: **"PUTTING THE EYEBROWS ON IT."** This usually refers to vocal parts, although you can *put the eyebrows on* just about anything.

After *"the eyebrows,"* the ultimate tweeze inflicted on the composition is determining **The Attitude** with which the piece is to be performed. The player is expected to comprehend **The Attitude,** and perform the material with **The Attitude AND The Eyebrows,** *consistently,* otherwise, to me, the piece sounds **'wrong.'**

Since most Americans use a personal version of *eyebrowsage* in their conversational speech, why not include the technique as a 'nuance' in a composition?

A musician may give the 'illusion' during rehearsal that he knows what I want on a certain passage, but the hard part is getting him to do it correctly, night after night on the road—because after a while, most musicians forget **why** I told them to do it **that way** in the first place, which brings us to . . .

## The Anthropology of the Rock and Roll Band

Very few people *choose* to play the bass. There are people in the audience who like to *listen* to the bass, because they like those low frequencies, and the way they make their bodies feel —but the role of the bass player in the band is not usually the most *exciting* role, because he has to play **repeated figures.** We have a viola parallel here: electric bassists are often failed guitar players, demoted to this duty after a band meeting in a garage when they were thirteen.

Drummers often exhibit an attitude which advertises: *"I play the drums because I am* **an animal**—*watch me* **beat these!** *Girls,* *are you paying attention now? I'm beating* **very hard!***"*

Keyboard players project an aura of frustration because they are not *guitar players.* (In fact, many musicians are convinced that in order to get The Blow Job after the show, they have to play **LEAD GUITAR.**)

They believe that if they imitate certain *guitar noises,* it will automatically guarantee them The Big Payoff—which is one of the reasons you now see keyboard players wearing those *'things'* around their necks that kind of look like guitars but have keys on them (like an accordion that's been hit by a truck, with a nozzle on the end), as if to say: *"What?! You'd rather blow* **the guitar player?** *Hah! Look at this high-tech dork* **I'm** *wearing!"*

Most of the people who play keyboards in rock bands are not really skilled musicians. They're usually there to play droning string synthesizer pads or punches, fills and mannerisms that aren't very demanding, providing the chordal accompaniment while the guitar player goes *"weedly-weedly-wee."*

Unless the keyboard guy is working in a bar band, where you're usually cramped for space and the setup goes wherever you can fit it in, his stuff generally resides in *'the back line.'* Because of this, denizens of *'the back line'* believe that the closer you are to the *front* of the stage (especially when cavorting with a phallic-looking appliance, illuminated by a blue spotlight), *the better the chances for the ol' you-know-what*—hence the desire of performers in **all categories** to move *"closer to the people"* (in spite of the fact that they might grab you by the ankle, pull you off the stage and mutilate you).

## How Did They Manage to Do That?

I don't give musicians a 'questionnaire' when they join the band about where they've been to school or what kind of technical information they possess—I'll hear during the audition whether they can play or not.

For the ones who pass the audition, as soon as I find out what they **don't** know, I attempt to devise 'language' that will describe my musical intentions, in shorthand form, if they don't know the standard technical terms or if (in spite of the fact that they might be great players) they have never been asked to try some of the things the band veterans have been doing for years from *muscle memory*.

For example—say I'm talking to Chad Wackerman. I'll tell him, *"The* **Quaalude Thunder** *goes here."* That's the shorthand description of a drum fill you hear on certain heavy metal albums—where the guy plays as many notes as he can on all of his thousand tom-toms before he ends with The Big Crash.

There's an assortment of 'stock modules' used in our stage arrangements. It helps if the guys in the band appreciate the musical humor of what's going on. Sometimes they do—and sometimes they don't. (If a guy can't willingly *'put on the lamp-shade'* and play stooge rock, he's probably wrong for the job.)

These 'stock modules' include the *"Twilight Zone" texture* (which may not be the actual *Twilight Zone* notes, but the same 'texture'), the *"Mister Rogers" texture,* the *"Jaws" texture,* the *Lester Lanin texture, Jan Garber-ism,* and things that sound either **exactly like** or **very similar to** "Louie Louie."

Those are **Archetypal American Musical Icons,** and their presence in an arrangement puts a spin on any lyric in their vicinity. When present, these modules 'suggest' that you interpret **those lyrics** within parentheses.

We evoke Mister Rogers with a celeste or bells playing some permutation of: *"It's a lovely day in the neigh-bor-hood."* We use that all the time. Another one is the *Fake Devo texture*—anything absolutely squared off, mechanical, dry and dead-sounding. Invocation of this plasticized mantra adds **another** dimension to a lyric.

The audience doesn't have to know, for example, who Jan Garber or Lester Lanin is to appreciate those textures—the average guy is not going to say *"Hey, Richie! Check this out! They're doing Lester!"*—he knows what that style **means**—he's groaned over it in old movies on Channel 13 for years.

This technique has been used in the band since 1966 on *Absolutely Free,* our second album. There's a twisted reference to Charles Ives at the end of "Call Any Vegetable." One of the things that Ives is noted for is his use of multiple colliding themes—the musical illusion of several marching bands marching through each other. In our low-rent version, the band splits into three parts, playing "The Star-Spangled Banner," "God Bless America" and "America the Beautiful" all at the same time, yielding an amateur version of an Ives collision. Unless listeners pay attention in that one spot—there are only a few bars of it—they might think it was a 'mistake.'

Then there's a place in "Duke of Prunes" where the "Berceuse" from Stravinsky's *Firebird Suite* is floated over another, more rhythmic theme from *The Rite of Spring.*

"I'm Losing Status at the High School" jumps into the opening figure of *Petrushka.* The 1971 band had an arrangement that quoted the opening trumpet fanfare from Stravinsky's *Agon.*

Then there are cues used on stage like twirling my fingers as if I'm piddling with a Rasta braid on the right side of my head —that means: **"Play reggae."** If I pretend to twirl braids on both sides of my head, it means: **"Play ska"** (as if it were double-time reggae). During any song, no matter what style it was **learned** in, on a whim I can turn around and do something like that, and the band will restyle the tune.

If I want something played 'heavy metal,' I put both hands near my crotch and do **"Big Balls."** Each guy in the band understands what the norms and 'expected mannerisms' are for these different musical styles, and will instantly 'translate' a song into that musical 'dialect.'

## Verrrrrry Scarrrrry

Science hasn't told us yet why some people find it amusing when they hear an old-time car horn go *"Ah-**roooo**-gah!"* I'm waiting for the answer—because I'm one of those idiots. I like sound effects A LOT (percussive and vocal), and use them often in my arrangements.

The ending of the 1988 Deluxe Version of "Peaches en Regalia" uses them, along with multiple, superimposed A.A.I.M.'s (Archetypal American Icon Modules).

When the melody comes in after the second intro, we use *"Fake Devo,"* superimposed on *"Twilight Zone"* in the rhythm section, while the 'nice little melody' is reharmonized with an ugly chord traveling parallel. Then there's a short break, and Ike says, **"Whooo-oo!"** like Count Floyd from *SCTV*. It doesn't mean anything, but to see Ike Willis pretending to be Count Floyd for one or two beats in the middle of all that is something I find enjoyable—and then, just to make sure that you didn't miss it, when the melody repeats the next time, it stops *just a little bit longer* and he says, **"Whoooo-oo, whoooooo-oooo!"** Of course it's **mega-stupid.** That's why I like it.

The first time I saw Count Floyd, I almost strangled. I was drinking a cup of coffee, lying in bed watching television, and it was a complete surprise. Joe Flaherty nailed **the essence** of TV monster movie *cheese* without even using a real word from the English language—**Big Eyebrows,** Joe—**real Big Eyebrows.**

## Road Rats

Musicians' 'priorities' change on the road. In rehearsal, they're struggling to get the piece learned; on the road, they're struggling to get a peep at the front row before the lights go down, to see whether there's any interesting 'vegetation' out there. Every band does that. I've never been on the road with an orchestra, but I'm sure they have their *trawl-meisters* too.

I respect musicians' idiosyncrasies—they add 'texture' to a performance. Musicians tend to generate better 'texture' when they get **'The Blow Job.'** Yes, I **want** them to find that elusive cross between a waitress and an industrial vacuum cleaner.

One of the more boring chores I am required to perform as a bandleader is maintaining 'corporate discipline' during the show. While the performance is in progress, I know that *the radar is on*—everybody is looking for the *(you guessed it)*.

That's okay. They should all get The Blow Job—but they should get it *the honest way*—they should **earn it**, by playing the songs right. Sometimes they try to cheat . . . and, folks, it is not a pretty sight.

For instance, there are a lot of reasons why musicians like to play solos on stage—but the usual reason in rock and roll is to get The Blow Job. One way to ensure that you look like the greatest thing going when you play **your big solo** is to make sure that you end your solo by going *up the scale*, then grab that last note and repeat it as fast as you can.

The statement is the same on any instrument: **"Oh, I'm squirting now!"** ⟨*Clever subtext to the audience.*⟩

In the case of violinist Jean-Luc Ponty, who was with the band briefly in the early seventies, no matter what the solo was, after a certain period of time on the road he always ended with the same passage—he'd wiggle up to the top of the instrument and squirt all over the place on the last note . . . **and the crowd went wild!** But if you're another guy in the band, and you see that happening every night, you go, *"Ho-hum."*

To a certain extent, Alan Zavod, our 1984 keyboard player, would do the same thing—he would end his solo with this thing that everybody called *"The Volcano."* He held the sustain pedal down and churned and smashed away to get a big blur going, and then topped it off at the end with a flourish. It worked every time, but it got to be a band joke. In fact, Alan really is a great pianist (and film composer). It's just that maybe—because he was working in a rock and roll band—he thought **that** type of solo was the appropriate vehicle to *project his aura across vast continental areas.*

I find it especially disturbing if, when the band is walking onto the stage to get the equipment ready, a musician cranks off a tiny, unaccompanied 'solo-ette' in order to draw attention to himself while piddling with his amplifier.

In Norway, we have played several times in a place called the Drammenshallen, or, as band vets refer to it: *the Drammin-drammin-drammin-drammin-hollin-hollin-hollin-hollin.* The last time we performed there was in the fall of 1984.

Some months before that date, Ike had used the word **'spoo'** —roughly the equivalent of *jizz*—in a conversation. I don't know where it came from, or if he made it up. In any event, 'spoo' turned out to be 'the mystery word' onstage that night.

When we came back to do the encore, Ike arrived first, and was kneeling down in front of his amplifier, doing kind of a low-rent Jimi Hendrix *"wee-wee-wee-wee."* As I walked out and witnessed this act of near desperation, I said *"Spoo!"* to him— he got it right away. [Translation: *"You're jerking off in front of your amplifier, Dr. Willis, and I know it."*]

# Does Humor Belong in Music?

What academicians regard as 'humor' in music is usually stuff along the lines of "Till Eulenspiegel's Merry Pranks" (remember, in 'Music Appreciation class,' when they told you that the E-flat clarinet is going *"ha-ha-ha!"*?). Take my word for it, folks—you can do **way better** than that.

I've stated elsewhere that "Timbre **Rules**"—*rules* **what?** For one thing, it rules in *'the humor domain.'* The minute you hear a trumpet with a Harmon mute going *"Fwa-da-fwa-da-fwa-da,"* you register 'something'—a *'humor* **something.'** (There aren't any technical names for these **'things'** because they don't give foundation grants to study this kind of stuff.)

Likewise, a bass saxophone, playing in its lowest register, conveys another sort of **'H.S.'** (Humor Something)—and how about our ol' buddy, *The Slide Trombone*—surely this graceful, expressive piece of machinery has its own little **'H.S.'** radiator built into it.

I've developed a 'formula' for what these timbres *mean* (to me, at least), so that when I create an arrangement—if I have access to the right instrumental resources—I can put sounds together that tell **more than the story in the lyrics,** especially to American listeners, raised on these subliminal clichés, shaping their audio reality from the cradle to the elevator.

We crack up during rehearsal because some of the stuff is *so stupid.* When building an arrangement, every time I have an opportunity to insert one of those modules I cram it in, and since rehearsal is a daily two-hour occurrence while we're on the road, the arrangements often change overnight, based on the daily news or some morsel of tour-bus folklore.

During the pretour rehearsals, the band members pencil these 'extras' in next to 'the real notes' so, when they finally have the show learned, they know not only the *song-as-originally-written* but also, superimposed on it, a flexible grid which will support a constantly mutating collage of low-rent Americana.

I owe this part of my musical existence to **Spike Jones.**

## La Machine

Most of my compositions today are *written on* and *performed by* a machine—a computer musical instrument called the **Synclavier.** It allows me to create and record a type of music that is impossible (or too boring) for human beings to play.

When I say too boring, I mean that in most compositions, someone has to play the *stuff in the background.* If you've ever been in a band or know anything about musicians, you know that no musician ever liked to play a background part. His mind wanders.

Much of today's music involves an ostinato bass line or some other type of repeated figure, and if the figure isn't played accurately, with conviction, whatever is laid on top of it doesn't work. To save the sanity of musicians who can't keep their minds focused when assigned to accompaniment duties, this machine will play ostinatos—cheerfully—until it's blue in the face (except it never gets blue in the face).

Anything you can dream up can be typed or played into the Synclavier. One of the things I use it for is writing blocks of complicated rhythms, and having them executed accurately by *groups of instruments.* With the Synclavier, any group of imaginary instruments can be invited to play the most difficult passages, and the 'little guys inside the machine' play them with *one-millisecond* accuracy—every time.

The Synclavier allows the composer not only to have his piece performed with precision, but to *style* the performance as well—he can be his own conductor, controlling the dynamics or any other performance parameters. He can bring his idea to the audience in a pure form, allowing them to hear **the music,** rather than the ego problems of a group of players who don't give a shit about *the composition.*

Obviously, there are things you can do with live musicians that you can't do with the Synclavier, and vice versa. I view them as separate mediums.

Some of the things live musicians do that machines don't do are good, and some are bad. One of the good things that live musicians do is *improvise.* They *respond to the moment,* and can play more expressively than the machine. (The machine is not devoid of expression, but I really have to type a lot of numbers into it to approximate the type of expression that I can get instantaneously from a well-rehearsed live ensemble.)

But musicians tend to be lazy, and they get sick and skip rehearsals. In fact, they do the kinds of things that other people do in normal jobs. If they were working in a shoestring factory, it might not make that much difference. In a live concert, everything is pressurized because all you have to work with is that single, living, two-hour hunk of time.

Machines don't get loaded, drunk or evicted and don't need assistance moving their families around in 'emergency' situations. On the other hand, machines don't decide to say things like *"We're Beatrice"* in precisely the 'wrong' place in the middle of a song, and make people laugh (one of Ike Willis's specialties). Subtracting the bullshit and the mistakes, if I had to choose between live musicians or La Machine, I must admit, from time to time I'm *almost* tempted to opt for the "human element."

## My Job! My Precious Job!

Every so often you hear someone from the Musicians' Union complaining about the possibility of devices like the Synclavier putting musicians out of work. I don't think that will ever happen. There are still plenty of people who believe that the only <u>real music</u> is music played by human beings (wearing leather and <u>large hair</u>).

Other union people seem to be under the impression that if you 'sample' a musician into a Synclavier, you magically (don't laugh) *suck the <u>music</u> out of the <u>musician,</u>* depriving him of some intangible dignity and/or potential income.

**Music comes from composers—not musicians.** Composers think it up; musicians perform it. If a musician *improvises* when he is performing, he becomes, *during those moments,* a *composer*—the rest of the time, he is the interpreter of a musical design originated by a composer. Composers don't have a union —and the Musicians' Union actually makes life more difficult for **them** with certain rule-book technicalities. The Musicians' Union helped to create the market for *sampling machines,* but refuses to admit it.

Listen to the radio—a lot of what you think is being played by *Beautiful Rock Stars* is actually being played by machines like the Synclavier. I know of a group whose producer brought them in for ONE DAY and sampled all their instruments. Then **HE** put the song together using *the sounds* of their instruments —the guys never played on the song. The machine played their instruments *for them.* All they had to do was come back and sing on top of it and make the video.

## While You Were Art

Art Jarvinen is a percussionist and former instructor at Cal-Arts. He put together a chamber ensemble called the E.A.R. Unit: two percussion, two keyboards, clarinet and cello.

He asked me to write an arrangement of "While You Were Out," a solo from the *Shut Up 'n Play Yer Guitar* album, for his ensemble to play at one of the **Monday Evening Concerts** (remember the postcard with *"We will be unable to play your piece because it requires a left-handed piano"?*—those guys—they're still in business).

I created the arrangement on the Synclavier, and, using another of the machine's features, printed out the parts. When he saw them, he realized that it was a difficult piece, and worried that his ensemble wouldn't have enough time to rehearse it, as the concert was imminent.

*"You're in luck,"* I told him, *"because you won't even have to play it. All you have to do is learn to* **pretend** *to play it, and I'll have the Synclavier take care of the rest. Just go out there and do what all the 'Big Rock Groups' have done for years—lip-sync it and make sure you look good on stage."*

I made them a tape copy of the Synclavier performance and told him, *"The way to pull this off is to have wires hanging out of your instruments leading into amplifiers and effects boxes on the floor. Any sound the audience hears that might be deemed 'synthesized' will be overlooked because there's a wire coming out of your instrument."*

Final result? The man who ran the concert series didn't know the difference. The two classical reviewers from the major Los Angeles newspapers didn't notice anything either. Nobody in the audience knew, except for David Ocker, my computer assistant, who had helped prepare the materials. **Nobody knew that the musicians never played a note.**

It produced quite a scandal in 'modern music circles.' Several members of the ensemble, mortified by all the hoo-ha, swore they would never *"do it again."* (Do **what** again? Prove to the world that nobody really knows what the fuck is going on at a contemporary music concert?)

## Conducting an Orchestra

One thing the Synclavier can't replace is the experience of conducting an orchestra. The orchestra is the ultimate instrument, and conducting one is an unbelievable sensation. Nothing else is like it, except maybe singing doo-wop harmony and hearing the chords come out right.

From the podium (if the orchestra is playing well), the music sounds so good that if you **listen to it,** you'll fuck up. When I'm conducting, I have to force myself **not to listen,** and think about what I'm doing with my hand and where the cues go.

My conducting 'style' (such as it is) lurks somewhere between nonexistent and massively boring. I try to keep cues to the bare minimum necessary for the players to do their job by simply indicating where the beat is. I don't think of myself as a 'conductor.'

*"Conducting" is when you draw 'designs' in the nowhere—with a stick, or with your hands—which are interpreted as 'instructional messages' by guys wearing bow ties who wish they were fishing.*

## Life on Stage

At home, a normal day for me is spent working by myself and not talking to anybody, so I really have to change my life around to go onstage.

As much as I would like to walk out there and 'be myself,'

the fact is that the 'self' I am—when I am just 'being myself'—would be utterly boring and unwatchable on a stage.

I don't have the skill or the inclination to do the usual rock and roll gymnastics, so I try to strike a balance between being as *sedentary as I actually am* and doing *whatever has to be done* in order to add a modicum of physical movement to the show.

I also have to take care of the daily business of running the equivalent of a little circus on the road. Part of this job is to make sure that the band delivers what it's supposed to deliver for the people who bought the tickets.

No matter how much we've rehearsed, I still have to **steer** the show-in-progress *("Is this sequence working? Is this keyboard solo taking too long to develop? Is everybody watching so that when I give the cue to come in after the alto solo in 'Inca Roads' there won't be a train wreck?")*. The only time I can 'lose consciousness' is when I'm playing a guitar solo, and then I have to concentrate a hundred percent on that—or at least ninety percent—to do it right.

If I'm in a bad mood, I try not to share that with the audience —at the same time, I'm not the kind of guy who can put on the 'Mr. Happy Face' and pretend that "all's right with the world" —acting out a lie is even worse than telling it.

In a situation where the intention is to create some sort of *structured spontaneous entertainment* (involving audience participation), the audience attending **that** concert is the **only** audience that is going to experience it. The piece exists **only for them**— unless it's recorded and goes out on a live album—but, *on the moment,* it's **just for them.** If they want to be a part of it, great —if not? Next case.

We once played a horrible venue—some kind of sports hall —in southern Illinois. The band was set up on the floor, and our amplifiers were playing straight into a concrete wall about two stories high, with the audience at the top of it—looking down. *Can you visualize that?* It was the worst setup imaginable.

So, naturally, I decided to try some 'audience participation' (like we can barely see them, and I want them to **'participate.'** *Surrrrrrre you do*).

I divided them into five sections, according to the way the seats fanned out—each section was going to be a different part of a mass chorus of maybe five thousand people. I said, *"Now, you guys over here, you're going to sing* **'Harbor Lights.'** *"* They had never even **heard** of *"Harbor Lights,"* but we showed them how it goes.

Then I said to each of the other sections, *"You are going to sing* **'In-A-Gadda-Da-Vida.'** *You're going to sing the opening bassoon solo from* **The Rite of Spring.** *You're going to sing the Prelude to Act III of* **Lohengrin,** *and you lucky folks over there get* **'Ave Maria.'** *I'll show you when to come in."* What a noise **that** was.

I *try* to have a good time on stage—it helps to compensate for the unpleasant physical sensation of being forced to perform in halls with shitty acoustics after waiting for a couple of hours in a dressing room that smells like sports vomit (but that's what I get for choosing rock instead of the bassoon). Maybe I'd better talk about the guitar for a minute here. . . .

## Stuff About Playing the Guitar

My father kept his college guitar in the closet. I plunked around on it every once in a while, but I couldn't figure out how to make it work. It didn't make any sense to me. It didn't *feel good* when I touched it.

Then, my younger brother Bobby picked up a cowboy-style, arch-top, F-hole guitar at an auction for $1.50 and started playing it. At that time I was interested in R&B. I liked the sound of blues guitar solos, but guitar wasn't the featured instrument on most of the records out then—the saxophone was.

I waited for records that had guitar solos on them, but they were always *too short*. I wanted to be able to play my own solos —**long ones**—so I taught myself how to play the guitar. I didn't bother to learn any chords—just blues licks.

Stylistically, my approach is closest to *Guitar Slim,* a mid-fifties blues player who recorded for the Specialty label (check out the solo on *"Story of My Life"*) until somebody stabbed him to death with an ice pick.

When I first heard it I thought: *"What the fuck is he doing? He really gets 'pissed off at it.' "* His style of playing seemed to be 'beyond the notes'—it had more to do with the 'attitude' with which he was mangling his instrument. What came out was not just the sum total of *certain pitches versus certain chords versus certain rhythms*—to my ear, it was something else. Besides the 'attitude,' he also provided the first instance I can recall of a **distorted** electric guitar on a record.

Although I wouldn't say I could play a *Guitar Slim* lick sitting here today, his *mangle-it strangle-it* attitude provided an important aesthetic guidepost for the style I eventually developed. My two other influences were *Johnny "Guitar" Watson* and *Clarence "Gatemouth" Brown.*

I'm not a virtuoso guitar player. A virtuoso can play **anything,** and I can't. I can play *only what I know,* to the extent that I've developed enough manual dexterity to get the point across —but that has deteriorated over time.

With the 1988 band, I didn't have to play very much in the show, because the focus was on the horn arrangements and the vocals. I didn't have to play fifteen-minute guitar solos, and, really, there's not much of a market for that anymore—the interest span of the audience has shriveled to about eight bars, and in those eight bars, you are expected to play every note you know.

The concept of "The Rock Guitar Solo" in the eighties has

pretty much been reduced to: *"Weedly-weedly-wee, make a face, hold your guitar like it's your weenie, point it heavenward, and look like you're really doing something. Then, you get a big ovation while the smoke bombs go off, and the motorized lights in your truss twirl around."* I can't do that stuff. I still have to look down at the neck to see where my hand is when I'm playing.

One of the reasons people want to become guitar players is that they think there's more to it than there actually is. When I first started, I was very enthusiastic about the improvisational possibilities offered by the instrument, but this has been dampened somewhat by the fact that, in order to engage in the type of improvisational escapades that seem natural to me, I must be accompanied by a 'specialized' rhythm section.

A soloist choosing to work in this odd style ultimately winds up as a hostage—he can go only as far into the 'experimental zones' as his rhythm section will *allow* him to go. The problem lies in the polyrhythms. The chances of finding a drummer, a bass player and a keyboard player who can *conceive* of those polyrhythms—let alone identify them fast enough to play a complementary figure on the moment, are not good. *(The grand prize goes to Vinnie Colaiuta, the drummer for the band in 1978 and '79.)*

It's hard to explain to a rhythm section during rehearsal what to do if I'm playing seventeen in the space of fourteen *(or Monday and Tuesday in the space of Wednesday)*. I can't specify in advance *everything* that ought to happen in the accompaniment when the shit hits the fan in the middle of a solo.

Either a drummer will play steady time, in which case my line will wander all over *his* time, or he will **hear** the poly-rhythms and play **inside** them, *implying* the basic pulse for most rock drummers, accustomed as they are to life in the petrified forest of *boom-boom-BAP.*

Jazz drummers can't do it either, because they tend to play *flexible time.* Polyrhythms are interesting only in reference to a steady, metronomic beat (implied or actual)—otherwise you're wallowing in rubato.

Just as in diatonic harmony, when upper partials are added to a chord, it becomes **tenser,** and more demanding of a resolution—the more the **rhythm** of a line **rubs against the implied basic time,** the more **'statistical tension'** is generated.

The creation and destruction of harmonic and 'statistical' tensions is essential to the maintenance of *compositional drama.* Any composition (or improvisation) which remains *consonant* and *'regular'* throughout is, for me, equivalent to watching a movie with only *'good guys'* in it, or eating cottage cheese.

I want to know three things when I go on stage: **[1]** that my equipment is working, **[2]** that the band members **absolutely** know the material, so I don't have to worry about them, and **[3]** that the rhythm section can hear what I'm playing and that it has some 'concept' of it so it can help build the improvisation.

If those conditions are met, if the acoustics are reasonable, and if I'm satisfied with my amp sound *(I could probably write another small book on that topic),* then all I want to do is go on autopilot, wiggle my fingers and listen to what comes out.

During the 1984 tour, I would usually play eight solos per night (five nights a week, times six months), and out of that there might have been twenty solos that were musically worthwhile enough to put on a record. The rest of it was garbage. It's not that I wasn't *trying* to play something; most of it just didn't come off.

If you're working this way, the chances of doing it 'right' every time are not good—but I'll take the chance. I don't feel I have anything to apologize for, or any exalted reputation to uphold.

# My Splendid Voice

It has been my experience that writing for singers precludes certain options provided by instruments—and the options get even more limited if the voice being written for is mine, since I don't have much of a range.

I can easily *'talk a song'* or do *'meltdown,'* but I can **sing** only about an octave, with seventy-five- to eighty-percent pitch accuracy. Let's be honest about it, friends 'n neighbors: with specs like that, I couldn't even pass an audition to get in my own band.

I can't play guitar and sing at the same time. My brain can't handle it. I can't even play rhythm guitar and sing. It's hard enough for me to stay in tune just **singing.** For a while there, I couldn't find anybody to fill the position of 'lead singer,' so I **had** to do it myself.

This led to a desperate search for *professional-sounding singers.* *Voilà!* Ike Willis and Ray White—but a lot of other vocalists who auditioned, when confronted with lyrics like *"Andy Devine had a thong rind,"* decided to think twice about their careers. They didn't want anything like **that** to crawl out of their mouths.

# My Lyrics Are Dumb. So What?

Some of the stuff I write is in the *'musically uncompromising boy-is-this-ever-hard-to-play'* category. Then there's the other category—songs in which the 'intrigue' resides in the lyrics, rather than the music.

If a piece intends to actually **tell a story,** I don't build an elaborate accompaniment because it gets in the way of the words. Take *"Dinah Moe Humm,"* for example. The 'artificial

cowboy' setting was chosen because it seemed right for the story
—but a song like *"The Dangerous Kitchen"* is another deal altogether.

**THE DANGEROUS KITCHEN!**
If it ain't **ONE THING**, it's **ANOTHER!**

In the middle of the night when you get home
The bread-things are all dry 'n scratchy
The meat-things, where the cats ate through the paper
The can-things, with the sharp little edges
That can cut your fingers when you're not looking
The soft little things on the floor that you step on
They can all be **DANGEROUS!**

Sometimes
The milk can **HURT YOU**
(If you put it on your cereal
Before you **SMELL** the plastic container)
And the stuff in the strainer
Has a mind of its own
So be very careful
In the **DANGEROUS KITCHEN**
When the nighttime has fallen
And the roaches are crawlin'
In the **KITCHEN OF DANGER**
You can feel like a **stranger!**
(The bananas are black,
They got flies in the back,
And also the chicken
In the dish with the foil,
Where the cream is all clabbered,
And the salad is **FRIGHTFUL,**
Your return in the evening
Can be **LESS THAN DELIGHTFUL!**)

You must walk very careful!
You must not lean against it!
It can get on your clothing!
It can FOLLOW YOU IN,
As you walk to the bedroom,
And you take all your clothes off,
While you're sleeping
IT CRAWLS OFF!
IT GETS IN YOUR BED!
It could get on your face then!
It could EAT YOUR COMPLEXION!
You could die from the DANGER
Of the DANGEROUS KITCHEN!

WHO THE FUCK WANTS TO CLEAN IT?
It's disgusting and dirty!
The sponge on the drainer
Is stinky and squirty!
(If you squeeze it when you wipe up,
What you get on your hands then
Could unbalance your glands and
Make you BLIND or WHATEVER!)
In the DANGEROUS KITCHEN,
At my house tonight!

"The Dangerous Kitchen" from the album *Man from Utopia*, 1982

The words were completely written out, but the melody and the accompaniment were improvised nightly, in a style we call *"meltdown."* The accompaniment was designed to *provide rhythm, texture and sound effects,* not necessarily *chords, melody and a 'good beat'*—a sort of rock *Sprechstimme* setting, combining a parody of the 'poetry and jazz' aroma of *beatnikism* with an abstraction of the type of onomatopoeia found in those Beethoven meadowland movements—with the cuckoos and wind, etc. (except, in this case, there's no cuckoo—just the stuff in the strainer).

I don't have any pretensions about being a poet. My lyrics are there for entertainment purposes only—*not to be taken internally*. Some of them are **truly stupid,** some are slightly less stupid and few of them are sort of funny. Apart from the snide political stuff, which I enjoy writing, the rest of the lyrics wouldn't exist at all if it weren't for the fact that we live in a society where instrumental music is irrelevant—so if a guy expects to earn a living by providing musical entertainment for folks in the U.S.A., he'd better figure out how to do *something* with a human voice plopped on it.

## 'Deviation from the Norm'

One of the things I've said before in interviews is: *"Without deviation (from the norm),* **'progress'** *is not possible."*

In order for one to *deviate successfully,* one has to have at least a passing acquaintance with whatever *norm* one expects to deviate from.

When a musician comes into my band, he already knows *sets of musical norms*. The drummers know all the *drumbeat norms* (how to play disco, how to play a shuffle, how to play fatback, etc., etc.). Bass players know all the *bass player norms* (thumb pops, walking lines, 'traditional' ostinatos, etc., etc.). Those are today's *radio music norms*. Part of the fun in preparing touring arrangements is *nuking those norms.*

The place where one finds the least enthusiasm for *norm-nuking* is in the world of the symphony orchestra. If you hand an orchestral musician a piece of *new music,* his instant response is likely to be: *"Feh! This was written by some guy who is still alive!"*

Players come into the orchestra already *knowing* what's 'good'—because they've played it a million times in the conservatory. So, when a composer approaches an orchestra with a piece of music embodying techniques or ideas that weren't 'certified' during the musicians' conservatory days, he is likely to experience *rejection at the molecular level*—as a defense mechanism of the entire orchestra.

As soon as an orchestra attempts to play something they don't know, they run the risk of fucking up. There are only two ways for them to avoid this potential embarrassment. One is to rehearse—but who will pay for this precious rehearsal time? The other is to avoid playing **any** new music.

When a guest conductor comes to town, he is not usually giving a performance of something by a living composer. He's doing Brahms; he's doing Beethoven; he's doing Mozart—because he can warm it up in one afternoon and make it sound okay. This makes the accountants happy, and allows the audience to concentrate on his *choreography* (which is really why they bought the tickets in the first place).

Why is that any better than a bunch of guys in a bar band jamming on "Louie Louie" or "Midnight Hour"?

## Hateful Practices

I find music of the classical period boring because it reminds me of *'painting by numbers.'* There are certain things composers of that period were not allowed to do because they were considered to be outside the boundaries of the *industrial regulations* which determined whether the piece was a symphony, a sonata or a *whatever*.

All of the *norms,* as practiced during the olden days, came into being because *the guys who paid the bills* wanted the *'tunes'* they were buying to *'sound a certain way.'*

The king said: *"I'll chop off your head unless it sounds* **like this."** The pope said: *"I'll rip out your fingernails unless it sounds* **like this."** The duke or somebody else might have said it another way—and it's the same today: *"Your song won't get played on the radio unless it sounds* **like this."** People who think that classical music is somehow more *elevated* than *'radio music'* should take a look at the **forms** involved—and at who's paying the bills. Once upon a time, it was the king or Pope So-and-so. Today we have broadcast license holders, radio programmers, disc jockeys and record company executives—banal reincarnations of the assholes who shaped the music of the past.

The contemporary *'harmony textbook'* is the embodiment of those evils, in catalog form. When I was handed my first book and told to do the exercises, I hated the *sound* of the 'sample passages.' I studied them anyway. If something is *hateful,* you should at least know what it is you're hating so you can avoid it in the future.

Many compositions that have been accepted as "GREAT ART" through the years reek of these *hateful practices.* For example, the rule of harmony that says: *The second degree of the scale should go to the fifth degree of the scale, which should go to the first degree of the scale* **[II-V-I].**

Tin Pan Alley songs and jazz standards thrive on **II-V-I.** To me, this is a *hateful progression.* In jazz, they beef it up a little by adding extra partials into the chords to make them more luxurious, but it's still **II-V-I.** To me, **II-V-I** is the essence of bad *'white-person music.'*

(One of the most exciting things that ever happened in the world of *'white-person music'* was when the Beach Boys used the progression **V-II** on "Little Deuce Coupe." An important step forward by going backward.)

It's the instructor's job to make you learn how to do all the stuff in those books. To get a grade, you must write exercises proving that you are capable of accommodating the entertainment needs of deceased kings and popes, and, after you've *proved* it, you get a piece of paper that says you're a *composer.* Is that **nauseating** or what?

It's worse in the graduate courses that teach students how to do 'modern' music. Even modern music has *hateful practices—* like the twelve-tone business that says you can't play note one until you've cycled through the other eleven, theoretically thwarting tonality by giving each pitch *equal importance.*

The *Ultimate Rule* ought to be: **"If it sounds GOOD to YOU, it's bitchen; and if it sounds BAD to YOU, it's shitty."** The more varied your musical experience, the easier it is to define for yourself *what you like* and *what you don't like*. American radio listeners, raised on a diet of_____ *(fill in the blank)*, have experienced a musical universe so small they cannot begin to *know* what they like.

In radio music, **timbre rules** (the *texture* of the tune, i.e., "Purple Haze" played on accordion is *very different* from Hendrix playing it on a squealing feedback guitar).

On a record, the overall timbre of the piece (determined by equalization of individual parts and their proportions in the mix) tells you, in a subtle way, *WHAT* the song is about. The orchestration provides *important information* about what the composition *IS* and, in some instances, assumes a greater importance than *the composition itself.*

American listeners know very little about the ethnic music of other cultures, and the closest they get to contemporary orchestral composition is the latest film or TV background music.

It's amazing that schools still offer courses in musical composition. What a useless thing to spend money on—to take a course in college to learn how to be a *modern composer!* No matter how good the course is, when you get out, **what the fuck will you do for a living?** (The easiest thing to do is become a composition teacher yourself, spreading *'the disease'* to the next generation.)

One of the things that determines the curriculum in music schools is: *which of the current fashions in modern music gets the most grant money from the mysterious benefactors in* **Foundation-Land.** For a while there, unless you were doing *serial music* (in which the *pitches* have numbers, the *dynamics* have numbers, the *vertical densities* have numbers, etc.)—if it didn't have a pedigree like that, it wasn't a *good* piece of music. Critics and academicians stood by, waiting to tell you what a piece of shit your opus was if your *numbers* didn't add up. (Forget what it *sounded like,* or whether it moved anybody, or what it was about. The *most important thing* was *the numbers.*)

The foundations that provide grant money for people engaged in these pursuits occasionally decide to stop funding one style of music after becoming *entranced* with another. For instance, it used to be that they would fund only *boop-beep stuff* (serial and/or electronic composition). Now they're funding only *minimalism* (simplistic, repetitive composition, easy to rehearse and, therefore, *cost-effective*). So what gets taught in school? *Minimalism.* Why? Because it can be **FUNDED.** Net cultural result? **Monochromonotony.**

In order to gain status at the university, a professor or *composer in residence* has to be plugged into something that's **really hot**—something **FUNDABLE,** and, as of this writing, the secret word is **MINIMALISM.** So, after a busy semester grading the papers of their minimalist trainees, they adjust their berets and fill out the request forms for 'foundation assistance.' Students and instructors alike compete annually for pieces of this pie.

One day, these cultural institutions are going to stop funding *minimalist music* and fund *something else,* and the Serious Music Landscape will be littered with the shriveled remains of *'expert graduate minimalists.'*

## Bingo! There Goes Your Tenure!

The following section is excerpted from the keynote address I delivered at the 1984 convention of the *American Society of University Composers* **(ASUC).**

I do not belong to your organization. I know nothing about it. I'm not even interested in it—and yet, a request has been made for me to give what purports to be a *keynote speech.*

Before I go on, let me warn you that I *talk dirty,* and

that I will say things you will neither enjoy nor agree with.

You shouldn't feel threatened, though, because I am a *mere buffoon,* and you are all *Serious American Composers.*

For those of you who don't know, I am also a composer. I taught myself how to do it by going to the library and listening to records. I started when I was fourteen and I've been doing it for thirty years. I don't like schools. I don't like teachers. I don't like most of the things that you believe in—and if that weren't bad enough, I earn a living by playing the *electric guitar.*

For convenience, without wishing to offend your membership, I will use the word **"WE"** when discussing matters pertaining to composers. Some of the **"WE"** references will apply generally, some will not. And now: *The Speech. . . .*

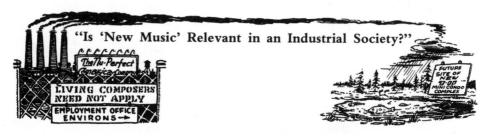

"Is 'New Music' Relevant in an Industrial Society?"

The most baffling aspect of the *industrial-American-relevance* question is: *"Why do people continue to compose music, and even pretend to teach others how to do it, when they already know the answer? Nobody gives a fuck."*

Is it really worth the trouble to write a new piece of music for an audience that doesn't care?

The general consensus seems to be that music by living composers is not only irrelevant but also genuinely obnoxious to a society which concerns itself primarily with the consumption of disposable merchandise.

Surely **"WE"** must be punished for wasting everyone's precious time with an art form so *unrequired* and *trivial* in the general scheme of things. Ask your banker —ask your loan officer at the bank, he'll tell you: **"WE"** are *scum*. **"WE"** are the *scum of the earth*. **"WE"** are *bad people*. **"WE"** are *useless bums*. No matter how much tenure **"WE"** manage to weasel out of the universities where **"WE"** manufacture our baffling, insipid packages of inconsequential *poot*, **"WE"** know deep down that **"WE"** are *worthless*.

Some of us smoke a pipe. Others have tweed sports coats with leather patches on the elbows. Some of us have mad scientists' eyebrows. Some of us engage in the shameless display of incredibly dramatic *mufflers*, dangling in the vicinity of a turtleneck sweater. These are only a few of the reasons why **"WE"** must be *punished*.

Today, just as in the glorious past, the composer has to accommodate the specific taste *(no matter how* **bad***)* of THE KING—reincarnated as a movie or TV producer, the head of the opera company, the lady with the frightening hair on the 'special committee' or her niece, *Debbie*.

Some of you don't know about Debbie, since you don't have to deal with radio stations and record companies the way the people from *The Real World* do, but you ought to find out about her, just in case you decide to *visit* later.

Debbie is thirteen years old. Her parents like to think of themselves as *Average, God-Fearing American White Folk.* Her Dad belongs to a corrupt union of some sort and is, as we might suspect, a lazy, incompetent, overpaid, ignorant son-of-a-bitch.

Her mother is a sexually maladjusted mercenary shrew who **lives** to spend her husband's paycheck on ridiculous clothes— to make her look *'younger.'*

Debbie is *incredibly stupid*. She has been raised to respect the values and traditions which her parents hold sacred. Sometimes she dreams about being kissed by a lifeguard.

When the people in the *Secret Office Where They Run Everything From* found out about Debbie, they were thrilled. She was **perfect.** She was **hopeless.** She was *their kind of girl*.

She was immediately chosen to become the *Archetypical Imaginary Pop Music Consumer & Ultimate Arbiter of Musical Taste for the Entire Nation*—from that moment on, everything musical in this country would have to be modified to conform to what *they* computed to be *her needs and desires*.

Debbie's 'taste' determined the size, shape and color of *all music broadcast and sold in the United States during the latter part of the twentieth century*. Eventually she grew up to be just like her mother, and married a guy just like her Dad. She has somehow managed to reproduce herself. The people in *The Secret Office* have their eye on her daughter at this very moment.

Now, as a serious American composer, should Debbie **really** concern you? I think so.

Since Debbie prefers only short songs with lyrics about boy-girl relationships, sung by persons of indeterminate sex, wearing S&M clothing, and because there is *Large Money* involved, the major record companies (which a few years ago occasionally risked investment in recordings of new works) have all but shut down their classical divisions, seldom recording *new music*.

The small labels that *do,* have wretched distribution. (Some have wretched *accounting procedures*—they might release your recording, but you won't get paid.)

This underscores a *major problem* with living composers: *they like to eat*. (Mostly what they eat is brown and lumpy—and there is no question that this diet has had an effect on their collective output.)

A composer's job involves *the decoration of fragments of time*. Without music to decorate it, time is just a bunch of boring *production deadlines* or dates by which *bills must be paid*. Living composers are entitled to proper compensation for the use of their works. (Dead guys don't collect —one reason *their* music is chosen for performance.)

There is another reason for the popularity of *Dead Person Music*. Conductors prefer it because they need *more than anything else* to *look good*.

By performing pieces that the orchestra members have hacked their way through since conservatory days, the rehearsal costs are minimized—players go into jukebox mode, and spew off *'the classics'* with ease—and the expensive guest conductor, unencumbered by a score with *'problems'* in it, gets to thrash around in mock ecstasy for the benefit of the committee ladies (who wish he didn't have any pants on).

*"Hey, buddy, when was the last time you* **thwarted a norm**? *Can't risk it, eh? Too much at stake over at the old Alma Mater? Nowhere else to go? Unqualified for 'janitorial deployment'? Look out! Here they come again! It's that bunch of guys who live in the old joke: it's YOU and two billion of your closest friends standing in shit up to your chins, chanting,* **'DON'T MAKE A WAVE!'"**

It's the terror of a *bad review* from one of those tone-deaf elitists who use the premiere performance of every new work as an excuse to sharpen their word skills.

It's settling for rotten performances by musicians and conductors who prefer the sound of *Death Warmed Over* to anything scribbled in recent memory (making them *'assistant music critics,'* but somehow *more glamorous*).

It's clutching the ol' *Serial Pedigree*, secure in the knowledge that *no one checks anymore*.

Beat them to the punch, ladies and gentlemen! *Punish yourselves* before *they* do it for you. (If you do it *as a group,* the TV rights might be worth something.) Start planning now, so that everything will be ready in time for the next convention. Change the name of your organization from *ASUC* to **"WE"**-SUCK, get some cyanide and swizzle it into the punch bowl with some of that *white wine* 'artistic' people really go for, and *Bite The Big One!*

If the current level of ignorance and illiteracy persists, in about two or three hundred years a *merchandising nostalgia* for *this era* will occur—and guess what music they'll play! (They'll still play it wrong, of course, and you won't get any money for having written it, but *what the hey?* At least you didn't die of syphilis in a whorehouse opium stupor with a white curly wig on.)

It's all over, folks. Get smart—take out a real estate license. The least you can do is tell your students: *"DON'T DO IT! STOP THIS MADNESS! DON'T WRITE ANY MORE* **MODERN MUSIC!***"* (If you don't, the little stinker might grow up to kiss more ass than you, have a longer, more dramatic neck-scarf, write music more baffling and insipid than your own, and Bingo! *there goes your tenure.)*

## Pierre Boulez

I met Boulez after sending him some orchestral scores, hoping that he would be interested in conducting them. He wrote back saying that he couldn't because, although he did have a chamber orchestra of twenty-eight pieces, he did not have a full-size symphony orchestra at his disposal in France (and even if he did, he probably wouldn't have used it, as he later stated that he didn't care for 'The French Orchestral Tone,' preferring the BBC Symphony).

I bought my first Boulez album when I was in the twelfth grade: a Columbia recording of "Le Marteau Sans Maître" (The Hammer Without a Master) conducted by Robert Craft, with "Zeitmasse" (Time-mass) by Stockhausen on the other side.

Within a year or so of that, I managed to get hold of a score. I listened to the record while following the score, and I noticed that the performance was not very accurate. I later acquired a recording of "Le Marteau" on the Turnabout label, with Boulez conducting, and was surprised to find that he took the first movement much more slowly than the tempo marked in the score. I razzed him about it when we met.

Boulez is, to use one of Thomas Nordegg's favorite phrases, *"serious as cancer,"* but he can be funny too. He reminds me a little of the character that Herbert Lom plays in the Pink Panther movies. He doesn't have the 'psychotic wink,' but he has some of that nervous quality about him, as if he might—given the proper excuse—start laughing uncontrollably.

I went to lunch with him in Paris, prior to the *Perfect Stranger* recording. He ordered something called *brebis du [fill in the blank]*—I didn't know what it was. It was some kind of meatlike material on weird lettuce with a translucent dressing. He looked like he was *really* enjoying it. He offered some to me. I asked him what it was. He said, **"The sliced nose of the cow."** I thanked him and went back to my pepper steak.

I saw him conduct the New York Philharmonic with Phyllis Bryn-Julson as soloist at Lincoln Center in '86 or '87. The audience was extremely rude. The first half of the program had pieces by Stravinsky and Debussy; the second half was a piece by Boulez. After the intermission, the audience came back in and waited for him to begin **his** piece—which was very quiet compared to the first two—and then about half the audience got up—noisily—and walked out. He kept on conducting.

I would have enjoyed the opportunity to grab a microphone and scream, *"Sit down, assholes! This is one of* **'The Real Guys'!**"

## *The Perfect Stranger*

Since releasing the LSO album, I have turned down at least fifteen commissions from chamber music groups of varying sizes from all over the world who offered me *cash* to write a piece of music for them. If I were a composer just starting out, I would think that was the greatest thing in the world—but I don't have the time anymore, and I shudder to think what would happen to the music if they played it without my being there during rehearsals.

Complicating matters, these commissions are offered in a way that requires my presence at the *premiere performance*—during which I would be expected to sit there and pretend it was terrific.

That's what happened to me when Boulez conducted the live premiere of "Dupree's Paradise," "The Perfect Stranger" and "Naval Aviation in Art?" It was underrehearsed.

I hated that premiere. Boulez virtually had to drag me onto the stage to take a bow. I was sitting on a chair off to the side of the stage during the concert, and I could see the sweat squirting out of the musicians' foreheads. Then they had to go into the IRCAM studio the next day and record it.

In the game of new music, everybody has to take a chance. The conductor takes a chance, the performers take a chance, and the audience takes a chance—but the guy who takes the biggest chance is the composer.

The performers will probably not play his piece correctly (bad attitude; not enough rehearsal time)—and the audience won't like it because it doesn't 'sound good' (bad acoustics; weak performance).

There's no such thing as a 'second chance' in this situation—the audience gets only one chance to hear it because, even though the program says *"World Premiere,"* that usually means *"Last Performance."*

Before an audience can tell whether or not it likes a piece, it needs to **listen** to it. Before it can listen to it, it has to know that it **exists.** In order for it to exist in a form in which it can be heard (not just on paper), it has to be **performed.** In order for a **large audience** to experience it, the performance must be recorded, released, distributed and given retail shelf space.

Interesting new music **does exist.** In spite of my rude comments earlier in this chapter, I know that sincere, optimistic people continue to compose it. Well, *where the fuck is it then?* Glad you asked! On the rare occasions when it does get recorded, it doesn't get **The Big Push** (or even the *Wizened Little Shove*), so any audience that **might** enjoy listening to it has difficulty finding it.

*Mr. Retailer* doesn't give a shit—he needs to move as many Michael Jackson records out the door as he can. *He too has a mortgage to pay.* **"Joe Blow's Super-Bitchen Concerto"** that used to wind up in *Bin 29*—way in the back—is not even **there** anymore.

If we expect to develop any kind of musical culture worth preserving for future generations in the U.S., we need to take a good look at the system which determines **how** things get done **why** they get done **how often** they get done and **who gets to do them**.

# CHAPTER 9

# A Chapter FOR MY DAD

My Dad had a top-secret security clearance when he worked at Edwards Air Force Base (1956–59). During that period I kept getting thrown out of high school, causing him to worry about a reduction in his classification––maybe even the loss of his job altogether. He told me at that time if I would just settle down and get good grades, he would send me to Peabody Conservatory in Maryland, probably thinking, *"Well, it's a music school—he wants to do something in music—he doesn't want to be an engineer—let's give him this to keep him quiet,"* but, by then, I had gotten to hate 'education' so much, I was so fed up with going to school—any school, conservatory or not—I didn't want any part of it.

I think my Dad was an interesting man—even if I didn't get along all that well with him. He was good at mathematics—he wrote (and published himself) a small book on gambling probabilities.

One thing that he always wanted to do was write a *History of the World*—**with Sicily as the hub.** (Can you imagine how a guy from Rome would laugh at that idea—the way people in Italy think of *Sicilians?* The way Romans think of **everybody else?**)

Mostly I tried to stay out of his way—and I think he tried to stay out of mine as much as he could. After I got into 'show business' and made some money, I bought a house for my parents, and, at that point, I guess they thought I was sort of okay.

My Dad died while I was on the road. We were working at the Circle Star Theater in Phoenix, Arizona, in 1973. Gail made the funeral arrangements in my absence, and still tells the story of the guy from the funeral parlor who had a silver shovel for a tie clip.

My mother seems to like it if she sees my name in the papers, and if she sees me on TV she thinks *it's good*—but she's a devout Catholic, so who can tell what she *really thinks* about what I do or the things I say?

I feel that if you live life in pursuit of 'certification,' 'appreciation,' or 'compensation' in any form from your parents, you're making a big mistake. The sooner you can say, *"Okay,* **they're them** *and* **I'm me,** *and let's make the best of it,"* the better off you're going to be.

We could improve worldwide mental health if we acknowledged that *parents can make you crazy.*

I believe that, to a certain extent, kids get weird because their parents made them weird. Parents have more to do with making their children weird than TV or rock and roll records.

The only other thing that makes them weirder than TV and parents is religion and drugs.

> *"All the old history was written for the amusement of the ruling classes. The lower classes couldn't read, and their rulers didn't care about remembering what happened to them."*
>
> My Dad (something he told me when I was a kid)

Over the years, my interest in history has grown to the point that I can *almost* comprehend my Dad's fascination with it. He never managed to write his **Sicilian History of the World,** but, since I've got a couple of hours here, let's try another approach —with rock and roll as the historical focal point. . . .

# The Entire World: A Short History

*Okay—we're pretending to be* **serious** *now—*

*Popular music* tells us something about *popular culture,* which then tells us something about *popular thought processes* (or the absence thereof).

When rock and roll first appeared, adults were completely hostile towards it. Today, they aerobicize to it.

The people who performed it—as well as its consumers—were thought of in the beginning as an undesirable social element. Then the sixties came along and, *wonder of wonders,* natives from a miserable little island off the coast of France reinvented this wheel and rolled it back in our direction (right over our foot). With a sickening crunch, *the Beatles* and *the Rolling Stones* became household words in America.

The British Invasion introduced us to the concept of the *self-contained* **singing band.** Singing bands who played their own instruments were not common in the United States at that time (we had surf music). Up till then, rock records were made either by soloists or groups of vocalists, backed by anonymous guys who attempted to operate musical instruments.

The success of the British groups forced a change in the way new American groups were put together. They now had to be *self-contained,* because every bar that hired live music wanted its own little U.S. version of *the Beatles* or *the Rolling Stones.*

During this period, it was discovered that millions—perhaps billions—of dollars could be made by selling circular pieces of black plastic in a cardboard sandwich with a stupid picture on the front.

In the beginning, **"The Big Bucks"** were made by low-life chiselers who screwed doo-wop groups out of their royalties. While the chiselers played golf, the singers vanished into the never-never land of *needles* and *cookers*.

The seventies came along. By then, the captains of corporate America had convinced themselves that **they had The Answer,** and so it came to pass that the world was introduced to the warmth and sincerity of *corporate rock*.

*Corpo-rock* mutated into *'disco'*—developed on the actuarial assumption that music by nonpeople is better and *cheaper* than music originating from *'the alternative source.'*

All those nice men who owned the bars and clubs where groups used to develop stopped hiring musicians, and replaced them with record players, big speaker systems and twinkling lights.

Disco satisfied social as well as musical needs. Disco people got to dress up all the time and go to places (if the guy at the door **let them in**) where everybody sort of 'looked good'—and later, after an evening of chemical alteration, everybody looked *even better*, and the next thing they knew, they were getting **The Blow Job.**

Punk, in the late seventies, purported to be a rebellion against that sort of silly behavior. Maniac bands started thrashing away in dingy little places with no decor, developing their own silly behavior. Yes, punk took us back to the energetic roots of rock and roll—and its mysterious accounting procedures. The guys with the safety pins in their noses probably netted less than their doo-wop junkie ancestors.

New wave evolved from punk, basically, by sterilizing its own safety pin. Newly glammed punkers sang *"Yum-yum!"* as they 'assumed the position' once again, sucking The Corporate Hooter (it's crusty nozzle emerging from a 'space-cloth' nursing bra this time).

## Listen to These Clothes

No change in musical style will survive unless it is accompanied by a change in clothing style. Rock is to dress up to. No musical innovation will ever succeed on a large commercial scale without the full involvement of the industries which profit tangentially from it: clothing and 'merchandise.'

## Death by Nostalgia

The really big news of the eighties is the stampede to regurgitate mildly camouflaged musical styles of previous decades, in ever-shrinking cycles of 'nostalgia.'

*(It isn't necessary to imagine the world ending in fire or ice—there are two other possibilities: one is paperwork, and the other is nostalgia. When you compute the length of time between* **The Event** *and* **The Nostalgia For The Event**, *the span seems to be about* **a year less in each cycle.** *Eventually within the next quarter of a century, the nostalgia cycles will be so close together that people will not be able to take a step without being nostalgic for the one they just took. At that point, everything stops. Death by Nostalgia.)*

## "I Dunno"

One of the **good things** that happened in the sixties was that at least **some music** of an *unusual* or *experimental nature* got recorded and released. So, who *were* those wise, incredibly creative executives that made this Golden Era possible? Hip young guys with Perrier breath? No—they were old cigar-chomper guys who listened to the tapes and said, **"I dunno. Who knows what the fuck it is? G'head—put it out there! Who knows? I dunno."**

We were better off with that attitude than we are now. The 'bright young men' are far more conservative—and more dangerous than the old guys ever were.

So, how did The New Guys get in there? Some got in because their Dad was one of The Old Guys. Some of them actually worked their way in—the guy with the cigar said one day: *"Sherman, look, I took a chance—it went out there—next thing I know, we sold a few million units. I* **still** *don't know what the fuck this shit is, but we* **gotta do some more.** *I tell you, Sherm—I need some advice! Why don't we get one of those hippie bastards in here?"*

So, they hire the hippie bastard—not to do anything 'big,' just carry the coffee; bring the mail; stand around and look *happening.* So one day the old guy says: *"Sherman, listen—I think we can trust him; he looks like he's* 'happening.' *We'll make him an A&R man—let* **HIM** *talk to these stupid fuckers with the tambourine 'n incense. He understands this shit—***he's got the same hair.*"***

From there, he's moving up and up; next thing you know **he's got HIS feet on the desk** and he's saying, *"Get rid of Sherman, Ms. Maxwell—and—oh, that 'new group'? We can't take a chance on them . . . it's just* **not** *what the kids* **really want—I know—I got the same hair.*"***

Things will not improve until these cocksuckers move back to Mister Rogers' Neighborhood.

There is something to be said for an executive who is willing to take a chance on an idea, even if he doesn't like or understand it. The new guys don't have that spirit. They are forever looking over their shoulder. (Remember when they used to have *the same hair?* All that shit they stuck up their nose made it fall out a couple of years ago.)

## The Economics of Artistic Freedom

*[Some parts of this section are derived from an edited transcription of a CNN interview with Sandy Freeman, October 31,*

*1981. Because of things which were said about the Reagan Administration, I feel that CNN tried to bury this interview. Instead of running it in the show's normal afternoon time slot, they ran it at midnight on Halloween—at the same time MTV was broadcasting our live concert.]*

When we talk about artistic freedom in this country, we sometimes lose sight of the fact that freedom is often dependent on adequate financing.

If you have an idea for an invention, for instance, you need the tools and the machinery to build it; you may have the freedom to think it up, but you don't have the financial freedom to construct it.

The same thing goes for artistic projects. You may have a great idea for an opera, but you won't be able to mount it unless you pay the graft to the unions which 'service' the arts. This is, for me, one of the most depressing aspects of contemporary American life—the negative way in which unions have impacted on the quality of the arts.

Unions, through their PR firms, perpetuate the myth that America is a *unionized country,* and that all the unions are there to *fight for the working man and woman.* Maybe in the beginning the unions did support the workers—but what they have turned into is a network of organizations that take money from working-class people to finance a banking scheme which often benefits organized crime.

In the case of the arts, I have experienced situations in which union stagehands were paid astonishing amounts of money for doing *nothing.* In some instances, they actually degraded the quality of the live shows they were hired to work on. Many locals operate by extortion, subjecting touring groups to interpretations of regulations that border on science fiction.

Let's say that you want to do a live recording at a

hall. A representative from the union will come up to you and say, *"You can't turn your recording equipment on unless you pay us three thousand dollars."*

*"For what?"* you say.

*"For extra union fees."*

*"Fees for what?"*

*"Oh, because we have to pay this special rate for these men who are standing around here."*

*"But for what?"*

*"Well, that's just what the union says—and if you don't pay, we'll stop the show."*

Would they stop the show? You bet.

In some instances, if I think the show is important enough to record, and there is no recourse, I pay. In other instances I don't pay—*and don't record*. This happened to us not long ago in Chicago. The union wanted to stick us with a three-thousand-dollar surcharge for recording. I was supplying all the labor for the recording from *my crew*—it was my recording equipment and my engineering staff. Why should I have to pay an extra fee to a bunch of guys who are sitting around eating sandwiches —who **care** *nothing* about what I'm doing, and will **do** *nothing* to enhance the quality of it? They're not putting in an extra second of work or an extra ounce of muscle power—and it's not just Chicago.

### Whatever Happened to Those Halloween Shows?

The last time we played the Palladium in New York City (before they made a disco out of it) was for a live simulcast, the MTV Halloween show, in 1981. (Westwood One was broadcasting it live on radio.) I was providing the audio feeds for MTV and the radio through my recording truck. MTV, Westwood One and I were each billed *one hundred percent extra for 'stagehand costs'*—

for yet another bunch of guys who did absolutely nothing. (My road crew moved the equipment in and out, and operated it.) I said, *"Okay, but that's it. I'm never coming back here."*

They weren't doing that many live events at the Palladium then, so I guess they thought it over for a minute, since my band had been a regular attraction there every year at Halloween and they wanted to keep the business —so they offered to give me a two-thousand-dollar 'rebate' (out of a stagehand bill that came to nine thousand dollars.) I said no, thanks. Remember, each of us— MTV, Westwood One and my company—was billed nine thousand dollars—a total of **twenty-seven thousand dollars for one night's nonwork.**

### Honesty, as a Quaintly Outmoded Concept

I realize that a lot of people feel that speaking out against unions is almost *'Un-American.'* I remind them: not all of America is unionized—in fact, the vast majority of Americans are **not**—and *glad about it.*

Some people fear that if the unions were to vanish, the labor situation would return to the way it was in the beginning, with child labor and sweatshops. **I agree with them.** Large employers *do* tend toward unscrupulous behavior when nobody is looking over their shoulder.

So, what's the bottom line here? I would like to see more honesty in business—at both ends of the table. Honesty in U.S. business appears to be at its lowest ebb in history.

There are a number of reasons for that. When political leaders do not demonstrate honesty, when people lie constantly in the media—everybody get used to **'The Big Lie'** as a way of life. At that point, honesty becomes a quaintly outmoded concept—nobody wants to be honest anymore, because if they are, they might *finish last.*

I would say that today, **dishonesty is the rule,** and honesty the exception. It could be, statistically, that more people are honest than dishonest, but the few that *really control things* are **not honest,** and that tips the balance.

I don't think we have an honest president. I don't think that he is surrounded by honest people. I don't believe that most of the people in Congress or in the Senate are honest. I don't think that most people who head up businesses are honest. We have let them get away with it because we're not honest enough to face up to the fact that we are **'owned and operated'** by a bunch of really bad people.

## Just Listen to That Budget

When the risks of creating a *successful* 'entertainment object' are increased by high production costs, committees (and the pitiful decisions they make) always flourish.

Committees make it possible for incompetent corpo-weasels to maintain their perks (and the fiction of *fiscal prudence*), while spending mega-budgets on 'sure-thing' movies, 'sure-thing' Broadway shows and 'sure-thing' recording artists.

The 'sure thing' is called a 'sure thing' because it has been outfitted with an 'insurance policy'—The Committee Itself. Nobody on it is EVER going to be held responsibile for ANY-THING—so WHAT CAN GO WRONG? Is it any wonder that project after project devolves into putrid nothingness—with more on the way?

In order to merchandise 'whatever it was that met with everyone's approval,' The Committee must spend **even more** time and money to make sure nobody finds out that there ever was such a thing as 'good stuff,' so, explaining that this is a matter of National Security, it enlists the aid of the Federal Government—perhaps a covert operation or two—to obliterate any criteria by which a customer might recognize how shitty the 'new stuff' really is. *[Fade up: "Battle Hymn of the Republic"; mass applause.]*

There are millions of people who love music, but have tastes which differ from the 'corporate ideal'—that's where independent labels come in. However, unless an independent is distributed through a major label, chances are the retailer is not going to pay on his ninety-day account—unless the independent has another hit coming in the door next month. The independent usually *doesn't,* but the major label *might,* and it is this leverage that gets the bills paid.

The major labels are more interested in merchandising than music. The idea is to get ONE *blockbuster monster motherfucker hit album* **every year.**

Corpo-wisdom dictates that if any one guy sells thirty million records, when the kids come into the store to buy The Big Hit, they'll also pick up something else. This is called a *"traffic-builder."* Ever wonder why every year at the Grammys *one guy sweeps up all the awards?*

# CHAPTER 10

# The One You've Been Waiting For

This is the chapter with the 'road stories' in it (*sanitized to protect the people who need protection, and/or people from whom clearances would be difficult to obtain*).

## Sometimes What Goes In Does Not Come Out

Once upon a time we had a road manager who used to work for a famous *'TV Teen Idol'* who decided to do a tour with a large backup band. One of the dates was Dallas, Texas—home of a *Famous Groupie Person.*

The afternoon before the show, Mr. Road Manager received a phone call from the F.G.P., who said, *"How many guys in the band? There'll be girls for everyone after the show."* The F.G.P. even volunteered to procure a specimen for Mr. Road Manager.

Sure enough, as the band was walking off stage, there stood the F.G.P.—and an entourage of A.G.P.'s *(assistant groupie person-ettes)*. The F.G.P. was ordering them: *"You go with him. You go with him. You go with him. You go with him,"* etc. Then there was a **BIG PARTY.** Mr. Road Manager wound up with an A.G.P. who stimulated him **greatly,** all the time thinking to himself: *"What a GREAT BAND! Even the road manager gets laid!"*—however, it was not to be. After the party, in his hotel room, the girl announced that she couldn't fuck him, because one of those **BIG ENGLISH GROUPS** had been in town the week before, and a **famous drummer** had *fucked her with a fountain pen—and it was still in her.*

## ⤛ Sleeping in a Jar

I couldn't tape the following story at the time it occurred (1971), but in 1987 I invited the protagonist to participate in a videotape interview. First: *my version, as I remember it.*

The star of STORY #2 is a girl named Laurel Fishman. (We'll use her real name because she is, in fact, proud of her accomplishments.)

She had been a regular attendee at our concerts in Chicago and other Midwestern cities in the 1960s, and in 1970 she won a contest run by a radio station in Chicago. The contest was to tell in twenty-five words or less how the Mothers of Invention had saved your life.

Her entry said that, since hearing the song "Call Any Vegetable," she had gotten in touch with her *friends in the vegetable kingdom* and, as a result of this, her body functions had been more regular.

The contest winner was to receive a backstage pass to our concert at the Auditorium Theatre, with one guest. I didn't even know the radio station was having a contest. At the gig, the promoter told us about it, and introduced us to THE WINNER —Laurel Fishman.

She had screaming orange-red hair, and makeup out to here, and was a little bit on the pudgy side. She walked in with a guy who looked like Carl Franzoni from the early *Freak Out!* days.

She had brought with her a 'present' for the band. It was a piece of *her own shit,* which looked like it had been *hand-molded into a perfect sphere,* sitting in a mason jar. She claimed that was *exactly how it had left her body.* I couldn't imagine how that could be true—I thought I saw *palm prints* on it.

Jim Pons, the bass player at that time, was *fascinated* by it. After the show, he took it with him. We got to the motel, got out of the car and were walking to the elevator. Pons couldn't stand it anymore—**he had to find out if it was real.** He unscrewed the lid, took a big whiff, and went, *"OOOhhhh my God!"* It wound up in the trash can just outside the elevator in the motel.

## Stuff Up the Cracks

In 1981, on one of Steve Vai's early tours, we were playing at Notre Dame University, and Laurel Fishman showed up. By some twist of fate, Steve wound up with Laurel in his motel room. They engaged in a variety of practices involving a hairbrush, and Steve drooling on his own dork while she jerked him off. (I got the **whole catalogue** of events the next morning during 'Breakfast Report.')

His name is Stevie Vai,
And he's a crazy guy
Last November, I recall
He needed a spanking

He decided then
A female specimen
Would be exciting for a night
To give him a spanking

Laurel was her name
She came to Notre Dame
(He told me just the other night
He oughta be thanking her for the spanking)

She was large and soft,
And she beat him off—
Made him drool upon his dork,
And gave it a wanking, after the spanking


Hairbrush! Oh! What a hairbrush!
(It's not that he requires grooming!
*Guys with light blue hair never do!*)


Then she did explain:
*"There's another game*
*That we can play with this device,*
*And then a banana!"*


It was slightly green—
Vapors in between—
Rising up to fill the room,
And *cook* the banana


Later in the dawn,
Laurel carried on—
Got right up and dressed herself and
Ate the banana

"Stevie's Spanking" from the album *Them or Us*, 1984


Since I'd known Laurel for years, and since she was being 'commemorated' in this 'folk song,' I thought that I should at least let her know *what* I was writing—and that if she had any objections to it, she should state them.

Not only did she *not have any objections*—she thought it was a good idea. She wrote out a release, in longhand, along with a list of all of the different objects she had been 'penetrated' with by Mr. Vai *(e.g., parts of guitars, assorted vegetables and the drummer's umbrella)*.

FRANK:

I think that you should say a few words—just *philosophically* about—you know—your *attraction to inanimate objects*.

LAUREL:

Well, they do *fulfill a need*—and I don't know how it began, really, or why I have this *attraction*; but I feel that many inanimate objects—sometimes common household objects or members of the vegetable or—well, I won't say *animal*—or fruit—kingdom—(*But that didn't sound right, so 'animal kingdom' certainly doesn't sound right. In fact,* **children and animals is where I draw the line.**) However, many objects can be very gratifying objects of *fulfillment*—and I think *that's what you wanted to know?*

FRANK:

Yeah. Right. I mean, that's fairly obvious—you'd be seeking 'fulfillment,' or you wouldn't be stuffing yourself with these things.

LAUREL:

That's true.

FRANK:

Okay. But let's say—you never can tell where this videotape will be on the air, or *who* will be watching; and they might not have tried *stuffing themselves with any doodads yet,* and you might want to give them the 'benefit of your experience.'

LAUREL:

Well, all I can say is: *it's worth trying* **once**—and I mean—surely there's some 'object' lying around the house that all of us have felt some sort of *attraction* to at one time or another.

Maybe it's that **spatula** you've been looking at for

years now—or maybe it's a **hammer** (actually, one of my favorite objects was a *black rubber-handled hammer*)— and these are fairly common objects that people use every day of the week—and every once in a while, I'll see a *particularly attractive male* carrying *one of these*, and I kind of have to hold myself back.

FRANK:

*Nudge, nudge—wink, wink.*

LAUREL:

But *anything'll do*, really—I mean, I've had many enjoyable afternoons in the grocery store that have resulted in *enjoyable evenings*.

FRANK:

Now, considering that you tried to convince us that you have 'personal machinery' that is capable of delivering a *payload of that magnitude,* and, theoretically (nature being what it is), people want to *have a good time*—if you're equipped with **that**— (how can I put this *discreetly?*) — if you can plop a big **'thing'** out like **that**, then maybe the problems involved in putting other **'things' in** (for amusement purposes) are *compounded* by the *geometry involved*—which might have led you, at one point or another in your life, to adopt 'certain practices' which *Christians* may find 'unique.'

LAUREL:

Or anybody, for that matter.


## The Fabulous Musician

Once upon a time, in a town in northern Florida, a certain Fabulous Musician met three girls in the parking lot of the hotel. He found one of the girls—the blonde—to be the most appealing, and asked her to meet him for *recreational deployment* after the show.

The band was handled by a booking agency, and the agency representative happened to be staying at the same hotel.

Somehow, between the sound check and the end of the show, the agent had clamped onto the girl that the Fabulous Musician was interested in.

The Fabulous Musician, being a student of human nature, was not disturbed by this usurpation of his 'beloved.'

He was, however, *certain* of several things:

**[1] Because the agent was an** *agent,* **he wasn't going to fuck the girl all night.**

**[2] The agent's room was right next door to his room.**

**[3] The agent's room had an exterior balcony, right next to** *his* **exterior balcony.**

**[4] Since it was summer, there was a high probability that the agent's curtains and sliding glass windows would be open.**

He also calculated that, by the time he got back to the hotel, he'd only have to wait *a mere few minutes* for the agent to accomplish his evil mission.

The Fabulous Musician told the other guys in the band (sitting in his room, on the seventh floor) that something 'interesting' was going to happen, and that they should be 'standing by.'

Grasping his trusty Polaroid camera, he leaped from his balcony onto the next and, with the click of a shutter and the flash of the flashbulb, produced an instantly 'compromising photograph' of the agent, who opined, *"I certainly would like to have that photograph"*—to which the Fabulous Musician replied, *"I certainly would like to fuck that girl."*

A trade was made. The agent received the photograph and

retired, naked, to the corner of the room, reading *The Godfather*. The Fabulous Musician called across to the other balcony for the rest to join him.

The girl, menstruating vigorously, seemed delighted at the prospect of *further gratification*.

The band seated itself around the bed as if it were an operating theater, and watched in amazement as the Fabulous Musician lifted a bottle of 'complimentary champagne' from a nearby table, placed his thumb over the end, and shook it into a froth, finally plunging it into *the crimson tunnel*—releasing a torrent of purple spew.

The girl achieved what appeared to be an *immense* orgasm. The Fabulous Musician withdrew the bottle with a flourish, turned to the spectators, said: **"Cheers, lads!"** and drank the remaining liquid.

## The Not-So-Fabulous Musician

The Story Of The Fabulous Musician eventually entered the realm of 'classical folklore.' It's one of the road stories passed down, band to band to band, *and so it came to pass* that another musician—a very COST-CONSCIOUS MUSICIAN (with ungodly bad breath)—heard the tale, was inspired by it and set out to *surpass* it, through the medium of his own personal magnetism.

He scoured the countryside to find a maiden willing to tolerate the procedure. Eventually finding a 'suitable somebody' willing to utter the magic words *"Why not?,"* he took her to a small German hotel.

At this point, he was confronted with a *major economic decision*. Realizing the exorbitant price of **mini-bar champagne** (yet fervently seeking his niche in history), he opted for the *'low road.'* **"Forget the champagne!"** he said, taking a couple of Alka-Seltzer tablets out of his shaving kit, stuffing them up the girl, and pouring water in. The results were not the same.

# CHAPTER 11

# Sticks & Stones

*"One becomes a critic when one cannot be an artist, just as a man becomes a stool pigeon when he cannot be a soldier."*

Gustave Flaubert (letter to Madame Louise Colet, August 12, 1846)

*"Definition of rock journalism: People who can't write, doing interviews with people who can't think, in order to prepare articles for people who can't read."*

Frank Zappa (From an old interview. This was 'borrowed' by the screenwriter of the film *Rich and Famous*.)

The people most offended by my lyrics seem to be rock critics. The audience usually likes them.

I have been attacked in print, on a personal level, for years —by people I have never met, who appeared to be trying to punish me for having the nerve to write on certain topics. (One newspaper in Colorado described me as a *"degenerate"* and a *"menace to society."*)

Most album reviews sidestep the musical content, because writers with enough technical knowledge to discuss music do not usually cover rock and roll. Whatever image I may have in the marketplace has been based, to a certain extent, on the *opinions* of people poorly qualified to make the judgment in the first place. Some examples:

*"Mothers and Dads, you thought the Beatles were bad. You got up in arms about the Rolling Stones. Sonny and Cher made you cringe. Well, as the man said, you ain't seen nothing yet. The Mothers of Invention are here with an album called*

**'Freak Out!'** *(someone suggested it should have been called 'Flake Out!') They come from Hollywood. Their clothes are dreadful—and I dig mod clothes. Their hair and beards are filthy. They smell bad. You just can't believe it—So, Mothers and Dads, next time the Beatles, the Stones, or Sonny and Cher come to town, welcome them with open arms. Next to the Mothers of Invention the other groups come on like the Bobbsey Twins."*

Loraine Alterman, *Detroit Free Press* (July 15, 1966)

*"I guess you might call it surrealistic paintings set to music. Not content to record just two sides of musical gibberish, the MOI devote four full sides to their type of 'artistry.' If anyone owns this album, perhaps he can tell me what in hell is going on.*

*"The Mothers of Invention, a talented but warped quintet, have fathered an album poetically entitled* **'Freak Out!'***, which could be the greatest stimulus to the aspirin industry since the income tax."*

Pete Johnson, *Los Angeles Times* (August 1966)

## Why They Write That Stuff About Me

Rock 'journalists' did not exist in 1965 and 1966 when the Mothers started out. Anyone who put out an album back then ran the risk of having it reviewed by a person who wrote featurettes for the cooking section of the *Daily Whatsis*.

When an interview or review like the ones above got published, it got stuffed into a *morgue file* someplace, to await a reincarnation on the day the next album got released or the group made a subsequent concert appearance.

*Morgue files* allow a lazy journalist to quote massive chunks of somebody else's story (as if it were a *'researched fact'*), saving him a few hours of work, and providing a convenient certification for his 'premise' (never at odds with the opinions expressed by the *Ancient Incompetents* whose work fills those files).

Unfortunately, I started doing interviews *way back then*. Yes, I talked face to face with many of the original *Ancient Incompetents*.

When rock journalism, as a form, finally developed, the wit and wisdom of the *Ancient Incompetents* became the data base for all writing to follow—so the material that has accumulated over the last two decades relating to my work **begins** with the garbage in that data base—magnified, embroidered, embellished and tweezed in every conceivable way since then.

To illustrate at least part of this concept, I include here an 'electro-factoid' currently running on the Dow Jones computer information service:

Zappa, Frank
   (zap'-uh)
The rock music star Francis Vincent
Zappa, b. Baltimore, Md., Dec. 21,
1941, is a musical satirist and an
originator of what is known as freak
rock. After founding a group called The
Mothers of Invention in Los Angeles in
1964, Zappa and the other members of
the group devised a stage show that
combined experimental music, anarchist
satire, and surrealist comedy with
deafening sound and a dizzying light
show. His work has had wide influence,
and the first of his many albums, Freak Out!
(1966)—which many consider to be a
rock opera—inspired the Beatles'
thematically unified Sergeant Pepper's

Lonely Hearts Club Band. Zappa's
best-selling single, Valley Girls
(1982), features his daughter Moon Unit
(b. 1968) in an arresting monologue
that parodies the slang and life-style
of trend-gripped white upper-middle-class
teenage American girls, particularly those of
Los Angeles' San Fernando Valley suburbs.

*-End of Text-*

## Why People Don't Understand My Stuff

There are several reasons why my music has never really been 'explained' in the press. For one thing, the people who write the articles don't really care **how it works** or **why it works.** I think this applies in a general way to rock criticism of every group.

Also, in those instances where the **writer** might actually care, his **editor,** *convinced that the public* **doesn't care,** will either cut or modify the article.

The manner in which Americans 'consume' music has a lot to do with leaving it on their coffee tables, or using it as wallpaper for their lifestyles, like the score of a movie—it's consumed that way without any regard for **how** or **why** it's made. Then, when it's merchandised, the emphasis shifts to the *pseudopersonality* of the artist—a magnification of the stage persona. *Do we* **really** *want to know HOW Michael Jackson makes his music? No. We want to understand why he needs the bones of the Elephant Man—and, until he tells us, it doesn't make too much difference whether or not he really is* 'bad.'

## About Boredom

If one thing keeps rock and roll boring, besides the radio-station programmers and the record-company executives, it's the writings of rock and roll journalists. They decide if a group is 'good' by listening to a couple of cuts from the first album—then if the second album is 'different,' they write that the band is fucking up—it's not 'consistent.'

The rock press sends a message to performers that they should stay in their mold: *"Don't change. If you do, we're going to say that your new record is a piece of shit."*

Then the guy at the record company who knows nothing about music, except for what he reads in *Rolling Stone*, will read the review and think, *"This group is dead—let's put the bucks into the next one."*—whereas a kid who listens to the record might make up his own mind and say, *"Go fuck yourself, I like it."*

For each type of music, there are listeners who think that reviewers don't know what they're talking about. These listeners, when excited about a certain group or style of music, will fight for it in their hometowns.

**These are the people who have made it possible for me to stay in music through the years—and I thank them for it.**

## Am I a 'Sexist'—or What?

If you were to take all the lyrics I've ever written and analyze how many songs are about *'women in demeaning positions,'* as opposed to *'men in demeaning positions,'* you would find that most of the songs are about **stupid men.**

The songs I write about women are not gratuitous attacks on them, but statements of fact. The song *"Jewish Princess"* caused the Anti-Defamation League of the B'nai B'rith to complain bitterly and demand an apology. I did not apologize then

*225*

and refuse to do so now because, unlike *The Unicorn,* such creatures **do exist**—and deserve to be 'commemorated' with their own special opus.

The basic function of any ethnic protective PR organization is to do what Congressman Duncan Hunter (R-California) suggested on the *Larry King show*—**"maintain the fiction."** (He used it in the context of protecting the Reagan administration during the Iran-contra scandal, suggesting it was our duty as Americans to support The President by looking the other way.)

Italians have an organization which seeks to 'maintain the fiction' that *no Italians are in the Mafia, nor do they sell drugs while engaging in murder for hire.* If you want to believe that, fine—welcome to Fantasy Land. If you want to believe that **wrestling is real,** go for it—and if you want to believe that women are a wonderful species that: **[1]** never goes to the toilet; **[2]** can't possibly do *anything wrong;* **[3]** is *completely superior to men,* then **believe it**—whatever makes you feel good.

# Why They Don't Play My Stuff on the Radio

Sometimes a radio station will get **one** phone call from **one person** who screams that he is going to complain to the FCC. Instead of the guy at the station thinking about how many listeners love the song, want to hear it again, and will support the station for playing it, usually the guy panics—and takes **my record** off the air. I object to that.

It has never mattered to me that thirty million people might think *'I'm wrong.'* The number of people who thought Hitler was 'right' did not make him 'right.' The same principle should be applied to anyone who has an *individualistic attitude*. Why do you necessarily have to be **wrong** just because a few million people **think** you are?

# CHAPTER 12

# America Drinks & Goes Marching

During a lecture in San Francisco, someone asked: *"If you're against drugs, why do you smoke cigarettes?"*

I answered, *"To me, a cigarette is **food.** I live my life smoking these things, and drinking the 'black water' in this cup here. This may be a baffling concept to the people in San Francisco who believe that they will **live forever** if they stamp out tobacco smoke."*

**The Drug Question** comes up all the time in interviews because people refuse to believe that I *DON'T* use them. There seems to be a consensus in America—since so many people, in all walks of life, use drugs—that a person can't possibly be *'normal'* if he *doesn't* use them. If I tell them I don't use drugs, they look at me like I'm crazy and question me about it.

Between 1962 and 1968, on maybe ten occasions, I experienced the *'joys'* of socially circulated marijuana. It gave me a sore throat and made me sleepy. I couldn't understand why people liked it so much. (If I *had* liked it, I'd probably be smoking it today, since I like to smoke.)

Americans use drugs as if consumption bestowed a *'special license' to be an* **asshole**. Whatever heinous act they might have participated in the night before can be *instantly excused* by saying they were 'high' while they were *doing* it.

Through the magic of Altered Body Chemistry, America in the eighties has devolved into an enormous hatchery for consumers. Corporate policy (itself influenced by drugs and alcohol) has decreed the breeding and maintenance of hundreds of millions of helpless illiterates, destined to spend their lives buying useless shit. When the shopping spree is over, the victims of this policy will gather in sad little groups and show their 'treasures' to each other, discussing how they're going to keep them, since the government is always trying to tax them away.

So, how do they deal with this sort of stress? Sex would seem to be the most efficient natural solution, but these mutants have been driven to *'secondary sources'* by lunatic doctrines (religious and political) which propound that **sex is bad.**

People who don't have an outlet often turn to violence—like those All-American bubbas who can't get laid and express themselves by pounding the snot out of each other in the parking lot of the neighborhood bar.

I have a theory about beer: *Consumption of it leads to* **pseudo-military behavior.** Think about it—**winos don't march.** Whiskey guys don't march, either (sometimes they write poetry, which is often more horrible, though).

Beer drinkers are into things that are *sort of like marching*—like football.

Maybe there's a chemical in beer that stimulates the *[male]* brain to *do violence* while *moving in the same direction* as other guys who smell like them *[marching]*—**"We, as a group of MEN, will drink this refreshing liquid, after which we will get together and beat the snot out of that guy over there."**

Beer seems to produce behavioral results which are psycho-chemically different from those produced by other alcoholic beverages.

Alcohol (the part that *'gets you drunk'*) is only one ingredient. There are other things in beer, and those *[herbal and/or biological]* components could affect the *[male]* brain, creating this violent tendency.

Go ahead and laugh. One day you're going to read about some scientist discovering that *hops, in conjunction with certain strains of 'yeast creatures,'* has a *mysterious effect* on some newly discovered region of the brain, making people *want to kill*—**but only in groups.** (With whiskey, you might want to murder your girlfriend—but beer makes you want to do it *with your buddies watching*. It's a *buddy beverage*—for *buddy activities*.)

Think about it: *"Who* **IS** *this 'Mr. Coors'? What does* **HE** *do for a 'good time'—and why does a man who owns a beer company need a 'top-secret security clearance'?"* Did you see him during the Iran-contra hearings? He has a **top-secret security clearance.** Do the guys at Anheuser-Busch have the same clearance? And when you see a beer commercial, besides *'the buddy pitch,'* don't they also throw in a little jingoistic, bunting-encrusted, flag-waving hoopla—the *all-American beer* syndrome? Every major industrialized nation has **A BEER** (you can't be a **Real Country** unless you have **A BEER** and an **airline**—it helps if you have some kind of a *football team,* or some *nuclear weapons,* but *at the very least* you need **A BEER**).

I think the mutant behaviors exhibited by people *'under the influence'* should be studied more closely. Gin drinkers, for example, are a breed apart.

People choose an *allegiance* to a certain beverage. Like bourbon guys—they're *bourbon guys* and *that's it.* And scotch drinkers? Forget it. They don't want to know from *'pink gin.'*

In contrast to *Mr. Beer Guy,* picture a guy who is religiously devoted to *Château Latour.* Is he marching? He ain't marching.

# CHAPTER 13

# All About Schmucks

In the future, etiquette will become more and more important. That doesn't mean knowing which fork to pick up—I mean basic consideration for the rights of other animals (human beings included) and the willingness, whenever practical, to tolerate the other guy's idiosyncracies.

We live in a world where people preach at you constantly (like now, even)—telling you *not to be fat, you can't smoke, you can't eat butter, sugar will kill you,* **everything** *is bad for you—especially sex.*

Every natural human urge has been thwarted in one way or another, so that some cocksucker gets to make a dollar off your guilt.

Certain people buy into this because they don't want to rock the boat. Unfortunately, adaptation of this sort requires that the adaptee willingly destroys his own personality.

If you wind up with a boring, miserable life because you listened to your mother, your Dad, your priest, to some guy on television, to any of the people telling you how to do your shit, then **you deserve it.** If you want to be a schmuck, be a schmuck —but don't wait around for respect from other people—*a schmuck is a* **schmuck.**

I suggest we learn how to take anything bad that happens to us and *polarize* it. Instead of being overwhelmed by a negative event, dodge to the side like those t'ai chi guys and let it whizz by your pants. Maybe it makes a little breeze—big deal. *(Please, don't mistake this for optimism.)*

There is an organization in Texas called The Church of the SubGenius, devoted to the teachings of some guy with a pipe in his mouth named **"BOB."** I'm not a member, but part of their 'theology' parallels mine.

As the planet gets more crowded, we must realize that *'slack'* is precious, schmucks are plentiful, impingements are impractical and werewolf etiquette for self-defense is a personal necessity.

Techniques must be developed to enable each of us to escape the other guy's bullshit (just as he wishes to escape ours). Heaven would be a place where bullshit existed only on television. *(Hallelujah! We's halfway there!)*

People should be encouraged to look after their own self-interest, but avoid *inflicting* themselves on other people—especially don't inflict yourself on a schmuck. The guy has already made his choice. *Cut the schmuck some slack.*

## Secondhand Smoke

I think the whole issue of secondhand smoke as a health hazard is a fantasy, but if someone complains in a restaurant that my smoke is bothering them, I won't smoke near them.

I think the anti-smoking business is a yuppie invention—an extension of the concept that *"we'll always be young, rich, and healthy."* People who would ordinarily be chain-smoking, and loving every minute of it, are now eating salads and jogging till they puke.

If they want to live that kind of life, fine—I have other priorities.

I like tobacco. As a kid, I took cigarettes out of ashtrays and pulled them apart to see what was inside. I liked the way tobacco smelled; I didn't care whether it was fresh or stale. Some people like garlic; I like tobacco. I like pepper, tobacco and coffee. That's my metabolism.

I didn't smoke until I was fifteen because of my asthma— my mother always told me, *"If you smoke, you'll die."* One day, I had the opportunity to smoke a Lucky Strike, and I didn't die.

The only times I've stopped smoking were when I had a cold. Once, when I got a chest cold in the middle of a tour, I stopped smoking—but then a funny thing happened: I noticed I could smell things that I couldn't smell before. Some people would say that was terrific. I didn't like it. I didn't like the way things smelled.

I walked into a hotel room and I could smell the rug, the disinfectant—as for smelling 'the great outdoors,' I don't live outdoors. Outdoors for me is walking from the car to the ticket desk at the airport.

## Who's Yer Tailor?

I just saw Reagan's Surgeon General, Doctor Koop, on CNN, making the statement that (I'm paraphrasing here): *"The behavior of smokers is pharmacologically the same as that of* **heroin addicts** *and* **cocaine addicts.***"* Oh, really? Who is this geek with the bogus epaulets on his shirt? Since when does the Surgeon General get to wear a costume?

Throughout his tour of duty, this "Doctor" has dispensed to the American public what I consider to be unscientific information (from what appears to be a fundamentalist perspective) on a wide range of health matters.

His explanation of the origins of the AIDS epidemic on an HBO special, for example (paraphrasing)—*"It came from a green monkey in Africa—perhaps the native, who was skinning it to* **eat** *it, cut his finger by accident, and some of the tainted blood got on him. . . ."*

Folks, it is far more likely that the disease was spread in Africa (and Haiti) as the result of injections administered by evangelical 'medical missionaries'—either <u>on purpose</u> (as part of **"God's Republican Plan For The Advancement Of Rich American White People"**) or through incompetence (using dirty needles for multiple injections without sterilization). How did it get back to the U.S.? Is it possible that some of those nice little missionaries share Jim Bakker's blessed sexual preferences?

Then, of course, there was Doctor Koop's C-SPAN appearance at a *"PMRC SYMPOSIUM"*—providing 'certification' for the 'scientific conclusions' of fundamentalist lunatics, raving about *"backwards masking."* Does this guy need a song, or what?

<br>

The Surgeon General, Doctor Koop
S'posed to give you all the poop
But when he's with PMRC
The poop he's scoopin' <u>amazes</u> me

C-SPAN showed him, all dressed up
In his phony "Doctor God" getup
He looked in the camera, 'n fixed his specs
'N gave a fascinatin' lecture
'Bout anal sex

He says it is not good for us
We just can't be **promiscuous**
He's a doctor—he should know
It's the work of the Devil, so
Girls, don't blow!

Don't blow Jimmy, don't blow Bobby
Get yourself another hobby
(If Jesus practiced medicine
I'm sure he'd do it
Just like him)

Is Doctor Koop a man to trust?
It seems at least that Reagan must
(But Ron's a trusting sort of guy—
He trusts Ed Meese
I wonder why?)

The AMA has just got caught
For doin' stuff they shouldn't ought
All they do is lie and lie
Where's Doctor Koop?
He's standin' by

Surgeon General? What's the deal?
Is your epidemic real?
Are you leaving something out?
Something we can't talk about?
A little green monkey over there
Kills a million people?
Hey, that's not fair!

Did it really go that way?
Did you ask the CIA?
Would they take you serious,
Or have **THEY** been
**Promiscuous?**

"Promiscuous" from the album *Broadway the Hard Way*, 1988

# "Words That Start with 'B' That Remind Me of What Republicans Do"

The eighties can best be summed up by the TV image of red-white-and-blue party balloons, escaping into the atmosphere, the recurring Republican pictorial metaphor for—what? **Freedom?**

(And the Democrats, trying SO HARD to act like Republicans, occasionally adopted this same metaphor during the 1988 campaign.)

When the Republicans really go at it, they *"let off balloons."* What the fuck **is** that? We see the bunting draped down here, and then: *whoosh,* the balloons go up. Who makes those balloons? Who blows them up? Who makes the bunting? Who makes out on these contracts?

There's no question in my mind—the beer, the balloons *and* the bunting all start with **"B"** for some Cosmic Reason.

*Bullshit* also starts with a **"B."** If you took **Beer, Balloons** and **Bunting,** then stirred in the **Bullshit,** you'd wind up with a scientific description of how the Republican Party works its Special Magic on the American electorate. Oh—let's add **Bourbon, Blow Jobs** and the **Bohemian Grove.**

# Hydrogen

*"As you grow older in your observation of the peoples of this Earth world, it becomes more noticeable that stupidity is the reigning virtue. The masses are always willing that somebody take the responsibility of caring for them."*

Paul Twitchell, *The Far Country*

Some scientists claim that *hydrogen,* because it is so plentiful, is the *basic building block of the universe.* I dispute that. I say there is more *stupidity* than *hydrogen,* and **that** is the *basic building block of the universe.*

This is not a matter of 'pessimism' vs. 'optimism'—it's a matter of *accurate assessment.*

Not only is there more stupidity than anything else in terms of universal *quantity,* but there is a wonderful *quality* to this stupidity. It is so **intensely perfect** that it completely overwhelms whatever it is that nature has piled up on the other pan of the scale.

Stupidity is *replicating itself* at an astonishing rate. It breeds easily and is self-financing.

The person who stands up and says, *"This is stupid,"* either is asked to 'behave' or, worse, is greeted with a cheerful *"Yes, we know! Isn't it terrific!"*

When Hitler was doing his shit, a whole bunch of people thought **he** was terrific, too. How could they be wrong? There were so *many* of them; they thought they looked good together —their arms all went up at the *same time.*

It seems to me that Americans in the eighties exhibit a remarkable willingness to embrace Fascism, especially when it is presented to them on a TV tray with balloons and bunting all over it.

It would be easier to pay off the national debt overnight than to neutralize the long-range effects of OUR NATIONAL STUPIDITY.

Forget about Iranian stupidity, or Chinese, or Russian, or South American, or Canadian stupidity—our very own homemade incompetence gets The Grand Prize.

We're not talking light-hearted foolishness here—when we go for *stupid* we go for **BIG STUPID**—like people who shoot at you on the freeway, or the *Rambos* and *Rambo-ettes* who blow people away in shopping malls and fast-food restaurants with automatic weapons.

Here it comes, folks! Watch it grow! One day, the BIG STUPID goes to a PTA meeting, winds through the PTL Club, wends its way to the White House, spreads out from the Oval Office like a cow flop into the judiciary system, dribbles over onto the desks of BIG BUSINESS, and the next thing you know we've got THE **VERY BIG** STUPID.

*THE VERY BIG STUPID* is a thing which breeds by eating The Future. Have you seen it? It sometimes disguises itself as a good-looking quarterly bottom line, derived by closing the R&D Department.

I can't think of any developing nation with a genuine 'fondness' for America. People in these countries see America as a threat to **their** national security; they see **US** as an *'Evil Empire.'* Everything Reagan said in the early days about Russia is easily descriptive of *our country,* viewed by a developing nation.

Because we possess THE VERY BIG STUPID, they know there is always the possibility that we might **use it on them—** accidentally.

Folks, over the years we have developed a *first-strike capability* with this hideous weapon, and have already deployed it several times, disguised as Reagan Administration *'foreign policy.'*

Some people in the Imaginary Heartland of America might say, *"Who gives a shit? They ain't going to get us. They ain't coming over here. Why, some of 'em don't even have air-o-planes."*

That kind of guy has bought stock in the THE VERY BIG STUPID, and has reaped a philosophical dividend which states on its face that, as a *Special Christian Nation,* we have the right to stomp all over the other guys (Manifest Destiny). God is on **Our Side,** and we're **supposed to do this,** because we're the only creatures *sophisticated enough* to bring peace and sanity to the rest of the world. *Pheeeeeeeuuuuuuuuuuwwwwwwwww.*

## The Exaltation of Ignorance

Stupidity has a certain charm—ignorance does not.

It has been said that ignorance is bliss—I'm not so sure. Perhaps I have been deprived in this regard but, never having been *truly ignorant,* I find it difficult to speak with any authority on the topic of such a 'blissful state.'

I have, however, observed a lot of *other people* who were certifiably ignorant, and I wouldn't say they were in a state of 'bliss.' They were having a good time, but I wouldn't call it 'bliss.'

When we celebrate Ignorance, and make that the National Standard of Excellence, we embarrass ourselves.

We celebrate it in hit records, TV sitcoms, most films, most commercials and, to a great extent, in our schools.

Our school systems train kids to be **ignorant, with style**—functional ignoramuses. They do not equip students to deal with things like logic; they don't give them the criteria by which to judge between good and bad in any product or situation. They are groomed and launched to function as mindless buying machines for the products and concepts of a multinational military-industrial complex that needs a *World Of Dumbells* to survive.

As long as you're *just smart enough* to do some kind of job, and *just dumb enough* to swallow the bunting, you're going to be 'all right'—but, if you venture beyond that, you run the risk of mysterious stomach problems and migraine headaches.

I believe that U.S. schools have a Search and Destroy program, aimed at any hint of creative thinking exhibited by students. Somebody plans this curriculum. Somebody writes those textbooks. Somebody sets those standards. Somebody watches to make sure *it all goes well.* Somebody pays big bucks for this shit.

# CHAPTER 14

# Marriage
# (As a Dada Concept)

Civil or religious certification of marriage reduces your beautiful 'relationship' to a business contract (between the partners, between the partners and the government, or between the partners, the government and Mr. God).

Except in the most extreme (religious fanatic) cases, the ceremony and the contract have no bearing on what people have to do to stay together. I've never met anyone who felt that marriage was a 'special career,' at which he or she must **excel,** but, if we are to believe the drivel on CNN, such people do exist somewhere in yuppie-land—white-bread mutants who set out to breed that **one perfect little child-artifact-piece-of-furniture-combination snackpack.**

This will be a frightening bunch when they grow up—all the worst behavioral traits of their accursed parents, combined with the ability to play a violin at seven, speak four languages by nine and graduate law school by eleven. *(Picture a civil war between them and the children of today's homeless in a few years.)*

## Mr. Dad

No matter what fantasies you maintain regarding 'your personal relationship to The Universe At Large'—everything gets modified within the contexts of *'spouse-ism'* and *'dad-ism.'*

As I walked out the door in September of 1967, on my way to the mysteries of our first European tour, I told Gail, *"If it's a*

243

*girl, call it Moon, and if it's a boy, call it Motorhead."* About two weeks later, I got the call that Moon had been born.

Her first word was *"werp."* The reason it was *"werp"* instead of *"Mama"* or *"Dada"* was that I used to edit tape (the *Lumpy Gravy* talking sections) in the living room. When you're editing dialogue and moving the reels back and forth, the backwards voices sometimes sound like they're saying *"werp."*

Gail and I never sat down and said, *"Now we're going to have another baby."* When the first one arrived I thought, because of where we were living and how much money I was making, that it would be **really inconvenient,** but it turned out to be okay —especially when we moved back to California the following year.

Moon is proud of the fact that she was born in New York, but I don't think she would have been too happy if she had been forced to grow up in *The City Of Cubicles.*

When Dweezil was born, Gail decided to have 'natural childbirth.' At that time, the only hospital in Los Angeles that would allow this process to occur with a Dad in the delivery room was Hollywood Presbyterian Hospital.

When it was time for the Big Delivery, we experienced a slight delay—we had to fill out a mass of papers before they'd let us in, riddled with irrelevant questions like: *"What religion are you?"*

Gail looked at me and said, *"What do we put?"* I said, **"Musician."**

That was the *first* thing that upset the admitting nurse. The *second* thing to spoil her afternoon was when she asked: *"What are you going to name the child?"* Gail said, **"Dweezil."**

Gail's got a funny-looking little toe which had been the source of family amusement so often that it had acquired a 'technical name': it wasn't **really** a toe—it was a **"Dweezil."** I thought then, and continue to think today, that Dweezil is a nice name. Fuck the nurse if she didn't like it.

The nurse pleaded and pleaded with us not to name the child Dweezil. Labor pains and all, she was going to make Gail stand there unless we gave her another name to put on the form. I couldn't see letting Gail suffer just to argue the point, so I rattled off an assortment of first names of guys we knew: **IAN** *(Underwood)* **DONALD** *(Van Vliet)* **CALVIN** *(Schenkel)* **EUCLID** *(James "Motorhead" Sherwood)*. As a result, Dweezil's original birth certificate name was **Ian Donald Calvin Euclid Zappa**. The nurse thought that was okay.

In spite of this harrowing experience, we always called him Dweezil. He was five years old when he discovered the **real names** on his birth certificate.

(I was in my mid-twenties when I found out! Up until the time I had to get a passport for the first European tour, I thought my name was **Francis**—a name I had always hated. In order to get the passport, I had to present my birth certificate—a mysterious document I had never seen before. My mother mailed it to me from California, and on it, much to my delight, was a name *OTHER THAN FRANCIS*—well it wasn't that good— "Frank" isn't much of a bargain—but I had thought for years, even printing it on album covers, that I was *Francis Vincent Zappa Junior*. How could I be such a fool?)

Dweezil was very upset, and demanded that steps be taken to rectify this tragedy. We hired an attorney and had his name legally changed to Dweezil.

That may seem like an unusual kind of demand for a five-year-old, but Dweezil was a very unusual child. When he was very young, his main interest was cars. I've seen kids who like to play with cars, but not the way Dweezil was into cars. One of his first whole sentences was: *"What happened to the green car?"*

When we took him home from the hospital, we had a green Buick. We hadn't had it for a couple of years, and he wanted to know what had happened to it.

When Dweezil crawled, he didn't crawl on his hands and knees; he crawled on his back. He would arch his back, and he would move by kicking his feet, balancing himself on the back of his head. He had actually worn hair off the back of his head by crawling across the floor in this manner. One day, he just got up and started running—no walking, right away to running.

He hated long pants, and refused to wear them to school. He went to school in shorts no matter what the weather was. Then he got interested in Japanese calligraphy. He had a little friend at school who was Japanese, and they used to play together all the time. This friend was apparently quite an influence on him. Dweezil got mad at Gail once and wrote her a scathing note—in what appeared to be kanji characters—just handed it to her, without comment.

Moon at one time wanted to learn how to play the harp. She took lessons for a year and then gave up. Every once in a while, they all think they want to play drums.

Diva, our youngest, got her name because she was the loudest baby in the hospital. Ahmet was delivered by C-section, and when I first saw him he wasn't making too much noise. I said to the nurse who was wheeling his incubator out of the delivery room, *"What's going on here? He's not breathing!"* She said, *"Oh, it's probably just some mucus."* It wasn't. He had hyaline membrane disease; he was premature and one of his lungs was collapsed.

He would have died if I hadn't been there and noticed that there was a problem. The nurse was wheeling that wagon down the hall like she was pushing a piece of ham.

So Ahmet spent the first part of his life in intensive care. This was while I was making the *Apostrophe'* album. I would work all night in the studio and end my shift with a visit to the hospital. I could talk to him and cheer him up, stick my hand in the incubator and hold his finger and say, *"Come on and get it."*

He still has scars on his chest from all the needles and hoses they had to stick into his lung to take the fluid out and puff it up—but you'd never know how sick he was to look at him now. He's probably going to be eleven feet tall by the time he grows up.

People make a lot of fuss about my kids having such supposedly 'strange names,' but the fact is that no matter what first names I might have given them, it's **the last name** that is going to get them in trouble.

> *Since she was saddled with that awful name,* **Chastity Bono** *has given her parents much grief over it.* "It helps to get into a show or something, but most of the time it's a pain," *she told* McCall's. *The girl blames mama* Cher, *who was inspired by a movie ex-hubby* Sonny *made titled* **"Chastity."** *When his daughter complains, Sonny usually reminds her of* Frank Zappa's *progeny:* "Be thankful we didn't name you **Dweezil.**"
>
> (*New York Post*, June 9, 1988)

## You Name It

It has traditionally been my job to name things around the house. When somebody brings a cat or a dog home, everyone waits until I name it, and then that's what we call it—with very few exceptions. [*"Go find the grouchy guy and get him to name this damn thing."*]

We had a sheep dog named *Fruney.* He eventually turned into *Frunobulax,* the monster in the song *"Cheepnis."*

247

The oldest and most durable citizen in our pet collection was *Gorgo* (short for *Gorgonzola,* one of the *Grunt People* in the original *Captain Beefheart* screenplay), a vile-tempered Siamese, recently deceased.

We used to have a great bird—a cockatiel, which I named *Bird Reynolds.* He would sit on my shoulder and talk to me. *Bird* also liked to sit on the edge of our Ping-Pong table when it was folded up in the living room.

I don't know how or why Moon ever decided to do this, but one day we found her staring at Mr. Reynolds, with her arms out, flapping them, saying: *"Tidal wave! Tidal wave!"* For some reason, this caused Mr. Reynolds to dance sideways along the top edge of the folded table. It was infallible. All she had to do was stand in front of him, hold her arms out and say, *"Tidal wave,"* and we had *action.*

A raccoon, brought home for a visit, injured Mr. Reynolds, and, while he was recovering and incapable of defending himself, he met an untimely end when one of the cats stuck his paw into the cage and swatted him in the middle of the night.

The business of naming things had its heyday in the times of the ancient Egyptians. It was believed then that, in order to successfully negotiate the voyage to the afterlife, the deceased tourist was required to *know the names of everything he might encounter along the way,* as he would be required to ask **permission to pass** from *each and every one of these entities or inanimate objects.* This included things like door sills, doorknobs, paving stones, etc., etc. In other words, folks, some schmuck with a golden hat on had to dream up all the names, then *keep them a secret,* so that later, another schmuck who was dead would have to memorize them, just so he could qualify for the Egyptian equivalent of *Pee-wee's Big Adventure.*

## How Our Cottage Industry Works

The grim side of having your own record business is that you have to **finance yourself.** The average guy who wants to go into the music business is probably still better off getting a record contract and letting someone else pay for his production.

The 'business part' takes time away from the 'glamorous part' of making music, and I don't know many musicians who have the temperament to deal with that. I'm lucky; I don't have to do the mundane stuff because Gail seems to find it *fascinating*.

I get my share of drudgery though—like typing out liner notes, writing the ads, supervising the packaging and so on, then Gail gets to do all the follow-ups; calling the vendors for production services and meeting with the bankers and our accountant, the wildly amusing Gary Iskowitz. She grumbles about it sometimes, but I think that *deep down* she **likes** it.

*[She just read this part and said,* **"Oh yeah, I like it so deep-down much it's like an out-of-body-experience!"** *So maybe she hates it? What the fuck—she's still pretty good at it.]*

This division of labor works best when we see each other the least. Don't get the wrong idea from that—Gail is also my best friend. If you can't be friendly with your spouse, it's not going to be much fun to live together. Friendship (let's get maudlin now) is a *very important dimension*. I think that a marriage without a friendship has to be pretty dreadful.

Gail has said in interviews before that one of the things that makes our relationship work is the fact that we hardly ever get to talk to each other.

We talk about business when we have to, but the rest of the time we don't talk at all. The other factor that has kept things interesting is that when I'm touring—which has been almost every year since we got married except 1984 to 1987—I am gone from the house six months out of the year.

Even when I'm not touring, our work keeps us on different schedules. The Cottage Industry—getting out records, tapes, CDs and videos, the mail order business and everything that entails—is sufficiently complicated that, in order to handle all the chores, I have to work the night shift and she has to work the day shift. We see each other on the edges when the shifts change.

If I worked the same hours she does, nothing could get done. Gail has to be awake during the day because the kids have to go to school and she has to handle the telephone. My schedule sort of twirls around the clock. I can't stay on nights all the time because every night I work an extra hour or so, editing, or recording, or on the Synclavier, or, presently, on this fucking book—pushing it a little later each night—but then, once I go to sleep, I want to grab eight or ten hours, and so my "day" keeps changing around. Every three or four weeks I'm back on daylight—and I dread it, because I can't get anything done. The phone rings all the time. All those questions Gail was dealing with when I was sleeping on the day shift, now **I have to answer—live, in person.** I can't edit—I can't write—I can't do anything because of the constant interruptions.

Daylight is an ugly time of day. So many people are awake, and if I go outside, I know what they're all thinking. They are mainly doing **bad things.** White-collar criminals fucking up the world. *Phooey on them.*

Nighttime is better. It's not just that it's *quieter,* but I can feel **the absence** of daytime bullshit. People have stopped *scurrying.* (I don't mind them *scurrying* when I'm asleep during the day— I'll find out what they were up to when I wake up and watch the six o'clock news.)

## How to Raise Unbelievable Children

I don't have 'friends.' Anybody who is 'the boss' in a business does not get to have 'friends'—he gets to have employees and/or acquaintances—and no matter what he does, they will always dislike him because he has **the nerve** to sign their paychecks. (Let's get a famous doctor to figure **that one** out some time.)

I don't have any time for 'social activities.' I do, however, have a wonderful wife and four totally unbelievable children, and that, folks, is **way better.**

As far as rearing children goes, the basic idea I try to keep in mind is that **a child is a person.** Just because they happen to be a little shorter than you doesn't mean they are dumber than you. A lot of people make that mistake, and forget how much value there is in *raw intuition*—and there's plenty of that in **every** child.

They may not have verbal skills or manual skills yet, but that is no reason to treat them like they're inferior *little lumps* whose destiny it is to grow up to be inferior *Big Lumps* like you.

We do all the regular stuff, like trying to keep them away from danger and out of trouble, but, after that, we have the responsibility of providing them with the basic data they're **never** going to get in school.

To the extent that it is practical, we share with them our personal philosophies, and attempt to impart to them what we like and what we don't like—so that we at least have some basis for understanding each other—but, in the final analysis, we realize that they are 'organisms unto themselves.' Whatever they're going to do in life, *they're going to do* regardless of home instruction.

## My Bad Attitude

The worst aspect of 'typical familyism' (as media-merchandised) is that it glorifies *involuntary homogenization*.

Thanksgiving rolls around, and the kids want to have a Thanksgiving dinner—they lay out the dining room table with all kinds of food, just like in the movies. Folks, they have to **drag me,** kicking and screaming, out of the studio to go upstairs and join them.

I will sit at the table, and eat—because I like the food—but I hate sitting around acting 'traditional' to amuse the *'little folks who happen to be genetically derived from larger-folks-who-buy-them-sportswear,'* enduring a 'family meal,' during which I might be required to participate in some mind-numbing 'family discussion' with mashed potatoes dribbling out the side of my mouth. I eat, and get the fuck out of there as fast as I can. It's the same with Christmas dinner or any other 'traditional family gathering.' I can't stand it. I don't want to be rude, and I don't want to spoil their fun—but I think they realize by now that I have what they would describe as a **'bad attitude'** about those kinds of things.

The same is true if I have to **go out** to eat dinner. A three-hour dinner to me is a **miniature eternity,** no matter how good the food is. One of the reasons is that while I'm waiting for the food to come, I have to sit there and talk to people. I really don't like to talk. It's like exercise for me.

## More Food Stuff

Gail cooks *maybe* once or twice a month—the rest of the time she's on the phone, handling the business. I would like to have 'regular meals,' but very seldom do we have anything *interesting* to eat around the house.

Most of the time, the house is like a teenage hotel, featuring our four kids plus all their friends. It's like a dude ranch or something. Usually they order pizzas, or they all go out to dinner. If any groceries are brought in, and tons are, I can never get to the stuff fast enough before it is inhaled.

I work in the middle of the night so, when I get hungry, I wind up digging in drawers to find something a teenager would refuse to eat. If I know we bought hot dogs that day, maybe I'll find a couple of buns left. The hot dogs are all gone. There aren't even any in the freezer. So I eat peanut butter. Most of the time the bread is gone—so I just shovel some out of the jar with a spoon.

The pantry is usually full—but it's full of **things you have to cook.** The icebox is full too—with steaks and chickens. You have to cook these things. I don't know how to **cook these**

**things!** If I did, who the fuck's got time to stand around and deal with that? *Please God!* **Don't make me eat a salad!**

I like fried spaghetti. I like **Fried Anything.** Whatever it is, **FRY IT**—except if it's a hot dog. Then you stick a fork in it and burn it in the fire on top of the stove (yes, folks, the legendary Super-Delicious Burnt Weeny Sandwich). By the way, the best time to eat fried spaghetti is for breakfast.

The kids look at me eating this stuff and go *"Yuck!"*

I say, *"This is* **DAD food.** *One day you're going to have to learn how to eat this shit, because* **you're** *going to have a house full of kids too, and the food is going to be gone, and you're going to open the icebox and say,* 'Uh-oh, what is that stuff?' "

We've tried to get some sort of system so I don't 'suffer' in the middle of the night. None of them have worked. It's impossible. There's another little icebox downstairs, next to the studio. Periodically it gets stuffed with things-to-eat-that-you-don't-have-to-cook, but no matter what goes in there, it vanishes within a day or so—and there are no ghosts in *that* part of the house.

## The Giraffe Cafe

From time to time Diva operates something called *"The Giraffe Cafe."* First, she made a sign that says, *"The Giraffe Cafe* **—OPEN.***"* Then—on those SPECIAL DAYS—she hangs it on the door upstairs. This means **she has made Jell-O.** *"The Giraffe Cafe"* has provided many nights of elegant dining when there was nothing around to fry.

It was raining the other day. Diva walked in and said, *"Oh! Can I go out and play in the rain?"* I said, *"Of course."* She got **all**

**dressed up for it**—like it was a special event—and spent an hour singing at the top of her lungs in the backyard. I can imagine some parents saying, *"Now don't go out there, you'll catch a cold."* I think that would have broken her heart.

Kids have a natural sense of mysticism, and a feeling of being connected to nature. The natural world is very exciting when it's all brand-new. For example, kids have an appreciation for snow which is generally not shared by the guy who has to shovel a driveway. The older you get the more you take nature for granted (unless you're Euell Gibbons and you want to eat everything that's lying on the ground until you die from it).

Diva is a dear little girl. She just turned nine. She likes to do a lot of 'normal little-girl things,' but **(Praise Gawwwwd!)** she has her bizarre side too. She had a Barbie doll once, but Ahmet burned most of the hair off, so Diva finished the job by squeezing Duco cement on her face, deforming the nose and forehead. (I'm sure there's an organization somewhere that would protest that.) Diva called her **"Snot Woman"** *(not bad, sweetheart).*

Dada has remained alive and well in my household since . . . forever. Even though the kids don't have the faintest idea of what **it** is, **they're it.** The whole house, and everything connected with what goes on around here, **reeks** of it.

**INTERCONTINENTAL ABSURDITIES** (founded 1968) is a company dedicated to *Dada in Action.* In the early days, I didn't even know what to **call** the stuff my life was made of. You can imagine my delight when I discovered that someone in a distant land had the same idea—AND a nice, short name for it.

## Ahmet Meets the IRS

There are phases that kids go through to develop the social skills necessary to work and interrelate with other people. Somewhere along the line, you're either going to learn to be a 'good employee' or a 'good boss'; there's not much in between.

One of the things that will decide if you will be an employee or a boss is whether you are allowed to develop the creative streak that will enable you to start your own business, or enable you to progress as an employee to the point where you're responsible for the activities of others.

At the ages my kids are now, they want to have fun, so why should I be bothering them with little details? Well, we sneak it in there. For example, Ahmet got a small part in a TV sitcom recently. We had a discussion about it, and now he realizes that he will have to pay income tax. His response to this news: **"That sucks."** Knowing that it sucks is a good place to start when planning your career.

It is also useful to show kids 'what the guidelines are,' and tell them that you expect them to adhere to those guidelines. If they don't adhere to the guidelines, then you think of different ways to **reimpress** the guidelines on them.

It's different in every case. When you have a confrontation with a child, it might be that the child is momentarily obsessed with some new concept, and isn't taking into account the feelings of others, or any number of **real things** that might be going on in **the real world.** It's only about, *"Can I go over to Janey's house? And if I can't, then why not?"*

*"No"* is not a good enough answer. So, if you're trying to deal with situations like that, screaming and hollering is the **least** effective method. One of the principles that works most of the time around here goes like this: If there is a difference of opinion between me and Ahmet, for example, about something he wants to do, if he can give me a good **LOGICAL** reason why **HE'S RIGHT** and **I'M WRONG,** I'll let him do it.

## Cruel and Unusual Punishment

Sometimes, as a punishment, Gail and I tell the kids that they can't watch TV for a week—we found that preferable to beating them over the nose with a tire iron.

I used to tell Dweezil that if he was bad, I was going to make him watch *The Man With The Brown Suit On*. The rest of us may find televangelists entertaining, but eleven-year-olds generally don't.

Now, of course, Dweezil watches *Robert Tilton* for laughs, on his own 'media center' in his bedroom. He's got a VCR, a TV, a computer, a CD player and all the rest of it—bought with money he earned.

He has a unique little place in the house with a stairway going up the outside that leads right to his room, so he can come and go as he pleases, but most of the time he likes to stay home. He's not as bad as I am, because he'll actually leave once in a while and go to a movie or a concert.

Both Moon and Dweezil took the California high school equivalency test at fifteen, which is the earliest age the law allows, so they both have high school diplomas. We're going to do the same for Ahmet and Diva. I want my kids out of the California school system as soon as possible.

As far as their 'cultural education' is concerned—films and books and so on—I make suggestions, but I'm not the kind of Dad to sit there and badger them until they 'experience the splendor' of something that only I might find interesting.

We have made sure that they acquired all the basic skills—like being able to read and write, knowing how to do arithmetic, and having some basic knowledge of science—and also some manners. After that, they're encouraged to make it up as they go along.

Moon likes to read, so she keeps up with things; and Diva loves to read. They take after Gail, who is **The Big Reader** in this family. Dweezil seldom reads, and Ahmet can't stand it (Ah! My sons!).

I don't think any of them has the desire to go to college, nor would I urge them to go—but, if they ever decided to, I wouldn't stop them . . . so long as <u>they</u> wanted to pay for it.

## Children of the Darned

Okay, a few last points about the current state of childrearing in America. A lot of people who cry out for government intervention or, as Tipper Gore calls them, 'consumer tools' to help raise and control their children are people who are *just too lazy to do it themselves.* These are the *"Me" Generation* assholes who think that **their** lives are the most important thing going. Once they have reproduced themselves, they adopt the attitude that the little replicant crawling around on the floor mustn't be a 'burden' to them, taking up too much of their 'hard-earned leisure time.'

They want to make sure that while they're out running around, getting *really really healthy,* and keeping their tans and wearing those rags around their heads, somebody will take care of their precious 'child-creature' for them. WAIT A MINUTE! I'VE GOT IT! How about **The Government?** Or some nice **Christian Group?** Or somebody who says he's **"qualified"?**

Grandma never would have put up with this shit.

I am disturbed by the way people like that treat their children —especially the single-child **yuppo-family** that uses the child as a status object: *"A perfect child? Of course! We have one here— he's under the coffee table. Ralph, stand up! Play the violin!"*

It's as if they are saying, *"Yeah, just* **look** *at HIM.* **We** *fucked!* **This** *came out. Now he can do* **so much homework!** *Yeah,* **we** *have a* **good boy.** *How about* **yours?** *Those people over there—* **they** *have an ugly one with a* **Jughead hat."**

*"Oh, we got* **ours** *a* **coonskin** *one—he was* **so-o-o grateful."**

The more **boring** the child is, the more the parents, when showing off the child, receive adulation for being **good parents** —because they have a **tame child-creature** in their house.

That's why they'll bring their neighbors in, open the door to the kid's room and show him off: *"Here, look at* **this!** *Ever seen one of these up close?"*—and if the creature in the room isn't frothing at the mouth and listening to backwards masking with heavy metal clothes on, then the parents are considered a 'success'; to be *admired* in the community.

My best advice to anyone who wants to raise a happy, mentally healthy child is: **Keep him or her as far away from a church as you can.** Children are naive—they trust everyone. School is bad enough, but, if you put a child *anywhere in the vicinity of a church,* you're asking for trouble.

# CHAPTER 15

# "Porn Wars"

*"The man that hath no music in himself,*
*Nor is not mov'd with concord of sweet sounds,*
*Is fit for treasons, stratagems, and spoils;*
*The motions of his spirit are dull as night,*
*And his affections dark as Erebus:*
*Let no such man be trusted. Mark the music."*

(*The Merchant of Venice*, Act V, Scene i)

The background history of the Parents' Music Resource Center, or PMRC, would take up more space than it's worth to spell out in detail. There are several 'historical accounts' from which to choose. Let's arbitrarily choose this one:

One day in 1985, Tipper Gore, wife of the Democratic Senator from Tennessee, bought her eight-year-old daughter a copy of the soundtrack album to Prince's *Purple Rain*—an R-rated film which had already generated considerable controversy for its sexual content. For some reason, however, she was shocked when their daughter pointed out a reference to masturbation in a song called "Darling Nikki." Tipper rounded up a bunch of her Washington housewife friends, most of whom happened to be married to influential members of the U.S. Senate, and founded the PMRC.

On or about May 31, 1985, the PMRC sent a letter to Stanley Gortikov, then president of the Recording Industry Association of America (RIAA), accusing the record industry of exposing the youth of America to *"sex, violence, and the glorification of drugs and alcohol."* Maybe they hadn't been watching television lately. The letter went on to demand a rating system for rock records similar to the MPAA rating system for films. The signatories included Gore, Susan Baker (wife of Treasury Secretary James Baker), Pam Howar and Sally Nevius (wives of prominent Washington businessmen) and the wives of nine other U.S. Senators.

Within moments, Edward O. Fritts, president of the National Association of Broadcasters, wrote letters to forty-five hundred commercial radio stations, implying that if they broadcast songs with explicit lyrics they would risk losing their licenses.

As this frenzy for self-mutilation developed, people within the record and broadcast industry debated amongst themselves as to what the most 'prudent course of action' might be—in other words, they were all in such a hurry to bend over for these harpies that the only details left for them to decide were:

> When to bend over,
> How far to bend over.
> When we bend, do we spread?
> Who's got the Crisco?

So, in a music trade publication called *Cashbox, I wrote them an open letter.*

### "Extortion, Pure and Simple"
### An Open Letter to the Music Industry

With all due respect to Stan Gortikov and the RIAA, I would like a few moments of your time to express my personal feelings regarding the unfortunate decision to bend over for the PMRC on the issue of album 'identification.'

First, let me say that I appreciate the difficult position the RIAA is in, and sympathize fully with the organization's struggle to move legislation through Congress. The problem seems to be the Thurmond Committee. This is where the industry's proposed legislation will live or die. It is no secret that Mrs. Thurmond is a member of PMRC. What is apparently happening is a case of extortion, pure and simple: *THE RIAA MUST TAP-DANCE FOR THESE WASHINGTON WIVES OR THE INDUSTRY'S BILL WILL FEEL THE WRATH OF THEIR FAMOUS HUSBANDS.*

It is to the RIAA's credit that the bulk of PMRC's demands were rejected, however capitulation on the stickering issue will cause more problems than it will solve.

The PMRC makes no secret of their intentions to use *'special relationships'* to force this issue. In an interview on an Albany radio station, Mrs. Howar made reference to a Mr. Fowler at the FCC, suggesting that some intervention by this agency might be in order, should their other nefarious techniques fail. **Did somebody rewrite the FCC charter while we weren't looking? What's going on here?**

Extortion is still an illegal act, conspiracy to commit extortion is an illegal act, and this issue goes beyond First Amendment considerations. No person married or related to a governmental official should be permitted to waste the nation's time on ill-conceived housewife hobby projects such as this.

The PMRC's case is totally without merit, based on a hodgepodge of fundamentalist frogwash and illogical conclusions. Shrieking in terror at the thought of some-

one hearing references to masturbation on a Prince record, they put on their *'guardian of the people'* costumes and
the media comes running. It is an unfortunate trend of
the eighties that the slightest murmur from a special interest group (especially when it has friends in high places)
causes a knee-jerk reaction of appeasement from a wide
range of industries that ought to know better.

If you are an artist reading this, think for a moment
. . . did anyone ask you if you wanted to have the stigma
of *'potential filth'* plopped onto your next release via this
*'appeasement sticker'*?

If you are a songwriter, did anyone ask you if you
wanted to spend the rest of your career modifying your
lyric content to suit the spiritual needs of an imaginary
eleven-year-old?

The answer is, obviously, **NO.** In all of this, the main
concern has been the business agenda of the major labels
versus the egos and sexual neuroses of these vigilant ladies.

A record company has the right to conduct its business and to make a profit, but not at the expense of the
people who make the product possible . . . someone still
has to write and perform **THE MUSIC.** The RIAA has
taken what I feel to be a shortsighted approach to the
issue. The 'voluntary sticker' will not appease these creatures, nor will it grease the chute through the Thurmond
Committee. There are no promises or guarantees here;
only threats and insinuations from the PMRC.

The RIAA has shown a certain disregard for the creative people of the industry in their eagerness to protect
the revenues of the record companies. Ladies and gentlemen, we are all in this together . . . when you watched
the hostages on TV, didn't you sort of mumble to yourself, **"Let's nuke 'em!"**? The PMRC deserves nothing

less (and the same to the NMRC or any other censorship group with a broadcast blacklist in its back pocket).

For the elected officials who sit idly by while their wives run rabid with anti-sexual pseudo-Christian legislative fervor, there lurks the potential for the same sort of dumb embarrassment caused by Billy Carter's fascinating exploits. I do not deny anyone the right to their opinions on any matter . . . but when certain people's opinions have the potential to influence my life and the lives of my children because of their special access to legislative machinery, I think it raises important questions of law. Ronald Reagan came to office with the proclaimed intention of getting the federal government off our backs. The secret agenda seems to be not to remove it, but to force certain people to wear it like a lampshade at a D.C. Tupperware party.

<u>Nobody</u> looks good wearing *brown lipstick*.

These creatures can hurt you. Get mad. Fight back. Use the phone. Use the telex. Demand that Congress deal with the substantive issue of connubial 'insider trading' and power-brokerage. Demand censure for those elected officials who participate. Demand fairness for the record industry's legislation in the Thurmond Committee. Remind them that they have a duty to the people who elected them that takes priority over their domestic relationships.

Did anyone give a shit about this? No. So, I decided to write an open letter to The President, which read, in part . . .

Mr. President,

Even though I disagree strongly with many administration policies, I have never doubted that your *personal* views on Basic Constitutional Issues are sincere.

I would like to know your opinion of the record censorship program sponsored by the PMRC, an organization involving the wives of elected governmental officials. Do you support this effort? If so, have you considered the basic issue of fairness when a pet project, likely to result in legislative action that will restrain trade and affect the lives of millions of Americans, is promoted by the spouse of an elected official and rushed to a Senate hearing while important national business waits in the wings? Is it fair that people not fortunate enough to be married to a D.C. Superstar have to keep their mouths shut while 'THE WASHINGTON WIVES' diddle with the legislative machinery?

The PMRC is an unlicensed lobbying group, comporting itself outrageously. While threatening an entire industry with the wrath of their husbands' powerful committees, they blithely spew frogwash and innuendo with the assistance of an utterly captivated media. When the PMRC's proposal leaps to a full committee hearing September 19th, an unfortunate precedent will be set.

If you support the PMRC (or the NMRC or any other Fundamentalist Pressure Groups) in their efforts to perpetuate the myth that SEX EQUALS SIN, you will help to institutionalize the neurotic misconception that keeps pornographers in business.

In a nation where deranged pressure groups fight for the removal of sexual education from public schools, and parents know so little about sex that they have to call Dr. Ruth on TV for answers to rudimentary anatomical questions, it would seem infinitely more responsible for these esteemed wives and mothers to demand a full-scale Congressional demystification of the subject.

Are we headed toward a time when descriptions of sexual behavior in entertainment media can be obtained only by employing a lawyer to petition under the Freedom Of Information Act? Must all sexual practices in the United States be tested and approved by The Moral Majority? *When they test them, do we get to watch?*

The PMRC loudly decries the label of censorship when it is applied to their plan. Jesse Jackson reminded Jerry Falwell in a recent CNN debate that *"You do not judge a tree by the bark it wears, but by the fruit it bears. . . ."*

Mr. President, if you are not serious about getting government off our backs, could you at least do something about getting it out of our nostrils? There seems to be a lethal cloud of brimstone and mildewed bunting rising from the Senate floor.

I do not expect a reply to this letter, however, any public statement from you on this matter would be greatly appreciated.

Thank you,
Frank Zappa

The President did not answer my letter. Instead, he gave a speech, a short time later, in Crystal City, Virginia, wherein he claimed that everybody in the record industry was a pornographer. Finally on September 19, 1985, the Senate Commerce, Technology and Transportation Committee held a day of highly publicized hearings to discuss the PMRC's proposal (a kangaroo court—five of the Committee's members had wives in the PMRC).

## FRANK ZAPPA: STATEMENT TO CONGRESS
### SEPTEMBER 19, 1985

These are my personal observations and opinions. I speak on behalf of no group or professional organization. My full statement has been supplied to you in advance. I wish it entered into the *Congressional Record*. Since my speaking time has been limited to ten minutes, I will read only part of it. I address my comments to the PMRC and the public, as well as this committee.

The PMRC proposal is an ill-conceived piece of non-sense which fails to deliver any real benefits to children, infringes the civil liberties of people who are not children and promises to keep the courts busy for years, dealing with the interpretational and enforcemental problems inherent in the proposal's design.

It is my understanding that, in law, First Amendment issues are decided with a preference for the least restrictive alternative. In this context, the PMRC's demands are the equivalent of treating dandruff by decapitation.

No one has forced Mrs. Baker or Mrs. Gore to bring Prince or Sheena Easton into their homes. Thanks to the Constitution, they are free to buy other forms of music for their children. Apparently they insist on purchasing the works of contemporary recording artists in order to support a personal illusion of aerobic sophistication. Ladies, please be advised: the $8.98 purchase price does not entitle you to a kiss on the foot from the composer or performer in exchange for a spin on the family Victrola. Taken as a whole, the complete list of PMRC demands reads like an instruction manual for some sinister kind of 'toilet training program' to housebreak ALL composers and performers because of the lyrics of a few. Ladies, how dare you?

The ladies' shame must be shared by the bosses at the major labels who, through the RIAA, chose to bargain away the rights of composers, performers, and retailers in order to pass H.R. 2911, the blank tape tax: A PRIVATE TAX, LEVIED BY AN INDUSTRY ON CONSUMERS, FOR THE BENEFIT OF A SELECT GROUP WITHIN THAT INDUSTRY.

Is this a 'consumer issue'? You bet it is. PMRC spokesperson Kandy Stroud announced to millions of fascinated viewers on last Friday's ABC *Nightline* debate that Senator Gore, a man she described as "a friend of the music industry," is co-sponsor of something she referred to as 'anti-piracy legislation.' Is this the same tax bill with a nicer name?

The major record labels need to have H.R. 2911 whiz through a few committees before anybody smells a rat. One of them is chaired by Senator Thurmond. Is it a coincidence that Mrs. Thurmond is affiliated with the PMRC? I can't say she's a member, because the PMRC HAS NO MEMBERS. Their secretary told me on the phone last Friday that the PMRC has NO MEMBERS . . . only FOUNDERS. I asked how many other D.C. wives are NONMEMBERS of an organization that raises money by mail, has a tax-exempt status, and seems intent on running the Constitution of the United States through the family paper-shredder. I asked her if it was a cult. Finally, she said she couldn't give me an answer and that she had to call their lawyer.

While the wife of the Secretary of the Treasury recites *"Gonna drive my love inside you . . .,"* and Senator Gore's wife talks about **"BONDAGE!"** and *"Oral sex at gunpoint"* on *The CBS Evening News,* people in high places work on a tax bill that is so ridiculous, the only way to sneak it through is to keep the public's mind on something else: 'PORN ROCK.'

The PMRC practices a curious double standard with these fervent recitations. Thanks to them, helpless young children all over America get to hear about oral sex at gunpoint on network TV several nights a week. Is there a secret FCC dispensation here? What sort of end justifies THESE means? PTA parents should keep an eye on these ladies if that's their idea of 'good taste.'

Is the basic issue morality? Is it mental health? Is it an issue at all? The PMRC has created a lot of confusion with improper comparisons between song lyrics, videos, record packaging, radio broadcasting and live performances. These are all different mediums, and the people who work in them have a right to conduct their business without trade-restraining legislation, whipped up like an instant pudding by The Wives Of Big Brother.

Is it proper that the husband of a PMRC NON-MEMBER/FOUNDER/PERSON sits on any committee considering business pertaining to the blank tape tax or his wife's lobbying organization? Can any committee thus constituted 'find facts' in a fair and unbiased manner? This committee has three. A minor conflict of interest?

The PMRC promotes their program as a harmless type of consumer information service, providing 'guidelines' which will assist baffled parents in the determination of the 'suitability' of records listened to by 'very young children.' The methods they propose have several unfortunate side effects, not the least of which is the reduction of all American music, recorded and live, to the intellectual level of a Saturday morning cartoon show.

Teenagers with $8.98 in their pocket might go into a record store alone, but 'very young children' do not. Usually there is a parent in attendance. The $8.98 is in the parent's pocket. The parent can always suggest that the $8.98 be spent on a book.

If the parent is afraid to let the child read a book, perhaps the $8.98 can be spent on recordings of instrumental music. Why not bring jazz or classical music into your home instead of Blackie Lawless or Madonna? Great music with NO WORDS AT ALL is available to anyone with sense enough to look beyond this week's platinum-selling fashion plate.

Children in the 'vulnerable' age bracket have a natural love for music. If, as a parent, you believe they should be exposed to something more uplifting than "SUGAR WALLS," support Music Appreciation programs in schools. Why haven't you considered YOUR CHILD'S NEED FOR CONSUMER INFORMATION? Music Appreciation costs very little compared to sports expenditures. Your children have a right to know that something besides pop music exists.

It is unfortunate that the PMRC would rather dispense governmentally sanitized heavy metal music than something more 'uplifting.' Is this an indication of PMRC's personal taste, or just another manifestation of the low priority this administration has placed on education for the arts in America? The answer, of course, is NEITHER. You can't distract people from thinking about an unfair tax by talking about Music Appreciation. For that you need SEX . . . and LOTS OF IT.

Because of the subjective nature of the PMRC ratings, it is impossible to guarantee that some sort of 'despised concept' won't sneak through, tucked away in new slang or the overstressed pronunciation of an otherwise innocent word. If the goal here is TOTAL VERBAL/MORAL SAFETY, there is only one way to achieve it: watch no TV, read no books, see no movies, listen to only instrumental music or buy no music at all.

The establishment of a rating system, voluntary or otherwise, opens the door to an endless parade of Moral Quality Control Programs based on 'Things Certain Christians Don't Like.' What if the next bunch of Washington Wives demands a large yellow 'J' on all material written or performed by Jews, in order to save helpless children from exposure to 'concealed Zionist doctrine'?

Record ratings are frequently compared to film ratings. Apart from the quantitative difference, there is another that is more important: People who act in films are hired to 'pretend.' No matter how the film is rated, it won't hurt them personally. Since many musicians write and perform their own material and stand by it as their art (whether you like it or not), an imposed rating will stigmatize them as INDIVIDUALS. How long before composers and performers are told to wear a festive little PMRC ARMBAND with their Scarlet Letter on it?

The PMRC rating system restrains trade in one specific musical field: rock. No ratings have been requested for comedy records or country music. Is there anyone in the PMRC who can differentiate INFALLIBLY between rock and country music? Artists in both fields cross stylistic lines. Some artists include comedy material. If an album is part rock, part country, part comedy, what sort of label would it get? Shouldn't the ladies be warning everyone that inside those country albums with the American flags, the big trucks and the atomic pompadours there lurks a fascinating variety of songs about sex, violence, alcohol and THE DEVIL, recorded in a way that lets you hear EVERY WORD, sung for you by people who have been to prison and are PROUD OF IT?

If enacted, the PMRC program would have the effect of protectionist legislation for the country music industry, providing more security for cowboys than it does for children. One major retail outlet has already informed the Capitol Records sales staff that it would not purchase or display an album with ANY KIND OF STICKER ON IT.

Another chain with outlets in shopping malls has been told by the landlord that if it racked 'hard-rated albums' they would lose their lease. That opens up an awful lot of shelf space for somebody. Could it be that a certain Senatorial husband-and-wife team from Tennessee sees this as an 'affirmative action program' to benefit the suffering multitudes in Nashville?

Is the PMRC attempting to save future generations from SEX ITSELF? The type, the amount and the timing of sexual information given to a child should be determined by parents, not by people who are involved in a tax scheme cover-up.

The PMRC has concocted a Mythical Beast, and compounds the chicanery by demanding 'consumer guidelines' to keep it from inviting your children inside its SUGAR WALLS. Is the next step the adoption of a 'PMRC National Legal Age For COMPREHENSION

Of Vaginal Arousal'? Many people in this room would gladly support such legislation, but, before they start drafting their bill, I urge them to consider these facts:

**[1]** *There is no conclusive scientific evidence to support the claim that exposure to any form of music will cause the listener to commit a crime or damn his soul to hell.*

**[2]** *Masturbation is not illegal. If it is not illegal to do it, why should it be illegal to sing about it?*

**[3]** *No medical evidence of hairy palms, warts, or blindness has been linked to masturbation or vaginal arousal, nor has it been proven that hearing references to either topic automatically turns the listener into a social liability.*

**[4]** *Enforcement of antimasturbatory legislation could prove costly and time-consuming.*

**[5]** *There is not enough prison space to hold all the children who do it.*

The PMRC's proposal is most offensive in its 'moral tone.' It seeks to enforce a set of implied religious values on its victims. Iran has a religious government. Good for them. I like having the capitol of the United States in Washington, D.C., in spite of recent efforts to move it to Lynchburg, Virginia.

Fundamentalism is not a state religion. The PMRC's request for labels regarding sexually explicit lyrics, violence, drugs, alcohol, and especially OCCULT CONTENT reads like a catalog of phenomena abhorrent to practitioners of that faith. How a person worships is a private matter, and should not be INFLICTED UPON or EXPLOITED BY others. Understanding the fundamentalist leanings of this organization, I think it is fair to wonder if their rating system will eventually be extended to inform parents as to whether a musical group has homosexuals in it. Will the PMRC permit musical groups to exist, but only if gay members don't sing, and are not depicted on the album cover?

The PMRC has demanded that record companies 'reevaluate' the contracts of those groups who do things on stage that THEY find offensive. I remind the PMRC that GROUPS are comprised of INDIVIDUALS. If one guy wiggles too much, does the whole band get an 'X'? If the group gets dropped from the label as a result of this 'reevaluation' process, do the other guys in the group who weren't wiggling get to sue the guy who wiggled because he ruined their careers? Do the FOUNDERS of this TAX-EXEMPT ORGANIZATION WITH NO MEMBERS plan to indemnify record companies for any losses incurred from unfavorably decided breach-of-contract suits, or is there a PMRC secret agent in the Justice Department?

Should individual musicians be rated? If so, who is qualified to determine if the GUITAR PLAYER is an 'X,' the VOCALIST is a 'D/A,' or the DRUMMER is a 'V'? If the BASS PLAYER (or his senator) belongs to a religious group that dances around with poisonous snakes, does he get an 'O'? What if he has an earring in one ear, wears an Italian horn around his neck, sings about his astrological sign, practices yoga, reads the Quaballah or owns a rosary? Will his 'occult content' rating go into an old CoIntelPro computer, emerging later as a 'FACT,' to determine if he qualifies for a home-owner loan? Will they tell you this is necessary to protect the folks next door from the possibility of 'devil-wor-ship' lyrics creeping through the wall?

What hazards await the unfortunate retailer who ac-cidentally sells an 'O' rated record to somebody's little

Johnny? Nobody in Washington seemed to care when Christian terrorists bombed abortion clinics in the name of Jesus. Will you care when the 'FRIENDS OF THE WIVES OF BIG BROTHER' blow up the shopping mall?

The PMRC wants ratings to start as of the date of their enactment. That leaves the current crop of 'objectionable material' untouched. What will be the status of recordings from the Golden Era prior to censorship? Do they become collector's items . . . or will another 'fair and unbiased committee' order them destroyed in a public ceremony?

Bad facts make bad law, and people who write bad laws are, in my opinion, more dangerous than songwriters who celebrate sexuality. Freedom of speech, freedom of religious thought, and the right to due process for composers, performers and retailers are imperiled if the PMRC and the major labels consummate this nasty bargain. Are we expected to give up Article One so the big guys can collect an extra dollar on every blank tape and ten to twenty-five percent on tape recorders? What's going on here? Do WE get to vote on this tax? There's an awful lot of smoke pouring out of the legislative machinery used by the PMRC to inflate this issue. Try not to inhale it. Those responsible for the vandalism should pay for the damage by VOLUNTARILY RATING THEMSELVES. If they refuse, perhaps the voters could assist in awarding the Congressional 'X,' the Congressional 'D/A,' the Congressional 'V,' and the Congressional 'O.' Just like the ladies say: these ratings are necessary to protect our children. I hope it's not too late to put them where they REALLY belong.

I testified before the Senate committee, along with John Denver and Dee Snider. My only regret about that episode is that, under the rules of the hearing, I was not afforded an opportunity to respond when I was denounced by a semiapoplectic Slade Gorton (former Republican Senator from Washington State) for my *"Constitutional ignorance."* I would have liked to remind him that although I flunked just about everything else in high school, I did get an 'A' in Civics.

If he wanted to tell me I was just an ignorant musician, why didn't he use the 'Ted Koppel method' and say, *"Now, Mr. Zappa, you're an intelligent man. . . ."* Anybody who gets that recitation from Ted twice in one episode of *Nightline* has surely been told how stupid he is.

One of the best lines of the afternoon came from Senator James Exon (D) of Nebraska—not exactly a liberal guy—who asked, *"I wonder, Mr. Chairman, if we're* **not** *talking about federal regulation, and we're* **not** *talking about federal legislation,* **what is the reason for these hearings?"** This received great applause, but was not carried by the network news.

Exon also pointed out that these hearings were better attended, by audience and media (thirty-five TV feeds, fifty still photographers) than any other legislative procedure he had been involved in, including hearings on the budget and Star Wars.

A few months later the RIAA caved in and, on November 1, 1985, agreed to place warning stickers on potentially offending albums, reading, *"Explicit Lyrics—Parental Advisory."*

The timing was interesting—the agreement was announced just a few days after the Senate version of **The Blank Tape Tax** received a committee hearing—October 30, 1985—and who was listed as one of the bill's cosponsors? Senator Albert Gore, of course.

When Jack Valenti, the president of the Motion Picture Association of America, asked Tipper Gore how many of the records released every year she would put into the objectionable category, Tipper said five percent. If five percent of the records are objectionable to the PMRC, and the process of stickering is further mitigated by the looseness of the agreement, it is not surprising that in the years since the RIAA's agreement with the PMRC was made, only a few albums have had stickers on them —placed on those albums either because the group thought it would be 'a sales tool' or because they had no clout and the record company stuck them with it.

Shortly after the second anniversary of that agreement, the PMRC asked for a *review of the agreement* because there had been *noncompliance*. The fact is, not many people do albums with lyrics that they would object to, and most of those who do are signed to record companies which are not members of the RIAA, and so are not covered by the ladies' pathetic little non-agreement.

The PMRC's list of people signed to member labels of the RIAA who were 'offensive' in 1985 was pretty ridiculous. The Captain and Tennille were on it for "Do That to Me One More Time." The Jacksons were on for "Torture." Bruce Springsteen was on for "I'm on Fire," and, of course, Prince, for the fabulous "Darling Nikki." Where was **he** throughout all this? He went apeshit and sued some spaghetti company for calling their product 'Prince,' but remained curiously silent during the record-ratings stuff.

None of the artists who made it onto the list which became known as *The PMRC's Filthy Fifteen* had anything in their lyrics **even close** to the stuff in my catalog, and yet, for some reason, I was never accused of being a 'violator.'


## You Want a Sticker? I'll Give You a Sticker!

Because of a dispute with MCA (Musicians' Cemetery of America) Records, which had contracted to distribute Barking Pumpkin Records in 1983, I invented MY OWN STICKER.

MCA planned to release *Thing-Fish*. The deal was done— they were up to the test-pressing stage. A woman in the 'quality control department' of their pressing plant listened to my album and became quite upset. Because she was offended, MCA backed out of the deal. So in 1984 I prepared this little item:

### WARNING/GUARANTEE

*This album contains material which a truly free society would neither fear nor suppress.*

*In some socially retarded areas, religious fanatics and ultra-conservative political organizations violate your First Amendment Rights by attempting to censor rock & roll albums. We feel that this is un-Constitutional and un-American.*

*As an alternative to these government-supported programs (designed to keep you docile and ignorant), Barking Pumpkin is pleased to provide stimulating digital audio entertainment for those of you who have outgrown* **the ordinary.**

*The language and concepts contained herein are* **GUARANTEED NOT TO CAUSE ETERNAL TORMENT IN THE PLACE WHERE THE GUY WITH THE HORNS AND THE POINTED STICK CONDUCTS HIS BUSINESS.**

*This guarantee is as real as the threats of the video fundamentalists who use attacks on rock music in their attempt to transform America into a nation of check-mailing nincompoops (in the name of Jesus Christ).*

*If there is a hell, its fires wait for them, not us.*

## Now What?

The agreement between the PMRC and the RIAA is, for all intents and purposes, unenforceable. Now the PMRC has moved into the world of video, complaining about television, home video and MTV. Paradoxically, Al Gore introduced legislation that would make it easier for people in Tennessee to get cable service, bringing MTV and slasher movies into entertainment-starved backwoods homes.

There were a lot of things that didn't add up during the PMRC episode. It seemed to me, and I stated it in interviews at the time, that the whole business looked like the ground floor of a presidential campaign for The Junior Senator From Tennessee.

### Making Gore-geous Music?

Off his Super Tuesday efforts, *Sen. Albert Gore Jr.* of Tennessee says he's now ready to rock 'n' roll to the Democratic presidential nomination.

Off the sales of his hit record "I Want Your Sex," George Michael says he's now ready to rock 'n' roll all the way to the bank.

Yes, folks, as strange as it may sound, *there is a connection!*

Michael credits Gore's wife, Tipper, with helping to push his album *Faith* (which contains the "Sex" song) way into the multimillion sales (3 million copies sold in this country alone). How so? Because Mrs. G. has been so outspoken against obscene lyrics in rock music, says Michael.

*"Perhaps now she can help sell a few thousand more records since her husband won big in the primaries,"* Michael said in Perth, Australia, where he is performing.

Gore won in six states in the Super Tuesday primaries.

*"As Americans like to say, there was much hoopla about nothing,"* Michael said about the lyrics in the song. *"It was, after all, just a pop record."*

New York *Daily News,* March 11, 1988

Following up on this—a CNN show called *Crossfire* covered the PMRC topic twice with me as a guest, the first time in 1985 (when I told that guy from *The Washington Times* to kiss my ass), and then again in 1987, when George Michael's sex song was 'controversial.' Believe it or not, ladies and gentlemen, the premise of that second debate on *Crossfire* was (don't laugh) **"Does Rock Music Cause AIDS?"**, with an opening bumper that included clips from Mr. Michael's video.

## The Blacklist

The first time I got involved with the PMRC issue was when I debated Kandy Stroud in Washington, D.C., on *CBS Nightwatch* in August 1985. It was supposed to be a one-hour taped debate in front of a live audience (which happened to include Stroud's young children, listening raptly as Mom recited the familiar litany of "oral sex at gunpoint," etc., etc.).

During the audience question-and-answer session, a Washington, D.C., disc jockey named Serf stated that the whole thing reminded him of the *radio blacklist* days—when certain artists and records were forbidden to be played on the air. That grabbed my attention. Several things were edited out of the show by the time it finally went on the air, and that was one of them.

The following week I was in New York doing a live radio interview on WNEW-FM. I was talking with the disc jockey about the blacklist days. I asked him, *"Have you ever seen one?"* *"Yeah,"* he said. *"I've seen it."* *"You've seen* **The Blacklist?"** I said. *"Would you go to court and say that you have?"* Then the guy started to get **really worried.**

After the Commerce Committee hearing on September 19, I began doing a lot of interviews on the PMRC topic. Sometime in November, right after the RIAA made their stupid agreement with the PMRC, I was back in New York, and one of the people who came there to interview me had been hired to write an article for *Playboy* magazine. She had heard the radio broadcast on WNEW with the reference to a blacklist and, through the Freedom of Information Act, had managed to actually get her hands on one.

She showed it to me and explained that the reason people haven't seen the blacklists before is that when you try to find one through the Freedom of Information Act, they don't help you. You have to ask **exactly the right agency** for **exactly the right documents,** or you don't get them. Who would ever think of asking the Department of Defense for a blacklist of pop songs? She did, and that's where it came from. It was dated April 1971 or 1972, and it had "Puff the Magic Dragon" on it along with maybe nineteen other songs.

The blacklist wasn't just the one piece of paper. It was a stack a couple of inches thick, and included all the corresponding FCC documents (it appeared that they were helping to implement the restraints—in violation of their charter)—and she was going to write an article about it for *Playboy*. It never appeared. I don't know where she is. I don't know what happened to the blacklist. Three other journalists were sitting in the room when she came in—a guy from *Cashbox* and two women from *High*

*Times*—and the list was shown to them. She thought she had a scoop, and she wasn't going to show the whole batch of documents to everybody, but a few of the people there saw it, as I did, and said, *"I don't believe this."*

## True Confessions

On February 14, 1986, the Maryland State Senate Judiciary Committee held a hearing on a bill proposed by delegate Judith Toth to modify the existing state pornography statute so as to include records, tapes and CDs. The bill had already been passed by the Maryland House of Delegates, and a Senate vote in favor would have placed it into law in Maryland, creating a dangerous national precedent.

Maryland has some funny ideas as to what constitutes pornography. Considering that it was my home state, I thought the least I could do was to help keep its citizens from making total fools of themselves, so I went there to offer my testimony.

The night before the hearing, the lobbyist hired by the RIAA, Mr. Bruce Bereano, threw a cocktail reception in Annapolis so I could meet a few of the state delegates. It was an evening of handshaking, autograph signing and posing for pictures. As I was introduced to each legislator, I asked which way he or she had voted. The bill, after all, had already passed the House by ninety-six to thirty or thereabouts. The delegates were honest and told me frankly how they had voted, and if they said they **had** voted for the bill, I gave them a pretty good razz. I said, *"This is your last chance to recant. All you have to do is fill out this piece of paper and say you've changed your position."* I got five of them to write confessions at that reception, and the next day at the hearing, I said, *"Here are the confessions of the delegates who realize that this bill is really bad and wish they had never signed it."* The next day, at the hearing, I read their names and confessions into the record.

## On Your Feet, or on Your Knees

I was able to acquire video tape of the State Senate proceedings in 1987, just as I was editing together the first of the Honker Home Video projects. I decided to combine parts of my testimony with the actual statements made by Ms. Toth and Delegate Owens in a way that would dramatize the issue, and included this in a one-hour show called *Video from Hell*. This is a transcription of the dialog-as-edited from that show. . . .

TESTIMONY BEFORE THE MARYLAND STATE LEGISLATURE, FEBRUARY 14, 1986. A BILL PROPOSED BY DELEGATE JUDITH TOTH TO MODIFY THE EXISTING PORNOGRAPHY STATUTE SO AS TO INCLUDE RECORDS, TAPES AND CDS HAD BEEN PASSED BY THE MARYLAND HOUSE OF DELEGATES.

F.Z.: It is my personal feeling that lyrics cannot harm anyone. There is no **sound** that you can make with your mouth, or **word** that will come out of your mouth, that is **so powerful** that it will **make you go to hell.** It's also not going to turn anyone into a 'social liability.' 'Disturbed' people can be set off on a 'disturbed' course of action by **any** kind of stimulus. If they are prone to being antisocial or schizophrenic or **whatever,** they can be set off by **anything,** including my tie, or your hair, or that **chair** over there. You can't point to the statistics concerning *'people doing strange things in the vicinity of rock music,'* because all you've got to do is look around at all the normal kids who listen to it and live with it every day who do not commit suicide; they don't commit murder, and they grow up to be, in some cases, **legislators.**

DELEGATE JOSEPH OWENS, CHAIRMAN OF THE JUDICIARY COMMITTEE: This is probably the worst type of child abuse we've got in this state, because it hits all the children. This is **mass child abuse,** and that's what it is. When they throw some of this *slime* at these children, it's abuse.

F.Z.: To say that rock music is 'the worst form of child abuse,' and 'mass child abuse,' is *sky-high rhetoric.*

DELEGATE JUDITH TOTH: We're not talking about references to sex. We're talking about references to incest. **Incest.** And it says, *'Do it, kids! It's fine.'* We're talking about rape and sexual violence. It's illegal in this state, but these records get out there and they say, 'Do it, kids! It feels good. It's fine. It's okay.' You've got to read this stuff to know just how **dirty** it is.

F.Z.: Did you guys **read** this? *[Laughter]* Or did you read the *'synopsis'?*

TOTH: This is **pornography.**

F.Z.: This is **censorship.** I oppose this bill for a number of reasons. First of all, **there's no need for it.** The idea that the lyrics to a song are going to cause 'antisocial behavior' is not supportable by science.

TOTH: This bill is **constitutional.** We're talking about minors in the first place. And stop worrying about their 'civil rights.' Start worrying about their *mental health,* and about the *health of our society.*

F.Z.: The bill seeks to keep people from seeing, renting, buying or listening to material described as depicting 'illicit sex'—and the description of what constitutes 'illicit sex,' as per this bill, includes *"human genitals in a state of sexual stimulation or arousal."* Is that **illicit** sex? Perhaps in Maryland. *[Laughter]* *"Acts of* human *masturbation."* Not *"animal masturbation"*; this is talking about **human masturbation** as an *"illicit sexual act."* *[Laughter]* *"Sexual intercourse or sodomy."* Why does the bill indicate that *sex-*

*ual intercourse* is **illicit sex,** and put it next to **sodomy** in the same line? The next line reads, *"fondling or other erotic touching of human genitals."* That is *"illicit"* in the state of Maryland according to the **law as already written?**

OWENS: The thing is, they *know* what they've got, they *know* what they're selling, and **that's what they're trying to sell.** Because that's the only thing they could sell to these minors.

F.Z.: Finally, on this list we find **"nude or partially denuded figures, meaning less than completely and opaquely covered human genitals, pubic region, buttocks or female breasts below a point immediately above the top of the aureola."** *[Laughter]* Now, *I like* **nipples.** I think they look nice—and if you take off the nipple, which is the characterizing, determining factor, what you've got is a blob of **fat** there. *[Laughter]* And I think that when you're a baby, probably one of the first things that you get interested in is the **nozzle** right there. *[Laughter]* You get to have it **right up in front of your face.** You 'grow up with it,' so to speak —and then you grow up to live in the state of Maryland, and they won't let you see that little brown nozzle anymore.

TOTH: I am not against artistic creativity. I am not for censorship. I think adults have the right to listen to and see whatever they want, but we're talking about **children** here. This is going to affect **children.**

F.Z.: When some people start talking about pornography and their desire to *"save the children,"* they sometimes choose strange ways to express that desire. Some of the statements made in support of this bill are absurd. I think you have problems in the law as it already exists, **let**

**alone amending it to include audio references to the so-called illicit sexual acts that are already in this document.** Because the bill talks about not being able to *"advertise matter containing these objectionable topics,"* it opens up the following possibility: a person wearing a *Mötley Crüe T-shirt—if Mötley Crüe was adjudged by whatever forum is going to make these decisions to be a 'pornographic' act—theoretically could be fined a thousand dollars or go to jail for a year because of* **his wardrobe,** *and if he wore it* **twice,** *it's* **five thousand dollars or imprisonment not to exceed three years, or both.**

The show ends with me talking over the credits, in an interview with a Maryland TV station, giving the final chapter to this silly story. . . .

F. z.: Do you want an example of censorship growing out of this bill? Censorship doesn't always work by someone taking a pencil and crossing a line out of a book, or forcing a record off the shelves. There are other forms of censorship.

I recently offered the Peabody Conservatory my services to teach for a couple of weeks—but they were afraid that if they brought me in to teach, they would *lose their funding from the state,* because the people who supported the censorship bill had the power to remove funding from the entire Peabody Conservatory.

JUDITH TOTH'S BILL WAS KILLED IN THE MARYLAND STATE SENATE JUDICIARY COMMITTEE. OTHER STATES HAVE CONSIDERED SIMILAR LEGISLATION. DELEGATE TOTH HAS VOWED TO REINTRODUCE HER BILL IN ORDER TO **"BRING THE RECORD INDUSTRY TO ITS KNEES."**

## More Initials to Watch Out For

Governmental agencies and groups like the PMRC find promotion easier when their bullshit is concealed behind an *acronym*. The 'aura' these organizations hope to generate from the use of the acronym could be scientifically described as **'The Acro-Nymbus'**—and any person believing that such an 'aura' certifies competence could be scientifically described as an **'Acronymbecile.'**

William Steading is the founder of **the NMRC, the National Music Review Council.** He runs two radio stations, one in Dallas and one in Salt Lake City, owned by the Mormon church. I received a flyer in the mail from this group, talking about **their idea for cleaning up lyrics.** The PMRC wanted to put The Scarlet Letter on **offensive LPs;** the NMRC wanted to put an **"Attaboy" sticker** on albums, indicating that it contains **nothing objectionable.**

At Steading's stations, when a new record came in, someone would listen to it, decide what he didn't like, transfer the record to tape, edit the tape and play the 'clean' tape on the air **instead** of the record.

That was rather deceptive. Some unsuspecting listener hearing the *Steading Version* might think it was a harmless little ditty, go out and buy the record, only to find out later it was about some leather weasel getting cornholed.

The NMRC plan gets it both ways: a station can play supposedly 'hot music' without worrying about losing its broadcast license to the FCC.

When groups like this go after 'SHOW BUSINESS ITSELF' —where so many people have 'skeletons in their closets'—they often go unchallenged. Albert Gore set up a committee to investigate **payola in the record industry,** and held his own little hearings, shortly after his wife's day in the spotlight, just to keep the pressure on—and then had the nerve to come to

Hollywood, meeting with the same folks whose livelihood he and his wife were threatening, and ask for presidential campaign contributions.

As I said before, nobody looks good with brown lipstick on, but Al looked RIDICULOUS.

## Who's Paying the Bills?

During a debate with Jennifer Norwood from the PMRC, Jello Biafra (of the Dead Kennedys) asked, *"Who's paying the bills?"* **Norwood blurted out that the PMRC was funded by Occidental and Merrill Lynch.**

Our pension plan is with Merrill Lynch, so Gail called and talked with the head man. If they were in fact supporting the PMRC, it was going to cost them our account. He insisted it wasn't company policy. Apparently, a call had gone out for people to 'donate' for a PMRC picnic. Somebody at Merrill Lynch in Washington, D.C., had noticed that Mrs. Packwood was a signatory to the PMRC letter, and, at the time, Senator Packwood was the chairman of the Finance Committee. So here's a guy at Merrill Lynch thinking that if he **makes a contribution to the PMRC,** he'll get to go to the picnic, meet Mrs. Packwood and thereby get his elbow into Mr. Packwood.

## Back in Control

*Back in Control* is an *"entity"* which, for a price, will take a child and remodel its behavior to suit the needs and desires of a 'concerned parent.' In her book, *Raising PG Kids in an X-Rated Society,* Tipper Gore recommends this group.

If you were to follow Tipper's advice and use the company's services, here's what you might expect—for example, if you think that your child is showing signs of becoming a *punker* or a *heavy metaler,* this *"entity,"* and others scattered around the United States, will **depunk** or **demetalize** your child (leaving you free to go sportfishing). Parents who find themselves baffled by the arcane behavior of *"today's young people"* can now just sort of ship the little buggers off to psycho-camp.

If you're interested in disposing of your kids in this manner, Back in Control offers a pamphlet, listing 'clues' as to what the **danger signs** are. One of them is (don't laugh) if the child is wearing *tennis shoes.* Yes, a sure sign of something **evil** developing at ground level.

The pamphlet includes a section on 'symbols' which indicate 'the possibility' of *satanic* or *demonic* behavior. One of the symbols <u>was</u> **the Star of David.** The Back in Control people said they saw the Star of David on an Ozzy Osbourne album. What a **jokester** that Ozzy is! (I understand they have been forced to modify that section of the pamphlet.)

For some reason, they don't like me very much. I got hold of a letter written by the head guy, putting **me** in the same category as *Joseph Goebbels* and *Senator Joseph McCarthy*—claiming that I was using <u>THE BIG LIE</u> technique against them. *Pheuuuuuuuuuuuuw.*

CALL OUR CONVENIENT 24 HOUR TOLL FREE NUMBER 1·800·666·6666 TODAY!

If the scare tactics of groups like the PMRC and Back in Control have not made an impact on musicians, they have certainly made one on the executives of the record companies who can tell artists what the labels **will** or **will not** accept as suitable material under the artist's contract.

If you make a record, you are not automatically assured that the song you wrote and recorded will reach the marketplace, because some coward in the record company may come up and say he can't allow it to escape for 'moral' reasons.

If the artist can't sing the song he wants to sing, release the record he wants to release, and earn the living he is entitled to earn from doing what he loves, he is cheated, and the audience is cheated—because they don't get to hear the best work of the artist—only that which he is allowed to release. Will the **artists** *ever get* **back in control?** Tune in again tomorrow, folks.

# CHAPTER 16

# Church & State

I know you've heard it all before, but, one more time, folks: **The U.S. Constitution specifies that the church and state be kept separate.**

Besides the Moral Majority, a lot of other entities in the TV religion industry claim to be conservative but are, in fact, the U.S. equivalent of the mongos blowing the shit out of the Middle East.

Anybody who claims that the Road to Righteousness is mapped out in some book (or pamphlet) he's waving around is an asshole (at least) or (more likely) a *fanatic,* in the clinical sense of the word.

 ## The Gipper as a 'Kept Boy'

Ever watch The Great Communicator addressing the *National Association of Religious Broadcasters?* Face it, folks: Ron is their **Kept Boy.** They've got him by the short ones—he **must** play ball or they'll cut the PR budget—for him and all the rest of the Helpful Republicans. Remember, a few years ago they were beating the bushes for Jimmy Carter—and if they ever found another Democrat to do their chores for them, they could easily switch back.

So, in order that the goods and services continue to be delivered, The Men Behind The Gipper insist that he surround himself with 'Qualified Advisers'—

[Insert sound effect of a large toilet flushing.]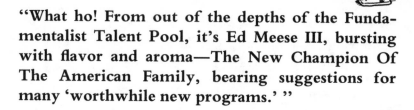

**"What ho! From out of the depths of the Fundamentalist Talent Pool, it's Ed Meese III, bursting with flavor and aroma—The New Champion Of The American Family, bearing suggestions for many 'worthwhile new programs.' "**

(Wasn't it sensational the way Ed-III kept everybody busy with his porno-mania, while Born-Again-Ollie cranked up that hilarious private-sectorized 'Secret Government'!)

" 'Junta'? What 'junta'? *This isn't a* **real** *'junta'—it's just a harmless little-bitty ol'* **'Jeezo-Junta.' "**

A deranged mullah with a rifle in his hand exhorting rows of prospective martyrs to Bite The Big One is not amusing, even at a distance of five thousand miles. Jerry Falwell suggested on a Larry King show (August 1988) that his followers be ready to *"die, if necessary"* when participating in anti-abortion *"civil disobedience."* We'd be wise to keep our eyes on the self-proclaimed Holy Men in our own backyard—including Jesse Jackson.

## Jesus Thinks You're a Jerk

In the early days of the Reagan Administration, we started seeing judicial test cases involving school prayer, creationist theory, and so on. One of the results was that, at the height of this frenzy to give the illusion of 'being fair' (one of our major faults, I might add) a decision was made in the California schools to order new science textbooks.

They were ordered to be written in a way that balanced *Creationist Mumbo-Jumbo* with *The Other Kind Of Mumbo-Jumbo.* When the books finally arrived, there was so little 'science' in them, they were rejected (and probably resold to somebody else's school system).

I hereby place a curse upon the cretins who assert that:

*"Americanism equals Christianity equals good fiscal policy equals fifteen minutes from Armageddon—but Armageddon is okay because **WE'RE** all going to Heaven and **THEY'RE** NOT!"*

**MY HUMBLE CURSE:**
**May your shit come to life, and kiss you.**

## C.A.S.H.

Once upon a time, I filed papers to start my own religion.

FOR IMMEDIATE RELEASE:

**"ZAPPA ANNOUNCES C.A.S.H.—CHURCH OF AMERICAN SECULAR HUMANISM"**

Thousands of years ago, wise men predicted a NEW RELIGION would appear at the time of a unique planetary alignment called The Harmonic Convergence—THE PROPHECY HAS BEEN FULFILLED!

The ancient writings didn't mention a Nixon-appointed judge named Brevard Hand, but they should have.

His ruling in the controversial Alabama School Textbook Case provided the Final Sign From On High which led the unpredictable Mr. Honker to file articles of incorporation in the State of Alabama for C.A.S.H.—CHURCH OF AMERICAN SECULAR HUMANISM.

In deciding the case, Judge Hand ruled that 'Secular Humanism' was, in fact, an actual religion, and that the tenets of its faith were dominating the curriculum of Alabama Schools, thereby violating the civil rights of decent Christian folks who demanded 'equal time.'

The problem with this historic legal interpretation, according to some, was that there really wasn't a 'religion' called Secular Humanism . . . and certainly no CHURCH of SECULAR HUMANISM.

Out of this desperate need, C.A.S.H. was created. Zappa reasoned that, if the Judge's ruling was upheld, Secular Humanism was entitled to the same benefits under U.S. law that every other religion enjoys: tax exemptions, awesome political power, unaudited expenditures of vast sums on real estate speculations, etc., so, in drafting the Tenets Of The Faith, he duplicated the actual language of the Judge's ruling, adding to it a few thoughts of his own. (THE COMPLETE LIST IS INCLUDED LATER.)

When asked to explain, Zappa paraphrased **Oliver North,** saying, *"As a result of Judge Hand's finding on this matter, I sensed a need for the creation of an* **'off-the-shelf, stand-alone, self-financing (religious) organization, capable of worldwide covert action.'** *"*

He also said, *"If the Judge's ruling is struck down . . . and, in fact,* **it should be,** *there is still a* need *for this church. The people of* **Our Faith** *refuse to be persecuted any longer by a fanatical fifth column, shoveling money in the direction of 'special friends' in Washington, D.C."*

unused press release, 1987

Here are some samples of the **Tenets of the Faith,** as listed in the actual documents filed in Montgomery, Alabama.

**That any belief in a deity or adherence to a religious system that is theistic is discouraged (but not forbidden), because of its emphasis on the unseen and transcendent.**

**That man is the center of the universe and all existence, and will act and be treated accordingly, unless evidence to the contrary be discovered through verifiable scientific inquiry.**

**That each man obey the secular laws, ordinances and regulations to which he is subject, after which he is responsible only to himself in the determination of whether his decisions are right or wrong.**

**That men have invented gods, and may continue to do so, utilizing these inventions for personal benefit.**

**That any man may choose for himself his own personal god or gods, and no adherence to any god at all is required for participation in this church.**

**That C.A.S.H. is the One True Church.**

Some of those were my additions—not part of Judge Hand's ruling, which was struck down a short while later. After hearing this splendid news, I un-filed the papers and 'dissolved the religion.'

I probably should have kept it going, since I came up with a few other nice 'doctrines'—for example: **THE DOCTRINE OF INVOLUNTARY INDUCTION,** which provided that, as *Founder of the Faith and Writer of the Rules,* there was no reason why I couldn't lay my hands on a map and *decree* that all human beings residing in whatever territory I might be fingering at the time were **Involuntarily Inducted into the Church of American Secular Humanism—whether they liked it or not.**

As you can see, ladies and gentlemen, this transcends mere *Mumbo-Jumbo,* sending us reeling into the realm of **Mumbo-Pocus.**

Think about the 'rules' of Christianity for a moment. Okay
—*What was it that Adam ate that he wasn't supposed to eat?* It wasn't
*just an apple*—it was the fruit of **the Tree of the Knowledge
of Good and Evil.**

The subtle message? *"Get smart and I'll fuck you over—sayeth
the Lord."* **God is the Smartest—and he doesn't want any
competition.**

**Is this not an absolutely anti-intellectual religion?**

# Section 501(c)(3)

In a 1987 C-SPAN broadcast, Father Robert Drinan stated
that, in 1979, the Republican Party made a deal to modify their
platform in order to gain the financial and logistical support of
The Religious Right.

Shortly thereafter, Ronald Reagan ponced into the Oval Office with a pat on the fanny from the NARB superstars who
organized the Jeezo-Minions to vote Republican with partisan
TV sermons and direct-mail fund-raising campaigns—**and
managed to keep their tax exemptions!** How did they pull
that one off?

The section of the IRS code that bestows this license to
pillage and plunder specifies that the exempted person or organization *may not lobby for (or against)* **any political candidate,
or for (or against)** **any specific piece of legislation**—if you
violate this, you lose your exemption and become liable for
criminal prosecution. Here is the actual tax code language:

**CODE SEC. 501.
EXEMPTIONS FROM TAX ON CORPORATIONS**

. . . (c) List of exempt organizations. . .

. . . (3) Corporations, and **any** community chest, **fund,
or foundation, organized and operated exclusively
for religious,** charitable, scientific, testing for public
safety, literary or educational **purposes,** or to foster national or international amateur sports competition (but

only if no part of its activities involve the provision of athletic facilities or equipment), or for the prevention of cruelty to children or animals, no part of the net earnings of which enures to the benefit of any private shareholder or individual, **no substantial part of the activities of which is** carrying on propaganda, or otherwise attempting to influence legislation (except as otherwise provided in subsection [h]), **and which does not participate in, or intervene in (including the publishing or distributing of statements), any political campaign on behalf of** (or in opposition to) **any candidate for public office.** *(emphasis supplied)*

The IRS is charged with the enforcement of this law—on the books since the thirties, virtually unchanged, in spite of many revisions in the rest of the tax code. Section 501(c)(3) has never been a secret.

The boss of this purported 'enforcement' is the Secretary of the Treasury—for most of Reagan's second term that was James (Born Again) Baker III.

Did he ever demand an audit of this multibillion-dollar con game? Were any of the regional IRS auditors Born Again, and reluctant to prosecute their church-mates at CBN, Oral Roberts University, or *'Water-Slide-For-Jesus-Incorporated'*? Should they not have been replaced with more objective personnel? (Did such personnel exist **anywhere** in the Reagan IRS?) I believe we have a classic case of *selective nonenforcement* here.

Would it be too extreme to suggest that in Baker's case, in the regional auditor's cases and in the case of the Televangelical Republican Protectorate At Large, this might be *an indictable offense?*

The payback for the 1979 agreement was to be delivered in easy monthly installments, throughout the Reagan presidency —legislative initiatives against abortion, in favor of school prayer, against homosexuals—all to be upheld by a bouquet of handpicked 'trustworthy' Supreme Court justices—in an atmosphere of *total immunity* from IRS interference.

Does anybody remember that Jim and Tammy Bakker were brought in as guests for Reagan's inauguration, and in 1983 Mr. Ron gave them a **humanitarian award?**

Didn't Falwell's 1988 fund-raising campaign to pardon Ollie North qualify him for a citation?

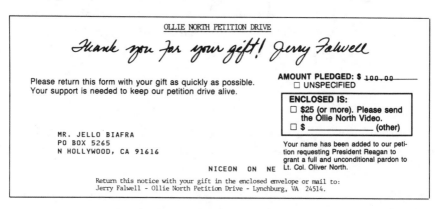

OLLIE NORTH PETITION DRIVE

*Thank you for your gift! Jerry Falwell*

Please return this form with your gift as quickly as possible.
Your support is needed to keep our petition drive alive.

AMOUNT PLEDGED: $ 100.00
□ UNSPECIFIED

ENCLOSED IS:
□ $25 (or more). Please send the Ollie North Video.
□ $ _____ (other)

MR. JELLO BIAFRA
PO BOX 5265
N HOLLYWOOD, CA 91616

Your name has been added to our petition requesting President Reagan to grant a full and unconditional pardon to Lt. Col. Oliver North.

NICEON ON NE

Return this notice with your gift in the enclosed envelope or mail to:
Jerry Falwell - Ollie North Petition Drive - Lynchburg, VA 24514.

How does this work? We send him money and then Ollie gets off the hook? What? Are we supposed to help Falwell **buy a pardon?** If the money is used for "lobbying purposes," do we have a little 501 violation on our hands? And how about those *Magic Mike* comic books he distributed at the Republican convention?

## Who Loves Ya?

People have a desire to believe in *'good luck,' 'angels'* of one sort or another, *'devils'* of one sort or another—*'mysterious forces'* which somehow link back to a *'godhead,'* or a *'controlling force,'* or a *'master plan,'* developed by some *'All-Knowing Consciousness'* that **LOVES THEM,** and wants to make everything *okay* for them.

Why do people want **that?** They're going to spend a lot of time trying to make things from The Real World fit that mold.

The minute something happens that doesn't follow the formula, they start worrying. It makes some of them psychotic—like the guy with the sword, hacking up people on the Staten Island Ferry because Jesus told him to do it.

One reason people **practice** religion is that participation creates the illusion of belonging to an extended family. Whatever the **Imaginary-Guy-In-The-Clouds** won't do for them *(sometimes he's busy—inventing crack; causing droughts; stirring up mischief here and there),* their fellow parishioners might.

> *"My mother didn't love me, my father didn't love me, but my friends at church think I'm a nice person—so we'll just climb on this really bitchen water-slide here, and love the jumpin' be-jeezus out of each other while we whiz downward . . ."*

If you want to stand on the steps of **any building** (or water-slide), all dressed up on a Sunday morning, for **whatever purpose** (a Christian business discussion, perhaps), **great**—go for it.

If you want to get together in any *exclusive situation* and have people *love* you, **fine**—but to hang all this desperate sociology on the idea of **The Cloud-Guy** who has **The Big Book,** who knows if you've been **bad or good—and CARES about any of it**—to hang it all on **that,** folks, is the *chimpanzee* part of the brain working.

One of the reasons these evil industries have survived throughout the ages is that the big guys have always made sure that the customers confuse the *'results'* of their *'prayers'* with *'the existence'* of **The Guy On The Cloud.**

What people call 'prayer' could just as easily be an unknown (or improperly described) psychic phenomenon which manifests a **tangible physical result.** Any group of people, focused on the same goal, might be able to aim an *unknown amount* of an *unknown energy* at some specific 'target.' Presto: *"Prayer That Works."*

## Robert Tilton: Under a Curse

I've been watching a televangelist named Robert Tilton, out of Dallas, Texas. He's the one who closes his eyes and says, *"Thank you, Jesus!"* as if Jesus were whispering to him throughout the show. Seen him yet?

At the end of one broadcast, Tilton announced that those viewers who didn't send in money were *"robbing God."* Because of that, he said, they were *"under a curse."* Naturally, the only way the curse could be lifted was for them to send **even more money than they might have previously considered.**

By this 'act of faith,' he said, **God would know that they were really sincere,** and, at that point, **financial benefits would flow into their lives.** In other words: **you** prove **you are** worthy of being prosperous **by sending an exceptional amount of money to the address at the bottom of the screen,** and that 'act of faith' triggers the **"This One's Okay"** blinker on the **Big Ol' Jesus Faith of Our Fathers Tally Board**—and, as soon as **"HE"** sees it, **"HE"** waves **"HIS"** blessed hand, and: **Voila!**

It's a variation on those real estate schemes they used to advertise on cable all night—sort of like *'solving your cash flow problems through Divine Intervention.'* (Was this the origin of 'Voodoo Economics?')

Ladies and gentlemen, here's Mr. Robert Tilton in action:

(Excerpts, transcribed from an actual broadcast.)

[TILTON enters a room full of POTTED PALMS and presents his profile. He is facing the wrong camera. An OFFSCREEN VOICE corrects him.]

VOICE:
*This one . . .*

TILTON:

*[Turning to face camera; laughing.]*

*Heh-heh.* Here, praise God, everybody was scrambling to get me here on time. Well, I'm here. And I believe Jesus is here. And I just believe *you're* here, and I can just tell already that this is going to be one of those *very extra special programs* today.

Why don't we just decide right now that today, during this program, it's going to be **your day** for a *breakthrough*, for a **miracle in your life?** Did you know *Psalms 45:1* says that **"your mouth can be as a pen of a ready writer"?** Do you realize that you can *write your own ticket with God?* You'll say, *"Now Bob, that's getting a little carried away!"*

Well, what do you think **prayer** is? If the old saying, *"Whatever will be will be"*—if that's **true** and **scriptural,** then why in the world did Jesus continually, consistently teach on the subject of prayer, the exercise of faith, **overcoming** and **changing** things? ⟨**Hora bassandah kitira dobosoyah**⟩, Jesus was constantly teaching us how to change things.

The mysterious group of syllables above is Mr. Bob 'speaking in tongues.' He reverts to this procedure at random intervals during the broadcast. A little later on we get . . .

*[TILTON faces screen, hands spread apart.]*
TILTON:

I want you to put your hand on top of mine *right now* on the television screen. I know it sounds foolish, but **God uses foolish things to confound the wise.** The Bible says—Jesus said, *"They shall lay hands upon the sick and they shall recover."* He didn't say **we couldn't do it through television!** If the little woman touched the hem of His garment and was healed, I think you can touch the hem of this television set. And I'm not Jesus, but I **know** Jesus, and **He's right here when we pray.**

*[Puts hands up to screen.]*

He said He's **there in the midst.** When two or more are gathered together in His name, He's **there in the midst.** And if you've got the faith to lay your hand on the television screen and agree with me as I pray, I know what God will do. It's time for **your healing,** it's time, *right now*—it's time, *right now*—for **your healing.** Let us pray.

Eventually he gets down to business and asks for money.

TILTON:

Al, what time is it? One and a half minutes. *Real quick!* Whoever you are—*real quick*—there's someone needs to make a vow of five hundred dollars. There's another person needs to make a vow of a hundred. You **need to do it!**

*[Picking up a pile of papers, reading through them one at a time; counting.]*

One, two, three, four, five thousand—that's a thousand—six thousand—here's that one five hundred—thirteen thousand—here's another five hundred. Here's that five thousand, **praise God!** I know there's somebody else supposed to do five thousand—*don't see the ten thousand.* Here's another thousand—what was that, thirteen or fourteen? How many—What do we have? Forty-five seconds. One, two, three, four, five, six, seven, eight, nine, ten, eleven, twelve, thirteen, fourteen, fifteen, sixteen, seventeen—three more people. Lord, in Jesus' name. IN JESUS' NAME! **ANGELS!**

*[Theme music comes up.]*

Thank you, Lord. Lord, I lay my hands on these

vows that have come in. We need three— Here comes the other three.

*[Takes papers handed in by assistant.]*

I'm gonna start **prophesyin'** now. You go and do the phone, real quickly. Even when we go off the air, we're still here, if you're 'that one'—and someone is with God, *trying to reason.* You're not reaping things you need in your life today! You never got 'in faith.' The devil came and stole faith out of the heart of Adam and Eve! That's what happened! Now the just shall **live!** By **faith!** Step out of the boat, out of life, and *go forward!* Here's that other five thousand, here's another thousand. There's someone supposed to call that ten thousand in. Father—right now, even when we go off the air, there's just a couple more missing. Father, in the **name** of Jesus, I **decree** into existence:

### Finances!

*[Pounds fist on table.]*

### Money!

*[Pounds fist.]*

### Deliverance!

*[Pounds fist.]*

**Healing** *flow into marriages!* Satan, I break your power, your curse, off of these families, off of their health, their mind, their finances, their job! You can't help it, if they are God's children—then they belong to God! In the name of Jesus, I pray, and **speak into existence.** Amen, and *Amen.*

Now this afternoon I'm going to mail you a letter, and a *prayer cloth* that **I've prayed over.** When we go off the air and you didn't call, and you were supposed to do, call when we go off the air—and if you want the free book, be sure and call.

Oh-ho, praise **God!** Thank you, Lord! Thank you!

*[Theme music up loud. Fade up ANNOUNCER's VOICE.]*

VOICEOVER:

Next time you're in Dallas, join us at **Word of Faith Family Church**, I-35 at Valley View Farmers Branch, North Dallas. Services are Sunday morning at eight and ten and Sunday evenings at six, with pastor Robert Tilton. You've been watching **Success 'n' Life.** On behalf of Bob and Marty, thanks for joining us, and God bless you!

On a really good show **he crawls**—he spreads the 'prayer requests' out on what he calls his 'ramp,' gets on his hands and knees, crawls over them, 'speaks in tongues,' and tells you that there are *lines still open.* You have to see him crawling through the 'prayer requests'—**rooting** through them, like a pig sniffing for truffles.

One possible 'scientific reason' for this unusual behavior might be that **more parts of his body touch the papers**—seated, he can only 'lay *hands* upon them,' but when you have knees, hands, the possibility of elbows—maybe even *shoes*—laid upon the correspondence, more parts of his 'anointed body' can be used to 'bless' them.

The other thing he does is squint his eyes and get silent for a while, and then he says, *"Thank you, Jesus!"*—as if Jesus just gave him a 'message.' Have you ever seen an **echidna?** It's an animal from Australia that's a cross between an anteater and a porcupine, and looks like it has venereal warts all around its eyes. When he squints, he looks like an echidna.

Right now, people around the world think America is all *Big*

*Macs* and *Levis*—but, if they **knew about this stuff,** they'd run away screaming every time an American landed in their country (the guy might have made one of those weird **vows** to Tilton, and the unsuspecting Berliner might be forced to witness the deranged tourist's **'seed'** multiplying all over the airport).

In Tilton's case, viewers who have 'released their faith' may be releasing something other than 'faith' (the way he defines it). They could be releasing a form of energy the Chinese have known about for seven or eight thousand years.

I don't think prayer in its *truest sense* is anything to scoff at, but the sad fact is that people are being manipulated, and their energy—their life force—is being usurped and used for the personal benefit of the *Video Energy Vampire* who leads them in 'prayer.' This is the essence of televangelism.

At its worst, it can lead to a suggestion that the whole congregation pray for the death of a Supreme Court justice. Reverend Hymers (the guy who led the protest against *The Last Temptation of Christ*) actually did this. He suggested that his followers wish the death of a certain justice because of his views on abortion.

We must be vigilant! Victims of this psychic manipulation could wind up haunting the mini-malls of America, like the zombies from *Night of the Living Dead,* stalking human *souls* in their sacred vehicles, marked on the rear bumper with the **'Sign Of The Fish.'** Forget about a Russian invasion—**these guys live next door to you!** Develop those reflexes, folks! Every time you see **The Fish**, think about using **The Harpoon.**

## Just Like Magic

Let's say you're a person of *not extensive education,* but you own a TV set—and let's say a preacher comes on and tells you to do something like that. Just because a man is uneducated does not mean he is without a life force. He might say to himself: *"Sounds good to me—let's go for it!"* Everybody has this energy, and the 'disposable' portion is not dependent on an individual's status in life, or how far he got with his education. (It might even be inversely proportional.)

Somebody watching Tilton, or Oral Roberts, or Swaggart, or any of the others, is told to 'release his faith'—and he says, *"Okay, I'm releasing my faith—Woo! Woo! Now what?"* **Poof!**— the *7-Eleven* blows up. You never know.

Or he 'prays' for money, and this 'influences the decision' of someone who hires him the next day—he gets a job and blames it on Jesus. He may think Tilton made it happen, and send ol' Bob a bag of money, paying off that seed faith gift of one-hundred dollars, one thousand dollars, or ten thousand dollars.

One man's 'prayer' is another man's 'unknown quantity.'

We might observe another man's 'successful prayer' and say, *"He's doing black magic. He's making shit happen without touching it."*

Or we might say, *"He's very religious; he's a dear, sweet, loving person!"*

We should say, *"Who knows what the fuck he's doing—but something happened. There's a Brown Thing in the kitchen! C'mere, Wanda! It's a goddamn poltergeist!"*

## Faith Healing

There is a parallel to this in kundalini yoga. I'm not sure it's related to *exactly* the same energy force, but, in situations where large amounts of sexual energy are released, strange things can happen.

Let's look at 'faith healing' in that context. I saw a woman on one of those shows who looked like she was *decorating her cookies* because the preacher 'laid hands on her.'

That wasn't Jesus making her squirt—she hit L-109 because a nice man with an expensive suit on was 'touching her.' He had her by the neck: *"Get into this position! Okay? Here comes* **The Lord!** *All warm inside now? You feel that* **warmth** *flowing through you now?"*

I believe **The Real Stuff** has *never* been called by **The Right Name.**

Everyone should have the opportunity to figure out their own 'name' for it, but remember: **If you name it wrong, you could wind up on your knees, snorkeling the philosophical sausage of some guy with a silk suit on.**

## The Dangerous Christians

One of the misconceptions about evangelicals in the U.S. is that they're all as extreme as Swaggart, Falwell and Robertson. They're not. Most of them just want to worship at their local church. They don't give a shit about those guys on television—they think they're clowns and that what they do cheapens *everyone's* religious experience. On this, we definitely agree.

I once received an anonymous letter, poorly typed and stuffed into a manila envelope, from a man who described himself as a *"highly placed person in the Fundamentalist Movement."* He said he was typing it himself, on his lunch hour, while his secretary was gone, because if would be *"dangerous"* for him if anybody knew that he was communicating with me. (All those nice Christians he's working with? **Dangerous?**) He told me in this letter that certain things I was saying about fundamentalists were not correct, and then proceeded to give me the information I needed to make my points properly. He was on my side. Whoever he was, I'd like to take this opportunity to thank him.

**Anybody who wants religion is welcome to it, as far as I'm concerned—I support your right to enjoy it. However, I would appreciate it if you exhibited more respect for the rights of those people who do not wish to share your dogma, rapture or necrodestination.**

## Missionary Foreign Policy

Missionary evangelism is the height of cultural arrogance. To go to somebody else's country and attempt, through trickery, food or medical treatment, to capture "souls" for Jesus, Buddha, Mohammed, L. Ron Hubbard, Sun Myung Moon—whoever—presumes that the guy with the travel budget and the hypodermic needle has a 'spiritual edge' over the 'native' he's going to 'save.'

The goal of U.S.-based evangelism has been, more often than not, to render docile a native labor force, so that it might be exploited later by a multinational company (perhaps a secret 'donor' to the crusade itself).

This is the worst kind of amateur foreign policy. *The Logan Amendment* prohibits such 'privatization,' and under it, the activities of U.S. missionary evangelists (as well as rogue NSC zealots) should be prosecuted.

# Form 211

Internal Revenue Service Form 211 **(APPLICATION FOR REWARD FOR ORIGINAL INFORMATION)** is an easy-to-read, one-page document provided to enable public-spirited citizens to report somebody, anonymously, for tax evasion:

> This application is voluntary and the information requested enables us to determine and pay rewards. We use the information to record a claimant's reward as taxable income, and to identify any tax outstanding (*including that on a return filed jointly with a spouse*) against which the reward would first be applied. We need social security numbers on this application in order to process it. Not providing the information requested may result in the suspension of the processing for this application. Our authority for asking for the information on this form is derived from 26 USC 6001, 6109, 6011, 7623, 7802, and 5 USC 301.

. . . . . . . . . . . . . . . . . . . . . . . . . . . . . . . . . . . . . . . . . . . . . . . . . . . . .

I am applying for a reward, in accordance with the law and regulations, for original information furnished, which led to the detections of a violation of the internal revenue laws of the United States and which also led to the collection of taxes, penalties, fines, and forfeitures. I was not an employee of the Department of the Treasury at the time I came into possession of the information nor at the time I divulged it.

. . . . . . . . . . . . . . . . . . . . . . . . . . . . . . . . . . . . . . . . . . . . . . .

Under penalties of perjury, I declare that I have examined this application and my accompanying statements, if any, and to the best of my knowledge and belief they are true, correct, and complete. I understand the amount of my reward will represent what the District Service Center Director considers appropriate in this particular case.

. . . . . . . . . . . . . . . . . . . . . . . . . . . . . . . . . . . . . . . . . . . . . . .

### TO BE COMPLETED BY THE IRS

In consideration of the original information that was furnished by the claimant named above, which concerns a violation of the internal revenue laws and which led to a collection of taxes, penalties, fines and forfeitures in the sum shown above, I approve payment of a reward in the amount stated.

Signature of Service Center Director _____

### PAPERWORK REDUCTION ACT NOTICE

The Paperwork Reduction Act of 1980 says we must tell you why we are collecting this information, how we will use it, and whether you have to give it to us. We ask for the information to carry out the Internal Revenue Laws of the United States. We need it to ensure that taxpayers are complying with these laws and to allow us to figure and collect the right amount of tax. You are required to give us this information.

It's **absolutely confidential**—no one can obtain a copy of your filled-out form, even through the Freedom of Information Act. In other words, they'll never know who did what to whom. The payoff? Usually, ten percent of anything the IRS collects.

Is it possible that somewhere in the depths of the PTL scandal, somebody filled out a 211?

Let's say that someone turned over documents that **proved** Jim and Tammy did something illegal—and let's say that because of this information, the government collects. The guy who filled out the 211 would then be entitled to a nice chunk— and not even *The Washington Post* would be able to *prove* who was behind it.

As Ollie North might say: *"That's a pretty neat idea!"*

A number of people were in a position to file this *APPLI-CATION FOR REWARD FOR ORIGINAL INFORMA-TION* on the PTL (including Falwell), so, if the IRS ever collects, it will be interesting to see who gets to open the Swiss bank account. (If it's Falwell, he can just funnel it through Ollie's, since they're so close now.)

## Making a Mockery of the Founding Fathers

Let me close out this chapter with a note about one of Pat Robertson's more reprehensible activities: *rewriting American history with a 'Christian' bias.*

His *700 Club* broadcasts have systematically disinformed viewers as to the **real** attitudes of the Founding Fathers on religion and its relationship to government. This seems to have been done in order to merchandise his peculiar vision of an

America under the thumb of religious regulators. (One broad-cast suggested the deployment of a **"Spirit-Filled Police Force"** that would just **know**—with the help of the Lord, of course—who the **real** criminals were.)

The revolutionaries who got this country started were not, as Robertson would have us believe, a bunch of wig-headed *Jeezo-Grovelers*, whimpering for guidance from *The Unseen Hand*. They had a First Amendment premonition about pimp-weasels like him. Speak up, boys . . .

*"The United States is in no sense founded upon the Christian doctrine."*
George Washington

*"It does me no injury for my neighbor to say there are twenty gods or no god. It neither picks my pocket nor breaks my leg."*
Thomas Jefferson

*"I do not believe in the creed professed by the Jewish church, by the Roman church, by the Greek church, by the Turkish church, by the Protestant church, nor by any church that I know of. My own mind is my own church."*
Thomas Paine

*"I do not find in orthodox Christianity one redeeming feature."*
Thomas Jefferson

*"The Bible is not my book, and Christianity is not my religion. I could never give assent to the long, complicated statements of Christian dogma."*
Abraham Lincoln

(Quotes as listed in *Salvation for Sale*, by Gerard Thomas Straub.)

313

# CHAPTER 17

# Practical Conservatism

Politically, I consider myself to be a (don't laugh) **Practical Conservative.** I want a smaller, less intrusive government, and lower taxes. What? You too?

Last tax season, I had a discussion with *(the wildly amusing)* Gary Iskowitz and *(the utterly fascinating)* Bob Kahan. Gary used to be the chief of the IRS audit division in Maryland and Washington, D.C., and Bob is one of the few decent Los Angeles attorneys.

Gary was providing the laughs with a recitation of Reagan's description of our new tax laws: *"Equity, simplicity and fairness."* Come! Let us experience the curious warmth of Irish humor.

### THE TIME IT TAKES TO PREPARE YOUR RETURN *

| Form | Recordkeeping | Learning about the law or the form | Preparing the form | Copying, assembling, and sending the form to IRS |
|------|---------------|-----------------------------------|--------------------|-----------------------------------------------------|
| 1040 | 3 hrs., 7 min. | 2 hrs., 28 min. | 3 hrs., 7 min. | 35 min. |
| Sch. A (1040) | 2 hrs., 47 min. | 25 min. | 1 hr., 1 min. | 20 min. |
| Sch. B (1040) | 33 min. | 8 min. | 16 min. | 20 min. |
| Sch. C (1040) | 7 hrs., 4 min. | 1 hr., 11 min. | 2 hrs., 9 min. | 25 min. |
| Sch. D (1040) | 1 hr., 2 min. | 45 min. | 54 min. | 35 min. |
| Sch. E (1040) | 3 hrs., 12 min. | 1 hr., 2 min. | 1 hr., 22 min. | 35 min. |
| Sch. F (1040) | 10 hrs., 53 min. | 2 hrs., 2 min. | 4 hrs., 10 min. | 35 min. |
| Sch. R (1040) | 20 min. | 16 min. | 22 min. | 35 min. |
| Sch SE (1040) | | | | |
| Short | 20 min. | 11 min. | 13 min. | 14 min. |
| Long | 26 min. | 22 min. | 37 min. | 20 min. |

*\* Department of the Treasury, Internal Revenue Service*

This eventually led to a discussion of a paper Gary wrote in college, about what would happen if the U.S. income tax were removed, and replaced with a national sales tax on all goods and services. Here're a few points he made (my paraphrasing):

[1] We'd save a fortune on the yearly budget of the IRS itself. The sales tax could be administered with approximately five percent of the current IRS staff.

[2] Because people would be taxed only when they **spent** money, the entire economy would get a boost as people received more of an incentive to **earn** money.

[3] Certain folks who always seem to avoid paying taxes (defense contractors and church-owned businesses, for example) would be allowed to make a glowing debut as Major Stars of the U.S. tax base.

[4] Drug dealers don't file tax returns, but they do spend money. As long as drugs are illegal, this is the only way to derive tax revenue from them.

[5] All of the cash in the 'subterranean economy' would now be part of the tax base.

I believe we are entitled to the benefits of large-scale services which only a Federal Government can provide—national defense, Social Security, high-ticket research, help for the homeless, etc.—*only so long as we are* **willing and able to pay** *for them;* however, **if** such services are requested and rendered, it should be the goal **and the responsibility** of the government to make the deal work at a bargain price, with the **least** amount of fuss—not with the *largest amount of paperwork, the highest payroll, and endless, insufferable layers of bureaucracy.*

Efficient Federal Government should present social policy choices to the electorate in clear language:

*"If you want* **these services,** *it will cost* **this** *much. Are you* **sure** *you want them now? Here is a list of ways they can be paid for—choose one. If you say you want these services,*

*we'll take care of it for you. If you say no—next case."*
That's right, folks: *Utopia.*

If we know we want services on a national scale, and if we know we have to pay for them *somehow,* who'd object to this plan?

Answer: **many of the people who claim to be 'conservative' today**—especially the ones who seem so eager to turn America into a place where morality is dictated by religious dogma, certified by bizarre judicial decisions, legislated by semantic chicanery *(Ever try to read a California ballot?),* maintained by 'emergency police measures' and, occasionally, implemented by selective enforcement of the tax code. These not-so-conservative—in fact extremely radical—varmints prefer to keep the IRS just the way it is, and don't mind paying a little extra to have it available as a tool for political extortion.

By the way, have you ever wondered what the specific 'mission' of the Internal Revenue Service is? Here's the 1964 version, still in effect:

### Statement of some principles of Internal Revenue tax administration.*

The function of the Internal Revenue Service is to administer the Internal Revenue Code. Tax policy for raising revenue is determined by Congress.

With this in mind, it is the duty of the Service to carry out that policy by correctly applying the laws enacted by Congress; to determine the reasonable meaning of various Code provisions in light of the Congressional purpose in enacting them; and to perform this work in a fair and impartial manner, with neither a government nor a taxpayer point of view.

At the heart of administration is interpretation of the Code. It is the responsibility of each person in the Service, charged with the duty of interpreting the law, to try to find the true meaning of the statutory provision and not to adopt a strained construction in the belief that he is "protecting the revenue." The revenue is properly protected only when we ascertain and apply the true meaning of the statute.

The Service also has the responsibility of applying and administering the law in a reasonable, practical manner. Issues should only be raised by examining officers when they have merit, never arbitrarily or for trading purposes. At the same time, the examining officer should never hesitate to raise a meritorious issue. It is also important that care be exercised not to raise an issue or to ask a court to adopt a position inconsistent with an established Service position.

Administration should be both reasonable and vigorous. It should be conducted with as little delay as possible and with great courtesy and considerateness. It should never try to overreach, and should be reasonable within the bounds of law and sound administration. It should, however, be vigorous in requiring compliance with law and it should be relentless in its attack on unreal tax devices and fraud.

* *Internal Revenue Cumulative Bulletin, 1964*

# The Color of Money

Even if we leave the IRS alone, there is a world of delinquent payments waiting to be collected. In order to identify the taxable dollars from drug dealing and other unreported income, it has been suggested that we **change the color of our currency.** Nothing *green* would be legal tender anymore—the government would trade everybody straight across.

At the point of the coupon exchange, Mr. Tax Man gets a good squint at your cash flow, and bills you accordingly. Personally, I'd rather dump the Federal income tax.

# National Defense

If you own something, you will fight to protect it. If you don't—who gives a shit?

The strongest defense any nation can have is a robust economy. What **is** that? Have we ever really seen one? The trickle-downers think it's 'robust' when the guys in the *Fortune 500* clean up. A nation is really strong when everybody's got a piece of the action. **Everybody.**

We have been criminalized by our own tax code—ninety-seven percent of the population has to chisel and scam to survive. This is not 'robust.' Are we too stupid to create a **real national defense?**

Thanks to our schools and political leadership, the U.S. has acquired an international reputation as the home of 250 million people dumb enough to buy *'The Wacky Wall-Walker.'* Let's face it: **Without us, everybody else who wants to sell stuff would be in Big Trouble.**

As long as we remain marginally literate, materially insatiable and stupid enough to *merger* away our future to the point that we become competitively impotent, we are covered by a *'Strategic Life Insurance Policy'*—with the premiums willingly paid by our trading partners.

It is only a slight exaggeration to suggest that if the Russians were to launch a U.S. invasion, Japan would gladly provide battalions of ninjas to take care of the 'problem' for us. If we get blown away, who's buying next year's Toyotas?

And the Russians? Considering how badly we're doing these days, can we afford to nuke **any nation** willing to spend one hundred dollars for a pair of Levi's? *(And what about all that Pepsi Nixon arranged for us to sell over there?)*

## Star Wars

Does anybody reading this *actually* believe America is prepared for a 'conventional war' with **anybody?** If trouble breaks out, what are we gonna do? Whatever it is—unless the guy in the White House is a lunatic—it's not going to involve our *Fabulous and Totally Expensive Nuclear Arsenal.*

We are not going to have a big-ass Mondo Nuclear War. Period.

Nuclear explosions under the Nevada desert? What the fuck are we testing for? We already know the shit blows up. We're building machinery for a war that is as **unlikely** as it would be **unwinnable,** and, in the process, creating environmental side effects that defy contemplation.

Defense money should be put into manpower and equipment appropriate to the kinds of conflicts we are **really** going to encounter in the next quarter-century. The manpower should be dedicated, the equipment should be easy to operate and maintain, and the management of military assets should be streamlined.

Let's say we have to make some 'show of force.' The most common scenarios involve small guerilla or terrorist groups. *Nuclear retaliation?* It has been suggested by others that Aerosol Pork Grenades would be a better deterrent—Islamic martyrs are denied entrance to heaven if they show up at the gate smelling like a pig. Denial of The Big Payoff removes a certain cachet from acts of voluntary self-destruction.

If we were to subtract that portion of the defense budget dedicated to **'weapons we will never use'** *(either because they could backfire on us, or guys with U.S. high school diplomas are sort of 'unqualified' to operate them—or maybe they* **never worked at all,** *but because they provided jobs in some guy's home district for five years, Congress kept the contract going)*, and apply it to education, low-cost housing and **non-military R&D,** we'd all be better off.

*But nooooooo!* We spent blobs of money on a start-up contract for SDI and find out later that the initial research reports that said *"It will work!"* were falsified by omission.

For those of us still stupid enough to desire ownership of this preposterous system, I suggest that it could have been paid for **fifteen minutes ago** with about ten percent of what this 'fiscally conservative administration' has already spent on balloons, bunting, straw hats, confetti and the rest of the detritus required to make a narcoleptic pinhead look 'presidential' for the last eight years.

SDI won't save us from nuclear suitcase bombs, poison gas, bio-weapons or cocaine smugglers—and it carries a trillion-dollar price tag. *Attention shoppers!* Let's take the trillion, divide it by our total population and pass out the results of the arithmetic —**in cash**—along with a bazooka and a box of grenades to every family in America. Given the choice between terminal taxation and this 'incentive program,' I think most Americans would opt to **defend themselves** *(and their exciting new bank accounts)* against anything as unlikely as a full-scale Russian invasion.

# Central America

Washington, D.C.: a city infested with statues—and Congressional Blow-Boys who **wish** they were statues.

Did these fine statesmen **really** think Nicaragua was a menace to our national security? Yeah? Then why the fuck did they hire an **amateur army** to look after our 'interests' down there? Wait a minute—what **are** our 'interests' down there?

We have just spent eight years being governed by dorks who acted like building a wall around Texas to ward off Sandinistas marching up through Mexico could be a super-bitchen strategic idea. *(Unless we used another amateur army of 'illegal alien' laborers, we couldn't even afford it—the Teamsters contract for hauling in the raw material could easily cripple the economy.)*

If we expect to protect our legitimate business interests on foreign soil, we are going to have to develop more efficient and **appropriate** tools for the job. These might include:

### PSYCHOLOGY

*Persuading the population of whatever country we're not getting along with this week that* **WE** *are the Good Guys—if the Russians can do it* **to us,** *think what we could do to everybody else with a little help from Madison Avenue.*

### DIPLOMACY

*Making honest and enforceable deals—and* **reliably** *living up to them.*

### ECONOMIC STRATEGY

*Help their economies to grow—don't just move in and rape the labor force. Besides, these developing nations could become* **important new customers.** *(It'll take 'em a while to find out how cheesy our products actually are, and, until they catch on—or we learn how to build better stuff—we can pretend to be* **The Greatest Nation On Earth** *for a few more years.)*

And, **if necessary,** pork spritzers or gunpowder—not plutonium or nerve gas.

## South Africa

It is a strategic necessity (as much as a moral one) for the U.S. to see that apartheid is brought to an end. You say you don't care? It doesn't matter that much to you? No big deal? If one of the competing black factions takes over, will you **really** sleep better knowing that whoever wins the inevitable inter-tribal war has an **H–bomb?** *And how about that growing segment of the white population marching around with a nouveau swastika flag, piling flowers on the local Hitler shrine, hoping to oust the existing government,* **so** <u>they</u> **can have the bomb?** Folks: Pork Cologne will not work on these people.

## The Middle East

It is absurd that people are dying over such a miserable piece of real estate. Israel has a right to exist **AND** the Palestinians are entitled to their own state.

The land issue would have been settled long ago if it weren't for the religious fanatics on both sides, the misguided efforts of the U.S. Israel lobby, the weakness and shortsightedness of several U.S. administrations, and our old friends in the weapons business. Guys who live on yachts purchased with the proceeds of bullet sales tend to feel awkward and out-of-place in the unemployment line. This often leads them to ingenious forms of 'product promotion.' Is it not a slight embarrassment that many of these gentlemen are of the American persuasion?

## Government in 'the New Perfect America'

I've said it before, and I'll say it again: *Politics Is the Entertainment Branch of Industry.*

C-SPAN's coverage of governmental proceedings is wonderful. **Caution! Buffoons on the Hill!** Wallowing in blabber and spew, regiments of ex-lawyers and used-car salesmen attempt to distract us from the naughty little surprises served up by deregulated corporate America.

Has it become impossible to govern the U.S. by reason or logic? America under Reagan saw the rise of governance by trickery, fear, disinformation and superstition. Oh Jesus! Here come those fucking balloons again.

## Nancy's War on Drugs

Speaking of superstition and balloons, let's examine the U.S. drug policy.

Once upon a time, we had a stupid law called Prohibition, based on the notion that alcohol was an 'immoral' chemical compound. Instead of saving the National Soul from demon rum, this policy was directly responsible for hundreds, perhaps thousands, of innocent people being murdered in gang wars or poisoned by severely unripened beverages.

Prohibition also made it possible for organized crime to develop and thrive on a scale never imagined by any of the legislation's sponsors. Have we detected any similarity to late-eighties America yet?

Illuminated by the rosy glow of a trillion-dollar global drug business, our covert war in Nicaragua looks like a badly directed snuff film, shot on location in a cocaine money laundry.

There has always been a symbiotic relationship between right-wing administrations and purveyors of 'sinful goods.' As long as the moralizers control the government, the purveyors' products remain *officially forbidden*. This keeps the price up and inflates their profits—a perverse system of international agricultural price supports. Would we really be surprised to discover that triple-rinsed coca-bucks have financed Republican campaigns at all levels for years?

Alcohol Prohibition gave us Eliot Ness. Drug Prohibition gives us Nancy Reagan, George Bush, Manuel Noriega, Oliver North, the jolly lads in the Medellín Cartel, and, of course, their local distributors over by the school yard.

Alcohol Prohibition introduced us to the thrilling exploits of wise-guy gangsters, supplying the entertainment needs of a booze-guzzling public—held hostage by a truly stupid piece of legislation. They dressed sharp, threw good parties, greased city hall and had enough money left over at the end of the day to buy a few unions and build Las Vegas.

Prohibition today has produced cartels of international party-boys who take in enough cash daily to finance the LBO of any corporation on the planet. Darlin', every crystal that crawled up your nose (at least since January of 1980) has helped to create the economic power base for a worldwide secret government.

## Suicide

The reasons why people opt for the dubious thrill of 'controlled substance consumption' vary, but one factor seems consistent at all social levels: *IN SPITE OF THE OBVIOUS PHYSICAL RISKS, PEOPLE WILL CONSUME THEM, NO MATTER WHAT.*

Party Chemicals, including alcohol, are usually consumed because Mr. Party Guy wants to achieve some variation on a condition we'll call *"blotto."* For some, this amounts to a slow death—and they *still* want to do it. **"Suicide—fast or slow? Should any government have the right to force an adult to stay alive if that individual chooses death—fast or slow?"** In some instances, perhaps. Generally, not.

I believe that people have a right to decide their own destinies; *people own themselves.* I also believe that, in a democracy, government exists because (and only so long as) individual citizens give it a 'temporary license to exist'—in exchange for a promise that it will *behave itself.* In a democracy, you own the government—it doesn't own you.

Along with this comes a responsibility to ensure that individual actions, in the pursuit of a personal destiny, do not threaten the well-being of others while the 'pursuit' is in progress.

## A Matter of Semantics

It disturbs me to hear news reports describing the "menace of drugs" sandwiched in between commercials for off-the-shelf painkillers, sleep inducers, diet capsules and beer.

Any societal "menace" involved would be more accurately catalogued as "substance abuse behavior"—a generic term to describe any chemically induced irresponsible conduct, whether derived from glue, nutmeg, dietary supplements, alcohol or the current list of compounds on the "controlled substances" list.

A drug is neither moral nor immoral—it's a chemical compound. The compound itself is not a menace to society until a human being treats it as if consumption bestowed a temporary license to act like an asshole.

There are many compounds which chemically alter human behavior. They pose individual health risks, and risks to the safety of third parties who might depend on the unimpaired competence of the user who is piloting a 747, performing open-heart surgery, judging a murder trial or writing federal legislation.

The fact is, no complete psychopharmacological 'behavior table' exists for the multitude of substances (controlled or otherwise) which humans might ingest—even accidentally—including foodstuffs, which could, based on an individual's body chemistry, produce hallucinations, psychotic episodes, or any number of other undesirable physical conditions leading to 'impaired behavior'—but, for some reason, we have fixated on "drugs."

The "drug problem" is real—but it has been muddled by

bad semantics. If we could eradicate every compound on the controlled substances list tomorrow, the "criminal" acts resulting from chemically altered states of human behavior (if we assume that people are basically well-intentioned animals, and only get weird when alien molecules attack them) would still continue.

Life could be described as a complex form of *electrochemical entertainment:* electrical charges modifying chemical compounds which recombine to make electrical charges which etc., etc., etc., eventually leading to **"Life As Behavioral Theater"** (with performances perceived via electrochemical sensors—which create charges, modify compounds, create more charges and so on). *Still with me?* In short, even before we had LSD, there were mushrooms—and before PCP, we had maniacs, robbers and murderers. Can we win **any** "war on drugs"? Are you kidding?

The biggest danger from the drug trade is not the occasional lethal blunders committed by users and street dealers—the real evils lurk in the financial and political power which flows upstream to the cartels' overlords. These guys have enough loose cash to snatch up a chunk of **any nation** on a whim.

U.S. drug users are financing the lower half of this equation, while our licensed representatives finance the rest by making life easy for the big guys with unenforceable pseudolegislation and a hilariously inept war on drugs. What do you say when U.S. Customs officers, asked to engage in *vigorous interdiction,* find it inconvenient to be tested for drug consumption themselves?

## Send In the Marines?

Should we declare that a state of war exists between the U.S. and each drug-producing, drug-distributing and/or money-laundering nation, in order to legitimize the involvement of all military branches? What do we do about China? They have an H-bomb and a fairly large army. *"Oh, well . . . heroin's not that* big a problem *anymore—let's just go after those bad cocaine dealers.*"

Are we to seriously consider armed international conflict because middle-aged men in the entertainment community need illicit pharmaceutical assistance in order to keep their dicks hard?

Are we gonna roll out the leftover Agent Orange and fuck up somebody's jungle because 'creative people at the network' rely on *native medicine* when making the complex aesthetic decisions which determine American television's fascinating content?

## Law and Order

Part of what we have licensed the government to do is maintain 'law and order'—first, to create enforceable laws to provide an outline for the practical aspects of social existence, coupled with a license to use force, if necessary, in order to apply them. What the fuck went wrong?

For one thing, we had a bumper crop of lawyers a while back, and every one of them wanted to earn a living—but, with so many lawyers competing for the *criminal dollar,* how could they expect to get **their** rightful hunk of American Pie? The answer was obvious: America *needed* more criminals. Not the really bad kind that do murder and rape and stuff—we needed regular, easy-to-defend, middle-class neighborhood criminals, with cash and equity. The lawyers of America set out to create a world where their services would be *indispensable.*

They ooched into the governmental machinery at every level, and, while we weren't looking, created a body of incomprehensible, contradictory, unenforceable laws (the IRS Code, for instance) which could be transgressed by anybody, anytime, *without their even knowing it,* thereby placing entire families in economically life-threatening situations—unless they knew a (don't laugh) **good lawyer.**

Then, the peculiarities of our **case law** system took over. **Case law** is what happens when a stupid judicial decision from one place gets cited as a "legal precedent," forming the basis for another stupid judicial decision somewhere else—like a computer virus.

Remember: In the beginning, we gave this *theoretical temporary license* to the *theoretical government* to create this *theoretically organized social system,* to be administered on a democratic basis —and part of the deal required that the *license holder* would create **law** for us and, with it, maintain **order.**

It was supposed to be done by guys who knew **something** about **how to do it** (and wanted to do it, because *we needed it*). They *said* they could do it. We believed them. We voted for them. But what did we get? A mutant subspecies that tells lies for a living, unwittingly assisted by semiliterate juries *(chosen by the lawyers themselves)* who do the rest of the damage to the system by excreting mounds of **case law.**

We could thin out the ranks of the legal profession a bit if it were required that everything lawyers **and** judges say in court be under oath, with treble punishment and property confiscation penalties for **them** if **they** lie—or if any of the documents generated or used as evidence are found to be *written forms of lies.*

## Zero Tolerance?

The new drug law that mandates the death penalty and confiscation of property connected with any drug-trafficking operation could lead to some intriguing conversations with Mrs. Thatcher. British offshore banking policy allows—even promotes—practices which assist in the laundering of drug money.

*Of all foreign governments involved in the current epidemic of LBOs and purchases of American assets—including the Arabs, the Germans and the Japanese—***Britain** (or unknown entities acting through British banking agents) **has grabbed the most.**

In many respects, the U.K. is well on its way to becoming a Third World nation—where the fuck are they getting all the cash to buy **us** up?

Is it an act of war to buy somebody's country out from underneath him? If somebody offers to buy your country (or what amounts to economic control of your country), and you sell it to him, does that mean your country plans to go into 'retirement'? What are we gonna do? Take the cash and move to Switzerland?

## Other Options

If we were to decriminalize and commercially 'recontrol' the "controlled substances" (dispensing them on a rack next to the alcohol in *State Stores,* or in chains of *Federal Party Pharmacies,* for example), benefits to the U.S. Treasury could be substantial, as would domestic 'cocaine brewery' profits.

At least one aspect of our agricultural problem would be solved *("What should we plant next year, Wanda?"),* the prison population would diminish, and, most importantly, we could put a crimp in the pipeline feeding cash to the guys in the jungle.

I don't know about you, but I have never issued a 'temporary license to govern' to **any guy** in **any jungle,** but, because they made so many friends in Washington during the last eight years *(just helping out with 'the war effort'),* they act as if it had been granted by proxy.

Would 'recontrol' put the cartels out of business? Probably not. What if RJR Nabisco decided to open a 'brewery division' —Dan Dorfman would report rumors of another big takeover, the stock would soar (a lot of church and pension-fund buying) and the cartel would wind up as a legit U.S. business—just like some of our most illustrious old-money families who hit it big when the booze trade got redignified.

What if a kinder, gentler CIA chose to produce a low-cost 'designer drug' with special 'social engineering characteristics,' and mount yet another covert civilian *test for profit,* arranging for this *New Buzz* to drive Traditional Flavors out of the marketplace? It worked with LSD. (And doesn't PCP—*makes you crazy; takes five guys to hold you down; etc.*—have a sort of 'militarily useful' aura about it?)

## Communism

Mr. Gorbachev has apparently stumbled onto one of the best-kept secrets in recent Soviet history: **Communism doesn't work.** *It's against a basic law of nature:* "PEOPLE WANT TO **OWN** STUFF."

*Perestroika* virtually certifies this as an axiom. You still want to call it *"Communism"*? Sure—g'head—call it what you want. We don't need to say, *"I told you so."* Leave a guy some dignity. The Cold War? Have another Pepsi—it makes you moonwalk.

In exporting their philosophy, the Soviets employed a technique reminiscent of U.S. evangelical TV ministries. They told people who were hungry and sick they'd give them food and penicillin. The evangelists forced them to read the Bible; the Communists made them read *The Little Red Book*—and if you couldn't read, the motherfuckers would recite it to you through a bullhorn.

The Soviets have spent many years (and a lot of money) marketing and maintaining a political Edsel, fueled by the assumption that *entire populations* will cheerfully endure Spartan conditions, then hand over the fruits of all labor to a benevolent bureaucracy which would redistribute the wealth in an 'equitable manner.' What?

In every language, the first word after **"Mama!"** that every kid learns to say is **"Mine!"** A system that doesn't allow ownership, that doesn't allow you to say **"Mine!"** when you grow up, has—to put it mildly—a fatal design flaw.

From the time **Mr. Developing Nation** was forced to read *The Little Red Book* in exchange for a blob of rice, till the time he figured out that waiting in line for a loaf of pumpernickel was boring as fuck, took about three generations. Television helped to speed up that cycle.

Decades of indoctrination, manipulation, censorship and KGB excursions haven't altered this fact: **People want a piece of their own little Something-or-Other, and, it they don't get it, have a tendency to initiate counterrevolution.**

Why, then, do so many Americans, while professing to adore Freedom and Democracy, support—even **demand**—that actions be taken by their own government which bear a striking resemblance to **Old-Style Evil Empire Communism?** *(Censorship? Disinformation? The Public Library Spy-Squealer Program?)* **Are we really that unspeakably stupid?**

## Use It or Lose It

Americans like to talk about (or be told about) Democracy but, when put to the test, usually find it to be an 'inconvenience.' We have opted instead for an authoritarian system *disguised* as a Democracy. We pay through the nose for an enormous joke-of-a-government, let it push us around, and then wonder how all those assholes got in there.

**Communism doesn't work because it is out of phase with human nature. Are we going to wake up one day to find this statement equally true when applied to the concept of Western Democracy?**

# CHAPTER 18

# FAILURE

Failure is one of those things that 'serious people' dread. Invariably, the persons most likely to be crippled by this fear are people who have convinced themselves that they are <u>so</u> <u>bitchen</u> they shouldn't ever be placed in a situation where they might **fail.**

Failure is nothing to get upset about. It's a fairly **normal** condition; an **inevitability** in ninety-nine percent of all human undertakings. Success is rare—that's why people get so cranked up about it.

Here are a few examples from my own personal collection of crumbled dreams. These are excerpts from actual business proposals, presented to guys with suits on, in The Real World.

Even though they all flopped, the very idea of walking into a corporate office and dropping one of these boogers on *Mr. Show-Me's* desk made it all worthwhile—a guy's gotta have a hobby.

The first example is a letter sent to a Chicago attorney, Arnold Silvestri, sometime in the early eighties. . . .

### I.C.A. GOES PUBLIC?

Here are some facts regarding I.C.A. (Inter-Continental Absurdities), and the possibility of taking it public.

I have an idea for a new device, potentially worth several billion dollars (patent search enclosed).

By using a modified version of the computer logic

currently employed in the generation of 3-D visuals for flight training simulators, in conjunction with an optical delivery system (yet to be designed), this device would make it possible to:

**[1]**

**Generate FREE-STANDING 3-D images, in any size (on your coffee table at home, or on a larger scale for theatrical use), 'folded out' from any two-dimensional source by PREDICTING and SYNTHESIZING the MISSING THIRD DIMENSION.**

**[2]**

**Create a service company which 'unfolds' existing 'flat' movies and TV shows so that they might be rereleased, viewable as FREE-STANDING 3-D OBJECTS.**

**[3]**

**Create a cable network which would broadcast material in this medium.**

**[4]**

**Sell hardware on a large scale to home and industrial consumers.**

This is not a 'holographic' process, and, as far as we have been able to determine, does not infringe on any existing patent.

The device is in three sections. The first one converts the picture data to a digital signal which can then be worked on by the math in section two (where the depth information is synthesized), finally arriving at section three which projects it to any desired size.

I have two partners in this venture: John Law, former VP, NATO Weapons Division, General Electric Corp. (his card and copies of correspondence enclosed), and Jerry Roth (card not available at this mailing).

John informs me that seventy percent of the materials (hardware and software) to do this project is available NOW, off-the-shelf, from within the aero-space industry. **None of it is secret,** and, through his industrial contacts, can be obtained without much trouble. It will also be his responsibility to locate R&D talent. Jerry's field of expertise is software and marketing.

By John's estimate, plans for a working prototype could be viewed within two years, at a development cost of 1.5 million dollars. There is no current estimate as to the cost of building the prototype.

The first person contacted for funding was Robert Armao (an attorney/PR man/investment adviser to Nelson Bunker Hunt, the Pahlevi family, etc.), who told me that the project was 'very speculative,' and, therefore, I must be willing to give up a seventy-five percent interest, PLUS pay his fee, PLUS pay his expenses.

In the most respectful way possible I informed him that these terms were located somewhere between science fiction and usury.

The next day I met with Tom Phillips and Archie McGill at Rothschild Venture Capital. They wanted a 'business plan' and other assurances (almost to the point of showing them a working model) before getting involved, and then stated that their limit would be no more than 2 million (which would create big problems when the device was ready to manufacture).

By coincidence, I had to make another stop at Armao's office to meet a friend after the Rothschild meeting (the offices are across the street from each other in Rockefeller Center). When I arrived, Armao asked me to come into his office, introduced me to a guy from some 'investment fund' and stated that he (Armao) would **no longer require a fee or expenses,** and that I would only have to give away forty percent for this first 1.5 million.

I told him I would think about it. Since that time he has tried to contact me in Los Angeles, but I was in New York.

Realistically, the deal is worth giving up no more than twenty-five percent (including the brokerage), which would then leave something further to bargain with when it's time to raise the heavy capital for manufacturing.

This brings us to the matter of 'going public' (which might or might not be the right move at this time, but is a possibility being given serious consideration).

If we agree that the earning potential of the **D.S.S.** (Depth-Synthesis System) is tremendous—although highly speculative by some standards—and that any film or stage venture is equally speculative *(but not as potentially lucrative)*, we might consider:

## [1]

**The plight of those unfortunate persons who, especially at the end of the year, need to 'dispose of money.' Surely these suffering wretches can be approached with a creative suggestion or two.**

## [2]

**We should also consider that the research facility which must be stocked and staffed to build the**

**D.S.S. has a continuing value and potential for the construction of other inventions once the primary objective is achieved.**

I mentioned a figure of 100 million to do all of this. That might be high . . . but, if it can be raised, why not? Other companies have raised more to do less.

The next document explains the meeting mentioned above at Rothschild Venture Capital, held at a time in the long-forgotten past, when CDs weren't even on the market. . . .

### A PROPOSAL FOR A SYSTEM TO REPLACE PHONOGRAPH RECORD MERCHANDISING

Ordinary phonograph record merchandising as it exists today is a stupid process which concerns itself essentially with moving **pieces of plastic**, wrapped in **pieces of cardboard**, from one location to another.

These objects, in quantity, are heavy and expensive to ship. The manufacturing process is complicated and crude. Quality control for the stamping of the discs is an exercise in futility. Dissatisfied customers routinely return records because they are warped and will not play.

New digital technology may eventually solve the warpage problem and provide the consumer with better quality sound in the form of compact discs **[CDs]**. They are smaller, contain more music and would, presumably, cost less to ship . . . but they are much more expensive to buy and manufacture. To reproduce them, the consumer needs to purchase a digital device to replace his old hi-fi equipment (in the seven-hundred-dollar price range).

The bulk of the promotional effort at every record company today is expended on 'NEW MATERIAL' . . . the latest and the greatest of whatever the cocaine-tweezed rug-munchers decide to inflict on everybody this week.

More often than not, these 'aesthetic decisions' result in mountains of useless vinyl/cardboard artifacts which cannot be sold at any price, and are therefore returned for disposal and recylcing. These mistakes are expensive.

Put aside momentarily the current method of operation and think what is being wasted in terms of **GREAT CATALOG ITEMS,** squeezed out of the marketplace because of limited rack space in retail outlets, and the insatiable desire of quota-conscious company reps to fill every available slot with this week's new releases.

Every major record company has vaults full of (and perpetual rights to) great recordings by major artists in many categories which might still provide enjoyment to music consumers if they were made available in a convenient form.

**MUSIC CONSUMERS LIKE TO CONSUME <u>MUSIC</u> . . . NOT SPECIFICALLY THE VINYL ARTIFACT WRAPPED IN CARDBOARD.**

It is our proposal to take advantage of the **positive aspects** of a **negative trend** afflicting the record industry today: **home taping** of material released on vinyl.

First of all, we must realize that **the taping of albums is not necessarily motivated by consumer 'stinginess.' If a consumer makes a home tape from a disc, that copy will probably sound better than a commercially manufactured high-speed duplication cassette legitimately released by the company.**

. . . . . . . . . . . . . . . . . . . . . . . . . . . . . . . . . . . . . . . . . . . . . . . . . . .

We propose to acquire the rights to digitally duplicate THE BEST of every record company's difficult-to-move **Quality Catalog Items [Q.C.I.],** store them in a central processing location, and have them accessible by phone

or cable TV, directly patchable into the user's home taping appliances, with the option of direct digital-to-digital
transfer to the F-1 (SONY consumer-level digital tape
encoder), Beta Hi-Fi, or ordinary analog cassette (requiring the installation of a rentable D-A converter in the
phone itself . . . the main chip is about twelve dollars).

All accounting for royalty payments, billing to the
consumer, etc., would be automatic, built into the software for the system.

The consumer has the option of subscribing to one or
more 'special interest category,' charged at a monthly
rate, **WITHOUT REGARD FOR THE QUANTITY
OF MUSIC THE CUSTOMER WISHES TO
TAPE.**

Providing material in such quantity at a reduced cost
could actually diminish the desire to duplicate and store
it, since it would be available any time day or night.

Monthly listings could be provided by catalog, reducing the on-line storage requirements of the computer.
The entire service would be accessed by phone, even if
the local reception is via TV cable.

One advantage of the TV cable is: on those channels
where nothing ever seems to happen (there's about seventy of them in L.A.), a visualization of the original
cover art, including song lyrics, technical data, etc.,
could be displayed while the transmission is in progress,
giving the project an electronic whiff of the original
point-of-purchase merchandising built into the album
when it was 'an album,' since there are many consumers
who like to fondle & fetish the packaging while the music
is being played.

In this situation, **Fondlement & Fetishism Potential [F.F.P.]** is supplied, without the cost of shipping
tons of cardboard around.

Most of the hardware devices are, even as you read this, available as off-the-shelf items, just waiting to be plugged into each other in order to put an end to the record business as we now know it.

Another miserable flop was a concept for a late-night TV show. In 1987, assisted by Danny Schrier, an aggressive young agent at ICM, I embarked on a depressing journey into the air-conditioned wilderness of TV-Land, pitching ideas to groups of individuals worthy of further anthropological study. It all began with a meeting in the ABC network office, on or about March 13, 1987. . . .

## NIGHT SCHOOL

A late-night adult program, sixty minutes, five nights per week. Show will be preceded by a warning:

*"This program deals with reality, using easy to understand colloquial American Language. If you fear (or have difficulty accepting) either of the above, feel free to change the channel. You have ten seconds."*

**NIGHT SCHOOL** will have a 'permanent faculty' and a pool of 'visiting professors.' Frank Zappa will host the show. Daniel Schorr has expressed interest in the position of 'PROFESSOR OF RECENT HISTORY.'

In that capacity, it would be his job to show raw, uncut news footage from the daily satellite feed, point out the material other broadcasters have deleted, speculate on the possible motivations behind the deletions, and refresh people's memories about recent events connected to each day's breaking stories.

A summary will be provided of what our elected officials really did for their paycheck in Congress each day. Votes on House and Senate business will be treated like sports scores.

Satellite interviews with political figures willing to take the risk will be a nightly feature.

Schorr will be based in Washington. Zappa will be in Los Angeles. Questions may also be asked by members of the live band in the L.A. studio.

Working on a twenty-four-hour delay, yesterday's news footage will be converted on a daily basis into three-minute rock music videos for a segment entitled **"NEWS IN HEAVY ROTATION."**

At least two brand-new music videos will be constructed each day, using Zappa's music (over three-hundred songs in the catalog, on digital audio tape, ready for synchronization), or those of any other artists willing to license their material at a special rate, and agree to ancillary usage, with rights controlled by the production company.

MTV has shown interest in a joint venture on this segment. The **"NEWS IN HEAVY ROTATION"** weekly summary would air on MTV each Saturday. MTV would split the cost of production for the clips, and promote **"NIGHT SCHOOL"** each day on their channel. **"NIGHT SCHOOL"** would cross-promote their weekend summary. Other details have yet to be worked out.

The live band will consist of ten musicians and three singers. Visiting musical guests will be encouraged to perform live. Studio facilities will make it possible to produce 'record-quality' stereo audio.

The members of the band will double as 'actors' in a purposely cheesey sitcom segment called **"THE FU-TURE FAMILY."**

Whenever a news item warrants it, **"THE FUTURE FAMILY"** will 'pre-enact' the possible social consequences, twenty years down the road.

Taking a cue from current news policy at KABC-TV, Los Angeles (during ratings sweeps, they either do a week-long 'special report' on *'Satanism'* or *BREAST CANCER*), our late night Psychology Course will deal almost exclusively with sexually related topics.

For at least the first month our study course will be **"THE HUMAN BREAST . . . WHY DO AMERI-CANS LIKE THEM SO MUCH?"** (If it is okay to show nude, diseased examples squeezed into a mammo-graphic apparatus at six and eleven o'clock, surely within the context of our home medical course, healthy ones ought to get on the air after midnight.)

Degrees will be offered for twenty-five dollars . . . call the **NIGHT SCHOOL** credit-card hot line and tell the nice lady you need to graduate in a hurry. By return mail you will receive a framed degree that looks better than a real one. For one hundred dollars you can graduate **cum laude.** Each individual **NIGHT SCHOOL** course offers a degree, so you might want several for your office. We expect that the completion certificate in *THE HUMAN BREAST* study course to be a favorite.

And now, one of the most ridiculous proposals of 1988. This was presented to *Mayor* Pelletiere (a Socialist), *Vice Mayor* and *Minister of Culture* Corbani (a Communist), and *Minister of Youth Affairs* Treves (an Anarchist) of Milan, in June of that year.

### PROPOSAL FOR A WORLD CUP FOOTBALL OPERA
#### *DIO FA*

Frank Zappa proposes to write, produce and direct a special entertainment event for the conclusion of the World Cup Football Finals in the summer of 1990, to be financed by the City of Milan and the Italian Football Committee. It will be an opera, with the premiere performance in La Scala, broadcast via satellite, worldwide.

The text will be in English, Italian, German, French, Spanish, Portuguese and Russian.

The performance will include dancing in many styles, special effects and a fashion show.

The musical accompaniment will include full orchestral settings, chamber music settings, ethnic choral and instrumental setting (executed via digital sampling and digital tape playback), advanced electronic music techniques and rock music (in styles ranging from doo-wop vocals to heavy metal). The music will be partly acoustic, partly amplified and, in some instances, mimed to digital playback.

Zappa will write the story and lyrics, supervise the set design, costumes and special effects.

The City of Milan, through its Sister City arrangement with Chicago, will engage the Chicago Symphony to provide the orchestral backing. (The La Scala orchestra will be represented by selected instrumental soloists.) The La Scala Chorus will be featured.

Zappa will select the stage director, orchestral conductor and featured vocal soloists. The negotiations for their fees will be the responsibility of the City of Milan. Their fees are not included in this proposal or budget.

A U.S. designer and staging company will be selected by Zappa to prepare the blueprints for the sets and special effects. The sets will be constructed in Milan, in the La Scala scenic facility under the supervision of the U.S. designer. The special effects will be constructed in the U.S. and shipped to Milan.

What follows is not a complete description of the event . . . only a collection of ideas to begin with. All material is subject to irrational modification.

The theme of the opera is:

**Millions of people believe football is God, but, it is said (at least in Torino), "God is a liar."—Dio Fa.**

To present this theme, we propose to use a large mechanical version of the marionette character shown in the logo of the Italian Football Committee in the role of 'FOOTBALL GOD.'

This FOOTBALL GOD marionette is afflicted with

an uncontrollable Nasal Growth Syndrome, pioneered by Pinocchio (perfected by Reagan).

Whenever FOOTBALL GOD tells a lie, a horrible soft nose grows out of the soccer ball which forms the head of the logo.

With each new lie, another monk appears (singing in Sardinian ethnic choral style), struggling to hold up FOOTBALL GOD'S repulsive nose with inexplicable religious machinery.

To conclude the production in a way that allows FOOTBALL GOD to have a tiny nose and live happily ever after, we propose:

> **As soon as the Italian National Team is selected, a rock video is made (in the style of "THE SUPER BOWL SHUFFLE") using the players in uniform to render an Anglo-Italian rap version of Michael Jackson's "I'M BAD." This will be made into an instant hit by all Italian radio and television stations.**

> **At the end of the opera, FOOTBALL GOD sings His Hit (assisted by the monks—who turn out to be the Italian National Team in disguise). And so, by singing "I'M BAD, I'M BAD, YOU KNOW IT, YOU KNOW IT!", GOD'S nose shrivels to Jacksonian proportions, and HE dances away.**

**"DIO FA,"** the logo for the opera itself, as it will

appear on posters and advertising, has been licensed (as part of the opera plot) to a mysterious Soviet clothing designer who plans to unveil the new line of Soviet fashions, via satellite, during the most dramatic part of the opera.

Zappa will attempt to make an actual licensing and manufacturing deal with the Soviets for REAL CLOTHES to be offered worldwide under the **"DIO FA"** label, with the garments making their debut as part of **a choreographed fashion show, with ballet and ethnic dancers as models, and the Soviet designer appearing on stage to be hugged by them after the clothing is shown.**

. . . . . . . . . . . . . . . . . . . . . . . . . . . . . . . . . . . . . . . . . . . . . . .

Other characters include: **Galileo, Tesla, Newton, da Vinci, Mussolini, Hitler, Stalin, and Elvis Presley as THE DEVIL.**

. . . . . . . . . . . . . . . . . . . . . . . . . . . . . . . . . . . . . . . . . . . . . . .

Great Britain is represented by dancers dressed as football hooligans, misinterpreting signals from the Queen (a waving mechanical cardboard arm, viewed through the window of a passing car).

. . . . . . . . . . . . . . . . . . . . . . . . . . . . . . . . . . . . . . . . . . . . . . .

America is represented by a group of tourists who line up at a phone booth with a sign on it that reads **"TALK TO GOD."**

Each one gets to ask a single question. The all-important questions are:

[1] **"Did I wake you up?"**
[2] **"What time is it there?"**
[3] **"How much is that in dollars?"**

[4] "Is that a castle, or what?"

[5] "What's the weather like there?"

[6] "When are you coming to America?"

# CHAPTER 19

# The Last Word

It is 5:30 A.M., December 25, 1988. I just finished reading the first set of galleys and have sprouted an eye-popping head-ache—nonetheless, this final material must be prepared in order to keep the 'recent history' part of the book up-to-date and make the deadline.

Since I submitted the manuscript, George Bush won *The Olympics of Banality*, Jim Bakker got indicted for tax fraud, Robertson is back on *The 700 Club*, the U.S. agreed to substantive talks with the PLO, and Congress passed a heinous piece of legislation designed to curb "audio pornography."

The 1988 CNN election coverage was biased beyond belief —every shot of Bush in the "bumpers" leading into news segments attempted to make him look "presidential" *(with Mickey Mouse?)*, while every shot of Dukakis was designed to make him look like a dork *(remember the one where he made that little weasel-face while catching a limply-tossed baseball in some supermarket parking lot? Pretty subtle, eh?)*

**"CNN—Your Network of Record"** has devolved into **"CNN—Your Network of Bullshit, Superficial Speculation and Calculated Innuendo."** They have a knack for dispensing "opinion-shaping" video-factoids disguised as "hard news." *(For example, the words "Star Wars" or "Strategic Defense Initiative" are seldom uttered on CNN without the viewer being subjected to a rerun of an animated clip showing nuclear missiles from* The Evil Empire *with big red stars on them being vaporized by what appears to be a Saturday morning cartoon ray gun. Clever subtext:* **"Who could argue with deployment of this wonderful family-saving defense system? Why, of course it works!**

See there! Just blew up another one!''*)*

Right around Christmas, CNN (with White House guid-ance, no doubt) began to pre-sell the concept of a sequel to the first Libyan bombing raid—a "surgical strike" against a new poison gas factory, **possibly** to be **carried out by** (watch the file footage, now) **cruise missiles, launched from subma-rines**—all of this accompanied by "hints" about when it might take place. Mr. Turner, you ought to be ashamed of yourself. Daniel Schorr got out just in time.

## Liberal Media Bias?

The concept of a "liberal media bias," spoon-fed to CNN viewers in talk-show blather and pompous 'news commentary' throughout the Reagan years, has at last been exposed for the pitiful manipulation it always was.

*"Liberal"* bias? Suppose a newsperson was some sort of frothing *"liberal"*—would he get a broadcast job in the first place? Not on CNN. But, **suppose he did,** and tried to sneak some form of *"bias"* into a story, do we think he'd last a week? Get serious. Frothing right-wing extremists are, however, prominently displayed and in plentiful supply on CNN.

The license holders for most broadcast outlets (especially the commercial networks) hardly qualify as *"liberal"* by any stretch of the imagination—and the guys on the board of directors? *Gimme a break.* This applies to all news outlets—electronic and print. The guy who owns the outlet determines policy and con-tent—that's why he owns it, so he can control it. This power to mold public opinion is bartered for 'favors' among 'friends'—it is the essential tool of *spin-control.*

The *"liberal media bias"* scam was a smoke screen, designed to conceal the squads of White House spin-doctors, sprinkling antiseptic on each morsel of "news" as it wafted past the rotor blades in The Gipper's backyard—all in the name of **balance** and **fairness,** of course.

Between 1980 and this writing, a news story could be deemed **balanced** and **fair** <u>only</u> if it had a hefty rightward spin. Certain types of stories got "special attention": *HEALTH-ENDANGERING GAY LIFESTYLES THREATEN EN-TIRE NATION* or *RISING INFANT MORTALITY RATE LINKED TO GROWTH IN ABORTION INDUSTRY*. Most of this shit sounded like it was drafted in "The Pastor's Study" at Falwell's *Old-Time Ministry of Gospel Propaganda*. Will the next four years be any different? What do **you** think?

The Gipper goes into private practice now—look for him as a TV pitchman for G.E. or some other defense contractor, and, perhaps, a born-again film career *(Bedtime for Bonzo II: Terror of the Green Monkey)*.

Would a *Kind And Loving God* let an asshole like that (and all his fabulous appointees) escape unpunished after eight years of Constitutional desecration?

(No, but one with a *way-sick* sense of humor is toying with the idea even as you read this.)

## Epaulet Update

As a follow-up to my comments on Dr. Koop: *CNN reported that of all the deadly diseases threatening America, AIDS weighed in at #7 (#1 was cancer with approximately 700,000 deaths per year; #2 was heart disease with approximately 500,000; #3 was diabetes with approximately 300,000; etc., etc.).* The total AIDS death toll **(since they first started counting)** was quoted in the vicinity of 40,000.

Another story reported that the age groups most frequently afflicted were people thirty years old and over, and infants *born infected*—**with little evidence of the disease among hetero-sexuals in the teens and twenties;** but, for some reason, the teen group gets targeted by the moralizers for admonitions: **"Abstain from sex unless you are married, lest ye perish from this righteous punishment (created, of course, by a**

**Kind And Loving God) in order that He might maintain penile discipline among naughty little libertines like you."**

Folks, take 250 million *live* people and divide by 40,000 *dead* people—what percentage is that? *Epidemic?* Have we just experienced semantic meltdown, or witnessed the birth of a new medical phenomenon: **The CNN Micro-Media Epidemic?**

## Poison Gas Again

Also on this topic, I obtained a copy of ***A Higher Form of Killing*** by Jeremy Paxman and Robert Harris, published by Hill & Wang. On page 240 you will find an excerpt from an Army manual discussing the feasibility of manufacturing and deploying **"ethnic chemical weapons"**—designed to kill people from *specific ethnic backgrounds*.

On page 241 you will find an extract from a 1969 Senate appropriations hearing, with testimony (speaker unidentified) regarding the development of **a new class of biological weapons** *(note the plural)* which would be **"refractory" to the human immunological system.**

Whose testimony was this? Was he asking for money to build a few of these diseases? What senators heard this testimony? Are they still in office? Did they appropriate any funds? If so, who got them? What did they eventually spend them on? The book doesn't say, but presumably some answers might be found in *The Congressional Record*.

*(I also recommend* **The Mind of the Bible Believer** *by Edmund Cohen, PhD.,* **Salvation for Sale** *by Gerard Thomas Straub and* **Holy Terror** *by Flo Conway and Jim Siegelman for any of you wishing to follow up on the Church/State issues discussed earlier.)*

Okay. That's it. **THE END.**

It's been a pleasure talking to you—and **don't forget to register to vote.**